Foreigners in the City of Silk

—

TORN CURTAIN PUBLISHING
Wellington, New Zealand
www.torncurtainpublishing.com

Second printing 2022
Third printing 2024

ISBN: 978-1-991299-05-5 (Softcover)
ISBN: 978-1-991299-06-2 (epub)

Cover photography by Agnieszka Malek
www.agnieszkamalek.com

Cataloguing in Publishing Data
   Title: Foreigners in the City of Silk
   Author: Anya McKee
   Subjects: Christian living, faith and spirituality, inspirational, personal memoir

Typeset in Berkshire Swash, Gidole and Minion Pro

A copy of this title is held at the National Library of New Zealand.

Foreigners in the City of Silk

—

ANYA MCKEE

To our Children
Eric, Joseph, Evangeline and Liberty
What we pulled off as a family
in Turkey is extraordinary.
We're so incredibly proud of you all.

and

To our Team of Friends
We couldn't have asked for a more
gracious, loyal and kind-hearted team.
For taking friendship to a whole
other level, thank you.

'Choose your friends before you choose your journey.'
-Turkish Proverb

Our story began when we flipped the way we prayed.

We'd always asked God to be with us. Whatever our family was doing, whether it was just Jeff or myself, or all of us together, our four young children included, we wanted Him in the mix. After all, when God shows up, significant moments happen. Lives get changed. Directions shift. Doors open. And so, nearly daily we prayed our default prayer: *Father, please come and be with us. We want Your presence.*

Sometimes we had an important meeting at work. Other times we were sitting in coffee shops sharing our lives with university students. There were occasions where we were praying with people or leading groups. But more often than not, we asked for God's presence simply because friends were coming for dinner or we were heading out the door to take the kids to school. 'Lord, please come. *Join us in what we are doing.*' And God generously, and sometimes extravagantly, turned up. Time after time.

And then, for no good reason except the subtle prompting of the Holy Spirit, we found ourselves less concerned about what *we* were doing and a whole lot more curious about what *He* was doing. We started wondering, 'Lord, what are *You* up to right now? Where are *You* working?' And then, we simply began to ask if instead of Him joining us, *we might join Him.*

Only, He caught us by surprise, because we never expected He'd respond with: '*Turkey. I'm working in Turkey.*'

At that moment, all we knew was that Turkey was a nation of about eighty million Muslims, and about as far from Australia as you can get.

It was also a country where we knew exactly *no one.*

But we'd asked, and He answered, and we weren't about to quibble, because somewhere deep inside, our hearts aligned with His and excitement rose within us despite the craziness of it all. God wanted to do more than simply join us in our human story. He wanted us to join Him in a God-story.

And this is how it happened.

Quite simply, everywhere we went, Turkey came up. *'I've just come back from Turkey.' 'We have friends serving in Turkey.' 'It's Global Pray for Turkey Day.'* And, of course, there was Gallipoli—the Turkish soil on which a generation of Australians and New Zealanders had fought, and lost, forging a bond with the Turks that remains strong to this day. Turkey, it seemed, was suddenly in the news, whether we were paying attention or not.

The next question we asked was, of course, *how?* 'God, if You are moving in Turkey and You want us to join You there, *how?*' How do two parents in their thirties transplant a family of six for who-knows-how-long and simply move to what might as well be a whole other world?

Thankfully, we weren't left in the dark. Just as the idea of Turkey had come up, so, gradually, did the details that would shape the years ahead. The simplicity of what God had in mind for us was striking: 'Go and live in Turkey with no agenda but to be a Christian family in a country where most people have never even met a Christian, and follow Me, just as you do back home.'

One thing, however, was clear. We needed people alongside us. There was no doubt God was inviting our family to join Him in Turkey, but we couldn't do it alone, nor did we want to. We started to wonder—were we meant to work for a foreign company in Turkey? Would we somehow link up with businesspeople over there? Should we join one of the teams of Christian expats living in the region? And then, in the midst of all the options, with amazing clarity, we heard these words: Team of Friends. *You need a Team of Friends.*

It was a God-idea from start to finish; our minds were suddenly flooded with names—people from across the years, old family friends, those we'd shared a childhood with, others who had been with us at school or university, men and women who had poured their love and wisdom into us, and others who we had poured our lives into. For a few amazing hours, we reminisced, wrote down names, enjoyed the memories, wrote an email, and then, with a sense of trepidation and excitement, sent it off.

The response blew us away. Our spirits soared as one reply after another came in. People who had been dear to us over the years were quick to rally to this new calling on our lives. And, they all agreed. They would commit to praying for us, one day a week, until this Turkey-gig was over.

We were only a month into our communications when one of our friends called. *'Jeff, I think you and Anya should consider taking a trip over to Turkey. Look around and get a feel for what you're getting into. I'll transfer the funds into your bank account. Book some tickets and do a reconnaissance trip.'*

That may have been the most valuable gift we would ever receive. Three weeks later, we boarded nine-year-old Eric and seven-year-old Joseph onto a domestic flight to Canberra where they would spend the next two weeks with family friends. Then we drove our two girls—four-year-old Evangeline, and Liberty, our eighteen-month-old toddler—across town to be looked after and doted on by Anya's parents.

And just like that, we were back to the two of us once again, boarding a flight of our own—one that would land us twenty-four hours later in Istanbul. We had a simple plan for our trip—visit a few cities and ask God to show us three things: where we should live, if there was a group of like-hearted people we could link up with, and what sort of work we should do. On the work front, we figured we had two options. Jeff could get a job with a multi-national company as a business consultant, or we could take Anya's small online editing company and expand it into the Middle Eastern market.

Those two weeks were some of the most fun weeks of our lives. Together we strolled the Izmir waterfront eating freshly steamed corn on the cob, we rode the Istanbul ferries, we toured the Blue Mosque and the Hagia Sofia, and we poked our heads around Turkish carpet shops and Middle Eastern spice markets. And, in ways we could never have imagined, some doors opened, and others closed.

It was obvious after three cancelled appointments that the idea of pursuing work with an international company was a non-starter. But every other environment we entered led to a stream of invitations. Foreign families asked if we'd join their expat communities, church groups welcomed us into their mix, and universities were excited about partnering with our academic editing company. Our thoughts began to solidify—online editing was one of the few viable ways for a foreigner to make a living in Turkey, *and* we were perfectly positioned to enter the market. Wherever we went, people wished us all the best and told us they were looking forward to our family's arrival.

We returned to Australia on a high. This wasn't so overwhelming after all. The only question left was, of all the options, which region would we choose to live in?

We eventually settled on Izmir, the most Westernised of the cities we'd visited and possibly the most liveable for foreigners. Within weeks we heard about an expat family who, for some reason, had very quickly returned to their home country, simply locking the door on their fifth-floor apartment in Izmir. Now they were looking for a family to take over the lease and buy outright the entire household of goods—an arrangement that suited us right down to the little details. We breathed sighs of thanks when we looked at the pictures of our new home. The apartment was decorated just the way we liked. The furniture was tasteful, the kitchen well-stocked with appliances and dishes. There was exactly the right number of beds—even a cot which would be perfect for little Liberty.

As the correspondence passed between us, the place only sounded more astonishingly suitable.

What size shoe do you wear?

Size 9, I replied.

It turned out that the closets even held clothing and shoes in the exact size of each person in our family. There were jigsaw puzzles and books and DVDs and Lego . . . the apartment waiting for us in Turkey could not have fit our unspoken wish-list more precisely.

Enthused by our housing miracle, we decided we would turn our attention to marketing our company to our newly-met contacts on the ground. We didn't want to waste too much time over the transition between Australia and Turkey. If there was one gut-level feeling we came home with, a sense we knew instinctively was from God, it was this: we needed to be there by the end of May. *Six months.* We had six months to get sorted and join Him in Turkey.

Our team of friends rose up in the most endearing of ways. With two hundred or so people now following our journey, we decided to divide the team into seven groups, allocating each group a day of the week. The plan was simple—once a week, we would write an update. We'd tell the team where we were up to, what the challenges were, what had transpired over the past week, and we'd send the same email out, every day for seven days. Each group would pray accordingly. Then we'd write the next email and another week would start.

We will never underestimate the value of our team of friends.

On the financial front, our plan was that within a year or so of living in Turkey our business would bring in enough income to fund our family, but until then, we would need help. Again, our friends were more than willing, quickly supplying our relocation and setup costs. Within three weeks of putting out the invitation, exactly half of the monthly sum we had been told we needed to live on as a foreign family of six in Turkey had also been pledged.

And that's where it plateaued.

What should we do about the other fifty percent? we wondered. *Go elsewhere to seek additional support? Sell our house to fund the shortfall? Approach people we didn't know, about joining us?*

The whisper from God seemed to be, *That's the amount I want you to go with,* and so we thanked our friends, decided we'd work hard to get as many editing clients as we could, and trusted God to bring in the rest.

~

It's a confounding thing to watch your nicely-laid plans unravel before you've even started out. It wasn't until much later that we understood that if we had known what was *really* on God's mind, or that the next two years would find us simply trying to keep up with what God was doing in a city we'd never dreamed of, there's a good chance all hell would have broken loose to prevent it.

The reality was, God was poised for a great work, we were about to be caught up in a story more significant than we had ever imagined, and *we just needed to get over there.* It was only then that we would find out that the city God had prepared for us was not Izmir after all. In fact, it was the one place we had ruled out from the very beginning.

Bursa. *The City of Silk.*

BUT FIRST . . .

Never again will I underestimate the importance of place.

We never anticipated living in the fourth largest city in Turkey, never expected to make a home at the end of the ancient Silk Road.

But we weren't there yet; we were still in Australia, on the other side of the world, sitting at the sturdy rubberwood table that had seen us through the first twelve years of married life, seen highchairs pulled around it, roast dinners served, and birthday cakes set upon it. Schoolwork was done at that table; there, little boys had disassembled mobile phones and folded paper planes. On its surface, freshly bathed babies had been lavishly sprinkled with powder and dressed. And it was at that table that we sat and read an email from our new acquaintances in Izmir.

> We are sorry to say we have had to finish up sooner than we expected. We have just about sold everything in the apartment, and we have finalised the lease. Unfortunately, we will be unable to hold the apartment for you after all.

I don't remember if we sat there in shock or whether we expressed our disbelief aloud. You see, the dining table was one of only a few things left in our house in Australia. In just three weeks, we were due to board an international flight that would take our family of six to live in Turkey.

If there had been one consoling thought as we'd packed a few special belongings and sold everything else, one thought to hold onto as our house in Australia grew emptier by the day, it was that there was an apartment ready for us on the other side of the world—a place that was perfect. It was the anticipation of our new home in Turkey that made this whole thing easier.

Easier to leave.
Easier to let go.
Easier to arrive.

So what do you do when it all evaporates? What do you do with the airplane tickets, and the kids now sleeping on mattresses on the floor, and the bikes being wheeled happily away to new homes? More significantly, what do you do with the strong sense that you need to be there before the end of the month? The month that ends in *three weeks' time?* What do you do with the feeling of disbelief when everything that had seemed so perfect, so like God going ahead and preparing a place, has just evaporated? What happens when it's suddenly all gone and the home you pictured isn't waiting for you after all?

There wasn't time to grapple with what had transpired. The most pressing question to sort out was, *what do we do now? How do you go about reconstructing a life you've just finished carefully and painfully disassembling?* And if you go ahead anyway, *what on earth do you do when you land with four tired children at Istanbul airport?*

The last thing we did at that table was to sit and drink tea together. We ranted awhile. There were tears. Fear nearly took us down. And then, we fell back on what we knew for sure.

'Tell Mummy something that is true,' I'd often said to my girls. I usually asked them the question when they felt scared, or when someone had said something hurtful to them. 'Can you tell Mummy something that is true?' And they'd reach deep into their little storehouse and find something. Anything. *My family loves me. I'm precious. My bed is warm.*

If there's one thing we've learned over the years, it's this: In the midst of trouble, there are always two voices. One is the voice of a liar; the other is the voice of truth.

I leaned back in my chair beside Jeff, slumped, exhausted, confused, and feeling *oh so alone*—because *who? Who in their right mind does what we've just done? Who resigns from the sort of job men dream about? Who gives away the Labrador puppy just when he's snuggled deep into their hearts and stopped destroying the laundry? Who leaves behind half an acre, and a garden wall laid block by block with their own hands, and maple trees that change with the seasons?*

The lies came thick and fast. We're irresponsible. Discontent. Got it wrong. Who do we think we are anyway? You've got *children*, for goodness sake. And parents. *Who does this to their parents?! Who takes someone's grandchildren to the Middle East for who-knows-how-long?*

Oh God.

I poured another cup of tea, and somehow, in the normality of that moment, something true found its way into the mess.

We need to be there by the end of May.

How does one call a feeling true?

Perhaps it had started only as a feeling, but it was a peaceful feeling nonetheless, and it came with a sense of conviction. Deep down we knew that we needed to arrive in Turkey by the end of May. It was the one thought that had remained and, in fact, grown stronger over time, and with it, other things had fallen into place.

A large university in Izmir had invited us to launch our editing company at their international fair in May. Summer began in May, meaning we could use our first few months in Turkey to build relationships and find our feet before the new school year started for our children. May made sense.

We like it when life's details tidily converge.

And so, in the moment of crisis, we held onto our plan. We were still going to Turkey, and we would still leave in just three weeks' time. We would keep believing that the direction we were taking was good, and we would arrive in May, as planned. As quickly as the email had upended our world, our confidence returned. The basics need not be thrown into question. The only real need was to find a new place to live, and we could sort that out in the week or two after we arrived.

Sometimes just pressing ahead brings relief.

～

As it turns out, seven of us landed at Istanbul's Atatürk International Airport. Seven of us, with exactly twenty kilograms of luggage each, not to mention the unseen baggage we all carried with us. My mother-in-law, somewhere along the line, had agreed to join us for the first few weeks of our venture. This was every bit as huge for her as it was for us. After all, she was in her sixties, had only ever travelled as far from Australia as New Zealand, and had as much fear of the Muslim world as I had of selling everything we owned.

I'm sure it's not easy being a mother-in-law to an exhausted wreck.

We got as far as Singapore airport before I stretched her too far. It's not important now, what happened. All I know is that I was tired, Liberty and the backpacks were heavy, and the sadness on my father's face as we had waved goodbye ten hours earlier was tearing me apart.

Bursa, Turkey

Population: 1.8 Million
First Capital of the Ottoman Empire
Historic trading hub at the end of the Silk Road

Yabanci

Turkish: foreigner, stranger, trespasser

Work for the peace and prosperity of the
city to which I have carried you.
Pray to the LORD for it, because if the
city prospers, you also will prosper.
Jeremiah 29:7

The First Year

1. Unexpected Comfort

I thought it would feel exhilarating, our first night in our new country. I thought that simply landing in Istanbul would make our spirits soar— that finally being in Turkey together would get us all exclaiming to one another about how *we'd made it!* About how we'd arrived, and a whole new wonderful life was beginning! I assumed the children would see the famous ruins of the city walls or the medieval castle on the hilltop and beg to be allowed to get out and explore.

What I didn't expect was the hollow in my heart. It never crossed my mind that all of us would feel so *absolutely drained.*

We collected our bags, purchased visas, and finally proceeded to the metro platform where we boarded an express train to the far side of the city. We had connected with another Australian family before we left and were thankful for their offer to spend our first night at their apartment. *'Our city is only a five-hour bus trip from Istanbul. Let's meet at the bus terminal, and you can travel with us back to our home in Bursa.'*

Bursa, of all places. The one city we had ruled out right from the start. But that's exactly where we were heading. The generous hospitality and familiar accents of our hosts had come as a relief, and after one night with them, we would move our family across town where another couple had kindly offered us the use of their apartment for a few weeks at least while we caught our breath and figured out Plan B.

We've always said with hopeful exuberance that if Plan A doesn't work out, Plan B will leave it for dead. Regardless, we arrived at the bus terminal on the outskirts of Bursa devoid of any emotion. Plan A was a lovely furnished apartment by the sea in Izmir where a thriving expat community was ready to welcome us, and now that it was gone, we couldn't imagine any kind of Plan B, let alone a better one.

Why on earth didn't someone just call for taxis?

We tried to board the local bus, but the driver wouldn't let us on. 'Too many bags, and they're too big,' he shrugged. We watched other travellers heave their luggage into the bus, and plonked ourselves down on the sidewalk, hoping we'd fare better on the next service in twenty minutes.

'They never do that,' my newly-met friend commented.

Well they just did, didn't they? I forced a smile but kept the thought to myself. *Obviously, this city is not for us. Did the bus driver have any idea we'd spent the last month tearing ourselves away from everything and everyone we love? Did he stop for a moment to ask how many hours the children had been awake, how many miles we'd just travelled?*

It was forty-eight hours after leaving our house in Australia that we finally arrived, and finally, there we were, in a small apartment belonging to a family we'd scarcely met. I wish we'd had it in us to be more sociable—and I wish we'd known in advance that they loved cats, because our ten-year old son, Eric, started wheezing and watering within five minutes of being there, I couldn't find his allergy medication, and in the end, he and Jeff went elsewhere to sleep for the night.

Maybe it's a blessing we were too ruined to care. Emotionally, physically, mentally—we had nothing left. I took the girls into the cosy little room that had been prepared for us and shut the door.

Oh the starkness of that moment.

After two or more days of travel, after all the goodbyes and the packing and the flights and the hauling of our lives across the globe, we were there, although truthfully, the girls had no idea where we were. How does a parent convey to a two-year-old that she has just traversed the world? What does *one* mile mean to a four-year-old, let alone *nine thousand* of them? I tucked the girls into bed and gently stroked their hair.

Oh, God.

I hoped that simple act comforted them, as once it comforted me.

And then I did the only thing that came to mind. I pulled back the curtains and sighed, '*thank you,*' because there, outside the window of our sixth-floor apartment, rising above mosques and minarets and balconies so unfamiliar to us, was the moon. The very same moon that had shone in the sky above us just the other night.

'Look at that, Vangie! See that moon, Liberty?!' I said. 'That's the same moon that was in the sky in Australia, and now it's here with us, and soon it will go back to where Nana and Grandad are again! The moon is the same everywhere we go.'

Whether the thought orientated our girls that night, I do not know, but at least in some small way, we were comforted. After all the upheaval, one thing had stayed the same. Maybe we were still in the same universe after all.

2. Moving Across Town

All it took was a good night's sleep for our enthusiasm to return. Jeff and Eric turned up early and we all regrouped around the breakfast table, lovingly laid out for us by our kind hosts. Joseph, our eight-year-old son, had already made friends with their boy, and as we thanked them for their hospitality, we promised that we would get together again sometime soon.

It was a mission, between six flights of stairs and a tiny elevator, but we left the boys and Jeff to the task of hauling suitcases, and soon a super-sized taxi arrived to pick us up.

The apartment we had arranged to live in for the next few weeks was situated in the old part of the city where the houses were built many centuries ago and still clung to the side of Mount Uludağ.[1] The streets on that side of town were narrow and winding and cobbled and the taxi driver honked his horn as we approached each corner because there was no way to see whether another car or taxi or dolmuş[2] might be coming in the opposite direction. But of course, every vehicle was doing the same; the air was filled with constant honking and beeping, and no one seemed to slow down or take notice anyway.

Before long, we all decided this was actually fun—the children sitting on our knees, Grandma holding on for dear life, our luggage packed in tight and Jeff nodding with great interest as the taxi driver talked the whole way in Turkish without seeming to realise that none of us could understand a word he was saying.

But we made it, and by the way the people on the streets looked at us, it was clear they were completely unaccustomed to seeing a foreign family in their part of town. We smiled politely, found the key exactly where we had been told it was, and the boys went to work once again, this time lugging one suitcase after another up a dark concrete stairwell all the way to the fourth floor, where we opened the door to the apartment of another expat couple, and stepped into what was for them, and now would be for us, a little sanctuary in this new land.

---

1 Pronounced: oo-lu-dah

2 Minibus with side-opening doors, used for public transport

A note lay on the kitchen table, and as soon as we saw it, we laughed.

Welcome, dear friends!
There's ice-cream for you in the freezer,
Love, Randy and Bonnie.

The children ran to the freezer, opened the door, and to their absolute delight, found tubs of ice-cream of all different flavours, packed in tight—litres of comfort food right there! In a moment, the tension dropped away, the fun returned, and as we scooped mounds of ice-cream into a bowl for each of us and watched the children snuggle next to Grandma on the couch, Jeff and I looked at each other with relief. For the first time in weeks, it was just us again, our little family, sitting in a lounge room, eating ice-cream.

Our hearts went out to Randy and Bonnie with profound appreciation. Months earlier when we visited Bursa, we had met this delightful couple. Jeff and I had joked with Randy about his love for ice-cream, but now we understood. After the huge effort of simply getting across town, the simple joy of eating a bowl of ice-cream brought us together and made us feel as if maybe we could pull off this whole crazy venture after all.

3. Old City Teacups

By our third day in Turkey, we were all in the mood to explore. What we didn't foresee, however, was that the moment we ventured out of our apartment, every one of our senses would spring to life; with so much to take in all at once, we felt as if we could literally burst. Everything was suddenly intriguing—the way shop owners called out to each other across the square, the way the cross-now signs started counting down the minute they turned green, how some women were covered from head to toe in black, while others wore skinny jeans and fashionable scarves . . .

Later in the week, I tried to capture it in my journal:

We've come to a country where absolutely everything is vibrant and exotic and new! Perhaps over time we will feel the heaviness that so many people describe when they live here, but right now, it's a sensory feast.

The Islamic call to prayer sounds haunting, compelling, ancient, and here we are, right in the middle of it all! We walk the stone streets, delightfully uneven yet masterfully laid—roads that have seen camels and carriages and the passing of conquerors and traders and a multitude of generations come and go—and suddenly we have a heightened sense of our place in history.

Children play and we are tuning into the syllables they use, to the sound of foreign words when they are shouted out in the streets. We notice the way two little boys stroll along like old men, their arms draped across each other's shoulders in this city of four million, without a parent in sight.

I'm fascinated by the speeding taxis and their ability to navigate blind corners and the strange but simple act of people signalling for a dolmuş. On the street, diesel fumes combine with the smell of fresh bread, and it doesn't matter if I look up, down or around, I'm at capacity, I'm full, I'm taking it all in and my soul is . . . well, joyful! I feel like a child in a new world, and I can hardly contain it!

We passed a little basement shop today. It looked like a quilt-maker's store because there was an old iron sewing machine inside, calico wool obviously sorted into grades, and a large set of scales. Rather than buying a factory-produced, packaged quilt, it seems here you simply select the quality and quantity of filling, have it weighed out and costed accordingly, then wait for it to be hand-made to your exact specifications.

I'm intrigued by the idea that the old man at the sewing machine has probably spent his entire working life making quilts like this, by hand, one at a time, each one unique, there in that little shop. Is he thumbing his nose at big industry, at mass production and faceless middlemen? His workshop is half-way above ground and half below, which means his windowsill is at the level of the footpath.

And that's what made me chuckle, because there, on the outside windowsill, right beside the flow of people walking down the street, sat a dainty glass tea-cup and saucer, with a small sip of tea remaining, and a fine silver teaspoon resting beside it.

It was like a scene from Alice in Wonderland. Why would a tea glass be there, of all places? Who left it there? Who stood in the main thoroughfare and sipped their tea with all the finesse as if they were at home in their own kitchen?! I was curious and baffled and amused all at once, but no one else seemed to bat an eyelid. And then, the moment which made me suspect we really have landed in another world entirely and might never be sure of anything again . . .

A boy of about fourteen, carrying a polished silver tray in his upturned *palm, walked briskly toward us, and, barely skipping a step, reached down, picked up the cup, saucer and spoon from the windowsill all in one flawless motion, placed it on his tray alongside three or four other glasses, and disappeared around a corner.*

And right now, I know that this life we have on earth is amazing. I don't know if I've seen it all, but this feels enough—this procession of transient moments, quirky and vibrant, where every corner and every culture seem to hold so much wonder.

I've had my head around my own little world for so long that barely anything surprised me or took my breath away, but suddenly we're here with the fresh realisation that our souls are made with far more capacity than we've realised, and for the first time since we arrived, we are starting to imagine the days to come.

4. Settling In

Though we had been in Turkey less than a week, we were acutely aware that the clock was already ticking—by the end of summer we needed to be in our own home and have the children ready to commence the new school year. It was time to lay aside our incredulity that the place we thought was all lined up, had fallen through, and to begin the search for another home. And so, we began making plans for Jeff to take a trip down to Izmir.

Only that plan too was disrupted, because the next day, Jeff woke up sometime during the early morning call to prayer with a strange but very clear phrase in his mind:

'*I've uncovered your feet.*'

We had learned over the years to discern God's voice amidst the cacophony of other thoughts that clamoured for space in our minds, and this was unmistakably Him. But, having woken not only to some rather cryptic words, but also to four cooped-up children, a still somewhat jetlagged mother and a wife ready to make plans and take on the world, there was no time for Jeff-style contemplation. Breakfast was on the table, everyone was tripping over suitcases, and Randy and Bonnie's two-bedroom apartment was already feeling too confined for the seven of us.

And then the phone rang.

It was the Australian woman who had met us in Istanbul. 'I was talking with my real estate agent this morning,' she said, 'and she has some houses for you to look at in case you might want to stay here in Bursa. If you like, I can come over with her this morning and take you to see them.'

The tinge of hope in her voice was the only thing that made me hesitate. You see, when Jeff and I had visited Turkey the previous year to get a feel for where we might live, there were only two cities we had instantly ruled out: Istanbul, because simply crossing the road with four young children could prove life-threatening, and Bursa, because . . .

5. Six Months Earlier

Before moving to Turkey, Jeff and I had flown over for a visit to make connections, figure out where we might live, and to see if we really did want to follow through with the idea of living there after all. It was a short trip, and now, after two weeks, we were getting ready to head back home. At the suggestion of a friend, we had decided to break the nine-hour bus trip from Izmir to Istanbul with a stopover in Bursa. There we would spend the night with a couple of American retirees who had lived in Bursa for a number of years.

We were travelling light—just a backpack each—and so, as we stepped off the bus in Bursa that afternoon, we immediately began looking for a sign that might indicate the direction to the city centre. Within seconds we were approached by a young man with an intent look in his eyes but a soft half-smile on his lips. 'Can I help you?' he asked. We showed him our hosts' address and he pointed us confidently in the direction we should go. 'Go up that hill,' he said. 'You will pass a covered market, but keep going straight until you come to the square with the statue in the middle . . .'

The young man spoke impeccable English; he had the vocabulary of a native speaker—nothing like the fumbled attempts to communicate that we had experienced so far on our trip. We shook hands and introduced ourselves. 'Jeff and Anya,' we said. He smiled in return. 'Pleased to meet you. My name is Ilir.'

'You're *Albanian*?' I asked, absolutely taken off guard, yet completely thrilled at the possibility. The name Ilir came from the ancient land of Illyricum—modern day Albania. 'Yes,' he replied with a large smile, 'I am here in Bursa to study theology at the university.'

Chance meetings mean different things to different people but for me, any mention of Albania, and we're practically family. You see, when I was seventeen, my parents had pretty much done what we were about to do—they moved our family across the world to live, not in Turkey, but Albania. Twenty years earlier, they too had sold everything, said their goodbyes, and joined the first wave of foreigners to enter Albania and bless a nation of people who were just coming out of decades of isolation from the rest of the world.

But it wasn't the right time or place to talk; more intercity buses were rolling in—the country, it seemed, was travelling on this particular day—and so we shook hands again and as we said goodbye, Ilir handed us his phone number. 'Call if you need anything,' he said, and then disappeared back into the crowd he'd emerged from.

There are times you wonder at how small the world is, at how we are all just a few degrees removed from one another once we begin to share our stories. Maybe this was more than a chance meeting. We didn't know. Still, we had been on the lookout for unforeseen yet heart-warming connections like this one, and as we turned away, Jeff and I half laughed, half exclaimed at the absurdity that the first person we should meet in Bursa was an Albanian theology student.

But the lightness of our steps and the grin on our faces didn't last. Within minutes Jeff and I found ourselves trying to keep from being separated, as the flow of pedestrians walking up the hill became a tight mass of humanity, all pressing against each other, leaning forward with determination and intent. To avoid being jostled about, we grabbed each other's hands, pressed in close together, and kept in step with the crowd. We had no idea where they were all headed, and the fact that it was early on a Friday afternoon baffled us. *Most people should be at work, shouldn't they?* But they weren't at work, and as we moved steadily towards the city centre, the atmosphere became increasingly tense.

A passing fear crossed my mind, one which I didn't have enough time or breath to articulate to Jeff. 'Where were all the women?' We were in the middle of a pack of men, obviously headed somewhere, for some reason; the intention in the air was palpable.

And then we saw the knives. Men, sharpening knives, were seated behind low tables off to the edge of the road. Men were purchasing knives. Some were carrying knives. And yet, there was no apparent feeling of violence, no sense of revenge or hatred. We had no idea of the scene we had stepped into until that night, when high on the hill of the city, Jeff and I lay in bed listening silently as one minaret after another began sounding the call to prayer followed by long, impassioned, Arabic words. Our American hosts had filled us in—we had arrived in Bursa on the eve of the annual sacrifice festival.

For the first time since coming to Turkey, we felt the presence of fear. What was going on outside our window? As the haunting summons from the mosques continued through the night, sleep evaded us. Whatever this religious festival was, the intensity was palpable. Our unaccustomed minds only had televised journalistic scenes to draw on, and none of them were reassuring.

The next morning, we decided we wouldn't delay—we appreciated the bed for the night and the chance to meet this wonderful couple, but we would continue on our way to Istanbul as soon as possible. *Good idea*, our hosts agreed, because later today, the slaughtering of animals would begin. All over Turkey, they told us, blood would flow; it wasn't a pretty time to be exploring a new city, besides, it could be difficult to get a bus ticket. This was the holiest festival in Turkey, and everyone was travelling as people from all over the country returned to their hometowns before the four-day holiday period began. On top of that, our friends explained, the sacrifice coincided with the end of the Hajj, and people who had made the pilgrimage to Mecca that year, were also making their way home. It seemed everyone was on the move; those who hadn't arrived at their village or city the previous evening would be taking whatever transport they could to get home by midday.

We took their advice, left for the bus terminal while it was still early, and with no small sense of relief, boarded a coach to Istanbul. The tension of the previous night had left us wrung out. Safely in our seats and mercifully out of Bursa, Jeff and I leaned against each other and before long, began to doze off. . .

. . . and then, suddenly, we were jolted awake, only to find that the bus came to a complete halt, right in the middle of a seven-lane highway. We tried to orient ourselves. We must have been asleep for a while, we figured, because ahead of us on the side of the road was a large green sign: Welcome to Istanbul. That perked us up. Soon we would be at our destination, where we would take a shower, wash off the nasty Bursa feel, and enjoy being in this incredible city for one last night. But why had we stopped? For that matter, why were all seven lanes of traffic, stopped?

That's when we saw the bull—*and* the men trying to wrestle the bull, because for some reason, the bull didn't want to be killed. Just why a group of men decided to sacrifice a bull right there on the highway, was beyond us. What was apparent, however, was that this particular sacrifice wasn't going according to plan. The men were plunging their knives into the beast, determined to finish the job they'd started, while trying to grab the rope that was meant to tether the animal but had now broken loose, and all the while, they were shouting—deep, panicked shouts—clearly desperate to keep the bull from charging through the barrier and into the holiday traffic.

Only it wasn't working. The bull was injured and angry; it was either going to turn on the men or run for its life right onto the highway, and all we could do was silently look on.

Eventually, the men won, the bull fell at the side of the road, our driver shifted the bus into gear, and the journey resumed. It was at that point we decided that Bursa was not for us; in fact, we would happily dismiss the entire experience of the past twenty-four hours from our minds.

~

Crazy, then, that now we were back in Bursa, back in our friends' apartment with the whole family this time, and my mind struggled to focus as I covered the phone with my hand and whispered to Jeff, '*Ros, the Australian lady, wants to show us some houses.*'

He shrugged. Sure. Whatever. Other than booking a bus ticket for his trip to Izmir, we didn't have any plans for the day, and if someone else wanted to take some initiative for us right now, that was fine by us. '*Why not?*' I replied, thanking my friend for her kindness.

Grandma had decided that a day at home would suit her well, so it was just the six of us who piled into the car with Ros and the real estate agent. 'I've got three houses to show you,' the agent said as we juggled children on our knees and headed off towards a suburb on the other side of town. *Conveniently close to Dave and Ros*, I realised. I braced myself for the inevitable disappointment we would have to inflict on their little family by the end of the day.

It was lovely to look, thanks so much. No, we're so sorry, but we're not staying in Bursa. We'd love to live here, of course, for your sake especially, but we just can't. There's nothing here for our kids. It's not the right environment for our business. Besides, we don't like Bursa. The people are rude. The city is ugly. Far too many mosques. No one speaks English. But we totally admire you guys; everyone agrees this is a tough gig. We feel for your kids too—we do hope they haven't got their hopes up. But it's been great to look around and we'll be sure to visit often . . .

My mental speech-writing was interrupted by our arrival at house number one, and so were my presumptions, because there, just over the lovely brick fence, through a low, wrought-iron gate leading to a pathway lined with freshly manicured lawns, was a cherry tree laden with fruit. To the left and right of the path were identical four-story townhouses, and before we'd all spilled out of the car and made it inside the gate (because our two little girls had squealed with joy and taken off towards the swing set just across the lane) before we'd all recovered ourselves and reminded ourselves that yes, this was still Turkey, still Bursa, and maybe there *was* more to the country than a bunch of dull, concrete apartments, a man with the kindest face in the world emerged from the house on the left, proceeded down the path, climbed up into the leafy tree and started picking cherries for our children.

What happened to the neighbours not liking foreigners? What about the time it takes for people to warm up to newcomers? Or the holding at arm's length we'd been warned to expect? And that smile! That grandfatherly smile. Oh, my heart.

But we were here to see a house, so with a '*thank-you*,' and a '*no, children, don't climb the tree just yet*,' we waited as the agent sorted through her keys and unlocked the front door.

I like wake-up-happy homes, and this one was lovely. I stood there taking it all in. *Clean. Fresh. Full of light. New kitchen. Beautiful wooden flooring. Marble staircase winding its way up one floor, up another, and that view—out over the whole city—but wait, there's a downstairs too—a fourth level just below ground, a big wide room with another bathroom. Yes, a Turkish squat toilet right at the entrance—that's important for guests, and . . .*

There were ten duplexes all the same as each other, positioned in pairs around a grassy square. Jeff and I glanced at each other. Neither of us wanted to be the first to say, 'What do you think?' because we weren't seriously thinking of renting a house in Bursa, *were we*? But now this house was messing with all our preconceptions, and the truth is, we didn't have to ask each other anyway, because the agent, with Ros at her elbow translating every word, was doing her job well.

'*What do you think?*' she asked.

Of course, there was another couple looking at the property; we'd need to move fast if we wanted it. *Places like this don't come up often. It only came to market last night. Yes, we can talk about the price. Why don't you come back to my office for some tea?*

And that's how Jeff and I found ourselves sitting on a nondescript footpath in the outer suburbs of Bursa, sipping tea from the same dainty glasses we'd seen everywhere by now, while Ros and the agent kept our children entertained inside the office.

'What do you think?' 'No, you first, what do you think?'

We stated the obvious. *It's nice. Great to have a playground right there. The neighbour was so lovely. It's way cheaper than Izmir. But . . .* and then, as we were about to rehearse the reasons we were not even considering Bursa, because, remember, we were going to live in a lovely, moderate, Western-style city on the Aegean Sea, five hours from here where there were plenty of expats and schools for our kids and even an international church, Jeff remembered the words from that morning.

'*I've uncovered your feet.*'

And in a flash, we knew what the Lord was saying.

Centuries ago, a young woman crept onto a threshing floor where men slept after a full day's work of bringing in the harvest. It was a simple but bold plan, but she was willing to follow the advice: '*When you find him, lie down and uncover his feet.*' The owner of the threshing floor and all the fields teeming with grain would then wake, and that would be her opportunity to *ask him a favour*.

Oh my goodness.

Our hearts and minds grasped the sweetness of the message. God wasn't telling us what to do. He wasn't saying we shouldn't go ahead with our intention to live in Izmir. He was simply asking us a favour.

'*Would you do me a favour, and live here in Bursa?*'

If he had told us to stay, we'd have obeyed, of course, but this was so much gentler.

Would you? For me? Would you do me a favour and settle in Bursa?

When he put it like that, it was easy.

You, God? Asking us a favour? Of course! That would be a pleasure.

But I like a deal, and the Lord knows that too, so we went inside and asked the agent if she might be able to negotiate a better price for us on the rent. 'Sure,' she replied, and picking up the phone, she called the owner, talked in Turkish for a few minutes, and, came back to us. 'Yes, no problem,' she said, 'he has agreed to drop the rent by two hundred lira per month.'

And that is how it happened. We signed the contract, though the only section we could make out since the whole thing was in Turkish was the address and the price, and then, still slightly bewildered at what we had just done, we shook hands with the agent and turned to leave. 'Oh!' she said as if she couldn't believe she had forgotten to mention it. 'My son has his circumcision party this weekend! Please, we'd love you to come!' and she scribbled the address and time on a scrap of paper.

Our enthusiasm quickly returned. 'Of course! We'd love to!' we replied. We might as well make that our default response, we figured, since this was obviously the day for it.

The agent offered to drive us back to our apartment, and as we made our way across town once again, we caught our breath in surprise. *Had our little family just stepped into a completely new city?!* Suddenly everything looked different—the people seemed happy, the sky was clear and blue, we noticed how clean and cared-for the streets were . . . and above all, we had a wonderful sense that we belonged, that *this* was our city. We were at home in Bursa.

6. Sunday

And then Sunday rolled around—our first Sunday in Turkey, and let's just be real, it was a disaster. Granted, we were still recovering from jetlag, seven people in a tiny apartment is high pressure, and the surprisingly hostile visit we had from two of the local church leaders that week had put us all on edge. Despite the population of nearly two million people, there was only one Christian church in Bursa where about forty people, as far as we knew, attended. Now, the rubber was about to hit the road.

We tried to dismiss the nagging reminder that in Izmir we could have easily slotted into an international church where we could at least worship in Turkish *and* English. But we were not in Izmir; we were in Bursa, and now it was Sunday and we would go to church, try to follow along in Turkish as best we could, and at least we could make friends with whoever the few local Christians were who attended.

To our credit, we did manage to get everyone dressed and ready to go. It was when we stepped out the front door that all hell seemed to break loose—confusion and fear and a great weight of homesickness seemed to be waiting for us on the doorstep, and in an instant, we all unravelled. Getting a young family out the door at any time is a feat for sure. But this was different. This *felt like* opposition, like some invisible force had come against us, causing us all to fret and squabble and break down in every imaginable way.

We tried to push through, but we couldn't even get a taxi to stop for us that day, and when it became obvious that we'd get to church awkwardly late anyway, we gave up. Better to be gentle on ourselves, we figured, and maybe we'd try again next week.

But now we were left with a question hovering in our minds. Was that a strange, unfamiliar sort of attack? Or could it possibly be that it was God, for some reason, holding us back?

Lord, help us.

We just presumed that we should attend the church wherever we lived. Why wouldn't we? But why did we feel so uneasy? Why had the leaders seemed so fearful? Should we come alongside them and help in some way? We hadn't factored in the possibility of bringing our family to live in Turkey and *not* attending a church, but really? Would we need to fight just to get there each week? Was this the sort of thing that Christians in Turkey were up against? Was this why churches around the country faced so much difficulty? Or were we missing something? For now, we had no idea.

7. The Mosque

If only Sunday had been a glitch along the way. Instead, it turned out to be just a small taste of what was to come. Over time, we would become more attuned to the invisible dynamics of our city, but in the meantime, it was a new week, and with five days until we could move into our new home, and Jeff's mum returning to Australia soon, we decided to make the most of our time together. When Monday morning rolled around, we decided we would get out and about and explore the city properly.

What better place to start, we figured, than with a stroll through the park, an ice-cream for us all, and then a quick peek inside the historic little mosque at the edge of the city square?—which is why we found ourselves standing under a towering 16th-century minaret where, like good, respectful tourists, we removed our shoes at the ornate entrance and quietly made our way inside. Jeff and the boys found a spot towards the back of the room and stood watching as a couple of men in front of them adopted one posture after another, alternately pressing their foreheads to the ground and then standing again as they recited their prayers.

Women, of course, were not allowed in the same space as the men. Their space was upstairs on a cramped and dull balcony with a curtain hanging from the handrail to ensure they were completely out of sight of the men below. I felt conflicted—the sense of unity among women in this culture was strong, yet I was provoked by the second-class treatment, the segregation that was implied, even among family members.

But we knew the system, and so, leaving Jeff and the boys behind, my mother-in-law, the girls and I made our way up the tight little staircase to view the mosque from the platform above. Only a few other women were there, one with her head lowered in prayer, and two others who sat cross-legged, quietly chatting as a baby girl crawled near them on the carpeted floor.

I knelt between Vangie and Grandma, holding Liberty in my arms, her blonde little head nestled under my chin. *'Precious child,'* I thought for at least the thousandth time, *'she's an absolute angel.'*

And right then, as if in violent disagreement, Liberty let out a horrific scream, arched her whole body back with unusual force, then flung her little head forward, hitting my cheekbone with an audible crack.

With Liberty's screams reverberating around the mosque, and my hand over her mouth to quiet her, I desperately tried to navigate the pair of us back down the staircase; and then, I felt it too—it was fear, but it was unlike anything I had experienced before. Our tiny daughter was shrieking now—only she wasn't hurt, she wasn't throwing a tantrum, all I could tell was that she was *terrified*. I could see it in her eyes. Crouching at the mosque door, trying to get my shoes on and hold Liberty, who was now thrashing about, I was thankful that Grandma had been there to gather up Vangie.

'*What happened?*' she asked.

'*Nothing,*' I replied, '*nothing at all. She was just quiet and still one moment and then . . .*' We looked at each other in helpless solidarity.

I was aware of the spectacle we must have been as we headed for home. Liberty screamed the whole way, like a child in a nightmare. Grandma was out of breath as we tried to hurry back up the winding streets. Jeff was carrying Vangie and calling the boys to stay close and keep up, and I was holding Liberty, whispering 'we love you, Liberty, we love you,' into her ear—but there was no letting up—her eyes were wild with fright, the screaming was causing everyone concern, and the swelling in my face was becoming more pronounced and painful with every step. We needed to get home, away from the mass of people.

With no way to pacify our tiny daughter, halfway up the hill we gave in and waved to the nearest taxi. Arriving back at the apartment, we shut the door behind us with unanimous relief. *What on earth had provoked the terror we were witnessing?* we wondered. We lay our not-even-two-year-old daughter on the bed and I began singing as I stroked her writhing, thrashing body.

'*How sweet the name of Jesus sounds . . .*'

It was a familiar tune, one that I had often sung over the children as they drifted off to sleep. But today this was no bedtime lullaby. Today we were dealing with an enemy we could not see, and I was determined that as I sang, the terror that had gripped Liberty should be driven away.

'*. . . it soothes his sorrows, heals his wounds and drives away all fear.*'

Liberty was slowly starting to settle when Jeff came into the room to take over, and as I turned to close the door behind him, I saw him kneel beside the bed, cradle our little girl in his arms, and begin to pray over her. Finally, Liberty fell into a deep sleep, and Jeff emerged, looking like a man who had fought an unseen battle and won, albeit in a wearying kind of way.

Our eyes had been opened to how sensitive our children were to the unseen realm but there was no time to stand blinking in the glare. Acutely aware of how foolish we had been to think we could simply walk into any and every environment unaffected, we tucked the children into their beds, bathed the family in prayer once again and settled down for the evening. We needed to turn our thoughts to other things—like furniture and appliances and getting set up. By the end of the week, we would move into our new home in Bursa.

8. The Market

As the sun rose the following morning, I woke up, aware that the socket of my right eye was throbbing, but unaware of the huge green bruise that had emerged overnight. I gasped as I looked in the mirror. *How could I ever go out in public like this?* I looked for all the world like a battered wife. This was no way to introduce ourselves to people out there! I didn't know what to do—the swelling and bruising glared even through layers of makeup, and it wasn't going to fade in a hurry. Life would have to go on.

So it was that we made our way back to the city centre in search of the second-hand furniture market we had heard of. With an entire house to set up, we figured a one-stop market would be a great help.

Eventually, we stumbled across a few streets lined with open-fronted stalls, all packed with a random selection of white goods and sofas, coffee tables, and small appliances, most looking like they'd been in circulation for decades. We walked from store to store overwhelmed with the decisions we needed to make so soon after our arrival—and underwhelmed at what was on offer.

The other issue was, should we focus on making our home a familiar place, a sort of sanctuary for our family, and therefore furnish it much as we would back home, or should we embrace a more Turkish style—which right now could mean anything from ornate Ottoman grandeur to gaudy communist-era bling to mass-produced Chinese imports? In any case, nothing especially caught our eye, and after an hour of sifting through stalls, one thing was clear—we would need to pull together whatever smattering of Turkish language we could and get ready to haggle.

'Come back tomorrow,' said one helpful vendor when he saw we were not ready to buy. 'Every day is different.' And we did. The following day we returned, only to spend yet another morning sitting in crude little stores, drinking endless glasses of black tea in the hope that our decisiveness would eventually catch up with us. In the end, we purchased a few small items which we could carry home on the bus, but now we were getting concerned. If we were going to have beds to sleep in or kitchen appliances to cook with anytime soon, we needed to fast-track our shopping.

On the third day, we had a breakthrough. A local doctor had just sold a household full of furniture to one of the vendors, we were in the right place at the right time! There, being unloaded into the store in front of us, was everything we needed—a fridge and freezer, washing machine, couches and a table and chairs, all in perfect condition. We couldn't have asked for an easier answer; a hundred little decisions had suddenly been rolled into one, and after a few minutes of haggling, we settled the deal over yet another round of tea.

'Can you point me to an internet café?' Jeff asked. 'Our phones aren't registered here yet, and I need to transfer some money from Australia.'

'No problem,' the store owner said, 'come with me,' and soon we were all weaving our way through the market—Liberty in our arms, Grandma keeping a tight grip on Vangie, and Eric and Joseph scooting in and out of the crowd until we came to the 'internet café' which turned out to be just a man with a laptop. Soon Jeff was perched on a stool between precariously stacked kitchen appliances and mattresses leaning against the walls, logging onto the computer of a total stranger.

Jeff smiled as he opened an archaic version of Windows, that is, until he realised that he needed to work with something else he'd never seen before—a Turkish keyboard. The next half an hour was a study in bewilderment as Jeff grappled with unfamiliar symbols and letters and tried to find the apparently missing keys he needed to simply access our bank account. Eventually, our Australian dollars were converted into a huge wad of Turkish lira, which felt like a momentous feat.

With everything paid for and the shop owner looking like he had hit the jackpot, we turned our attention to how we would transport the furniture to our new home. Again, the locals had it sorted. Without a word of consultation with us, one vendor nodded to another, who nodded to yet another, and thirty seconds later a truck emerged from who-knows-where, edged its way into the crowded market, pulled to a stop beside us, and suddenly a group of men gathered around and began piling our furniture, in no logical fashion, high onto the tray at the back.

We decided to hold our comments about how perilous the whole thing looked. Apparently, the amount of rope was what really mattered, and once everything was tied down, Jeff and our two enthusiastic boys promptly squashed into the cab beside the driver. It was time to deliver the spoils to our new home.

We had learned a few numbers in Turkish for the purposes of shopping at the market; we hadn't however, foreseen the need to give directions. 'No problem,' the driver said, making exaggerated gestures with his arms. 'Sol! Sa! Sol is right. Sa is left. Good, let's go!'

With a heaping plate of nachos and salsa pictured in his mind, Jeff led the way, Sol, Sa, Sol, Sa; and with that, our family was well on our way to setting up our home in Bursa.

9. Filling a Home

As it turned out, buying a truckload of furniture from the second-hand market wasn't anywhere near what it took to fill a house. I started praying, 'Lord, you don't leave empty spaces. You fill them. I'm trusting You now to fill our house. We've made a good start, but it still feels empty . . .' The next day, I heard there was an Ikea on the edge of town.

Thank God. Literally. Ikea we knew. Ikea we could work with; it made us realise how comforting a simple thing like a familiar brand can be to an expat. And so, after a sparse first night in our new home, we traipsed the family three or four blocks down the hill to the main road, where we caught a bus labelled 'otogar,' and forty minutes later arrived at the bus terminal on the edge of town, where Ikea had set up one of their typically enormous stores.

Walking through the doors of Ikea was as close to the feeling of coming home as we had experienced yet. The kid's playground at the entrance was a relief. The café at the top of the elevator was a relief. The all-your-household-needs-under-one-roof was a relief as well.

We bought each of the kids a free-refill drink and began winding our way through the different sections. Kitchen utensils–check. Chopping board–check. Water glasses–check.

Never underestimate what it takes to start over from scratch: pegs to hang out the laundry, a mirror for the bathroom, plates, saucepans, two folding tables—one for the kitchen and one for the balcony. . .

We would keep adding to the list for weeks to come, but the immediate issue was how to transport the day's purchases home. After three hours in-store, we loaded the kids with bags and, carrying a couple of flat packs each, hefted our stash onto the bus, gave our fellow passengers apologetic looks as they squeezed around us, then disembarked, coaxed ourselves back up the hill with our boxes, and eventually arrived home, elated and weary.

For all the effort, it didn't amount to much; once we'd put it all away into cupboards and unpacked the few pieces of furniture it became obvious that we still had a long way to go. Houses in Turkey come without fixtures of any kind—no kitchen cabinets, no oven or dishwasher, no curtains, no showerheads or towel racks. Our list seemed to grow as quickly as it shrunk. *A couple more beds, drawers for the clothes, mats for the front entrance, saucepans, light fittings . . .* we were far from finished.

It was the following week when, eager to move beyond furnishing a house, we made one last trek across town. By this time, we were on a first-name basis with nearly all the staff—in fact, the next time we walked through the double-door entrance, a young sales assistant recognised us and ran over to us, holding a shoe in his hand. 'Hello!' he said, obviously pleased to see us. 'We've been waiting for you to come back! Is this Liberty's shoe?'

Indeed, it was, and that greeting was enough to infuse us with momentum for the task ahead. With fresh enthusiasm, we offloaded Liberty to the now-familiar play area and picked out the larger items we were needing. *Another couch. A hall cupboard. Wardrobes.* We were on a mission to get the job finished, and this time, as we made our way through the checkout, an assistant took us aside.

'*Around the back of the building there are men who have trucks,*' he half-whispered. '*You can use Ikea delivery, but it is very expensive. Those men will take you and your parcels to your home for twenty lira.*'

If only we'd known that a week earlier! To our relief, the trucks were there, just as we'd been told. Seeing our family laden with trolleys of long, heavy, flat-packed boxes caused a momentary stir among the drivers. Who would have the good luck of a large, final delivery at the end of the day?

We chose one of the mid-sized vehicles, pushed and prodded until everything was in nice and tight, waved as Jeff and the boys clambered into the driver's cabin to ensure they could help unload at the other end, and with no spare seats for the rest of us, I took the girls by the hand and went in search of a taxi.

It was eight o'clock by the time we tucked the children into bed that night. And then, Jeff and I had what seemed like a good idea. *'Let's put something together before we go to bed.'* This was Ikea furniture after all, and assembling it, we figured, was best not done with four children in the mix. Besides, why leave our purchases sitting in boxes for days? We might as well get started while there was still some evening left.

So we did.

We laid out, in neat little piles on our lounge-room floor, the multitude of components that would make up our buffet cabinet.

Side A. Side B. Top Shelf. Bottom shelf. Middle Shelf. The list went on and on. *Little screws. Medium screws. Long screws. Cam lock screws. Washers. Hinges. Rails. Glass door 1. Glass door 2. Drawer handles. Small, medium and large wood dowels . . .*

We set about the task methodically, but somewhere into the eight-page assembly manual with its arrows and diagrams and tiny one-line instructions repeated in a multitude of languages, we came unstuck. Between us, it took every limb to simply hold the structure together as one of us turned the allen-key.

This particular piece of furniture had been a last-minute purchase, a feel-good buy after all the must-haves. After carefully carrying my six fine-china cup, saucer and plate sets in our hand luggage across the world, they deserved to be put on display, I figured, and a lovely teak cabinet with glass shelves and doors would be just the thing.

We had gone through the checkout without even considering paying the extra fifty lira for the piece to be assembled for us. Why, when we could do it ourselves? By midnight, though, when we realised that we were only halfway there, fifty lira seemed a scant amount to pay. 'Best not to calculate the saving as an hourly rate,' we told ourselves. 'Best to keep at it. Carefully. There's nothing worse than getting to two in the morning only to realise you've got your side pieces upside down and now the shelves won't slot in after all.

Perseverance ruled the day. Or as it turned, *the entire night,* because it was just as we snapped a cover on the last end-screw and stood back to appreciate a job well done, that we heard the call to prayer.

The *morning* call to prayer.

Stunned, we pushed the dresser up against the wall and looked out the window. The sun was beginning to rise. It was five a.m. Nine hours, it had taken us, to put this thing together; the children would soon be downstairs ready for breakfast, and there was nothing to be done but to sit on the floor and laugh as only those who are miles beyond the point of exhaustion, can.

10. Circumcision Party

By the end of the week, a sense of normality had returned, and our excitement turned to the circumcision party we were about to attend. Circumcision parties, who would have guessed, are lavish occasions! The hotel venue was decked out with balloons in the local football club colours, and family members, all dressed in ballroom attire, stood magnificently at the entrance to greet the guests as they arrived.

With a kiss on either cheek, we were ushered into a function room and seated at tables, while an 'uncle' was already well underway, chanting a lengthy reading of the Koran monotonously into a microphone.

We had naively presumed that Mert, the real estate agent's son, would be a baby, but, *no*, as it turned out, the boy in the centre of it all was a robust thirteen-year-old—the perfect age to have Eric and Joseph cringing at the very thought of what he was about to endure.

We gathered from the fact that the boy was in fine form when we arrived, that he had not yet been 'done.' Perhaps the party was meant to get him ready; bolstered by the cheering guests and a tiny bit dulled by his first taste of wine, he should be all set for his step into manhood.

Upstairs, two clowns played games with the children, and Eric and Joseph were hustled into the mix and left to join in as best they could. The problem that soon became apparent, however, was that our boys knew nothing of the Turkish rules that applied to what we thought were familiar children's games. On top of that, we'd obviously missed the memo about what happens when a foreigner gets competitive with a Turk.

It was when Eric won a game of musical chairs and found that no one was impressed, that he suddenly understood: the boy who is to be circumcised should have been allowed to win. Mert, the only other child left standing, was clearly upset, and there was no way we could see, to fix the situation. 'Just apologise,' we said to Eric, but the children upstairs didn't seem to be able to grasp the concept, or our fumbling Turkish. The only thing to do was to let the night move on.

And it did. The entertainers soon left, the children joined their parents in the hall below, and then, a hush descended and the guests stood and turned towards the door, at which point we realised that we had no need to worry—young Mert was about to be restored, in no small way, to the top of the pecking order.

What a triumphant entrance! As the doors flung open, in walked four men carrying on their shoulders a padded throne on which young Mert sat, now dressed in a lavish satin robe with a wonderful turban upon his head. Festive music broke out as the throne-bearers entered the room, and the crowd clapped and cheered and rose to form a long line of well-wishers who would greet the young man, and, most importantly, lavish gifts on him.

Thankfully, we had enquired about the custom at occasions like this and had come prepared. With the small gold 'Coin of the Republic' we had purchased at the local mall, we stood in line, waiting our turn as one by one, similar gold coins or notes of cash were pinned onto the sash around the young man's torso. The family hugged and kissed and thanked each person until every guest had given their gift and in so doing, provided Mert with a wonderful boost into adult life.

From that point on, the festivities really kicked in as a towering five-tier cake was rolled in on a cart, the periphery of the room was lit up by cascades of fireworks, and with a full-length Ottoman sword and a dramatic flourish, Mert proceeded to cut the cake. Then the dancing began! What a hoot!

Vangie, our four-year-old, had spent the past two hours consuming orange soda, and we could only watch in awe as our little girl came to life, mingling in with the crowd, delighting everyone with her energetic dancing, and very much looking as if this was the life she was born for. Jeff and I cast a quick look at each other. Yes, we may as well throw caution to the wind, ignore the fact that the last time we danced was at our wedding fifteen years earlier, and simply let loose as best we could!

As it happens, Turkish dancing is rather easy to get the hang of—raise your arms, take a few steps, click your fingers, and you're pretty much done. If in doubt, imitate the Grandma next to you—the one with the black trench coat and full headscarf—or the young woman in front of you in the skimpy dress and stilettos.

The contrast between backgrounds, beliefs and ages was on display for everyone to observe, and yet, as we bundled our children up at the end of the night and made our way back home, our hearts were full with the realisation that none of those differences matter when you're in Turkey and it's time to dance.

11. But First, Our Apologies

The weekend celebrations were a wonderful reprieve, but by Monday we were once again traipsing in and out like a parade of ants; back and forth to the key-cut man, the multiple utilities offices, the market to buy bed linen, the plumbing shop for an implement to unclog the bathroom drains, lightbulbs so we wouldn't be caught out every time the sun went down, the internet connection company, the mobile phone provider. . . and, of course, trips to the supermarket, where it seemed to take forever to simply work out what was what as I stood there in the aisle with my dictionary and exchange rate calculator, trying to figure out what the unfamiliar packaging contained and how much we were even spending.

Life doesn't stop while you're in transition, and we had to factor that in—kids still needed to be fed, people still had to be able to find their socks in the morning, and everyone still longed for a real shower or, heaven forbid, a moment to unwind and relax.

We'd reached capacity. We had overtired kids and strung-out parents, and we were tired beyond belief. Then one morning, it all got the better of us, spilling out in a horrid, angry, anxious mix that I'm sure floated through the open windows and into the hearing of anyone nearby.

I presumed that eventually we would adjust to the relatively dense city living we were now in, but right then, without our familiar half acre of land conveniently buffering our lives from those around us, all I could think was that there was a good chance the neighbours had already written us off.

I decided it was best to be real with them right from the start, and so, when I saw Arzu Hanım[1] through my kitchen window that afternoon, I ventured out to apologise. 'I'm sorry there's been a bit of shouting next door,' I said. 'We're all a bit tired and stressed.'

I liked Arzu and Omer. The way Omer Bey[2] had climbed the tree to

---

1 Mrs

2 Mr

gather cherries for our children showed the kind heart of the man next door, but his wife made me smile too. I had no way of knowing what she made of us, because she didn't speak a word of English, but she smiled with her eyes, and I liked that.

A few days after we had moved in, we had met Arzu and Omer's son, Fatih. Fatih was home from university for the summer and had endeared himself to us the moment we met him. He also understood English incredibly well. Fatih had already rescued us a number of times that week when we had been clueless about the language, and I didn't want to presume too much on his help, but when I spotted him coming out his front door, I decided this was an opportunity I needed to take.

'Can you help me talk to your mum?' I asked, and right then, I was thankful for every minute Fatih had spent learning English because I'm pretty sure his mother, until that day, had never experienced an apology in her life, and confusion about what we were trying to say was the last thing any of us needed.

'Can you tell her I'm sorry about this morning?'

There was no way to justify the whole thing. How could Arzu begin to imagine what we'd just left behind, how many details we'd worked through over the past six months, or how much of our life was still up in the air? Still, we're all human, I reasoned. Even quiet middle-class Turks must have the odd squabble here and there.

'We really lost the plot,' I said to Fatih, and then revised what I said in case he decided to translate my words literally. 'We were fighting,' I said, 'because we are tired and overwhelmed and moving across the world with four children is very difficult.'

Faith translated and Arzu nodded with motherly understanding. 'I'm sorry for the shouting,' I said again, but seeing her look of concern only made me keep on trying to explain. 'We're not perfect,' I said, 'but please don't worry about us. I just wanted to apologise. In our family, there's lots of grace for when we mess up. We got it wrong this morning, but we're okay, really!'

Thankfully, Fatih's command of English was unusually good. I'm sure it's not easy to find words like 'grace' when you're not accustomed to using them. *Grace.* Arzu's expression made me wonder if it were not just a new word, but a new concept. So I spelled it out. 'It's when we show kindness even after we've hurt each other.' Now Fatih had a smile on his face. *What a way to introduce the neighbours to his mother.* But there we had it, and at least now, Arzu Hanim could rest easy. The yabanci[1] were okay.

12. Ordering Water

When it came to the to-do list, it was drinking water that finally made it to the top. Tap water in Bursa, we had been told, was not fit to drink. All we had to do, though, was arrange a delivery of two or three fifteen-litre bottles each week, just as the locals did. Having diligently prepared the Turkish phrases he'd need, Jeff telephoned one of the water companies. '*Merhaba*,' I heard him say. '*Iki shishe su, lutfen.*' '*Two bottles of water, please.*'

Fatih had already prepped us. 'All you need to do is give your name and address, and the water will be delivered to your house' he had said. The problem was that Jeff was speaking in Turkish over the phone with an operator who obviously had no experience in communicating with foreigners and what should have been a simple conversation quickly turned into a debacle.

Nothing Jeff said seemed to help the man on the other end understand the simple request. The operator, on the other hand, seemed to believe that the faster he spoke, the more Jeff would understand, and ten minutes into the fiasco, with Jeff now a long way off his prepared script, he eventually hung up the phone, no more confident that our water delivery was sorted than when he'd started.

Something must have got through, however, because less than an hour later, a truck pulled up at our front gate and a wiry little man with an anxious look on his face lugged two heavy canisters to our front door and quickly retreated to his truck. *Success!* we thought, though we had no idea how it had happened.

By the following week, the call centre had devised a plan. Now that the company knew where the babbling foreigner lived, they would simply wait for Jeff to call, and when they heard it was him, the operator on the other end would interrupt and say, 'Okay, okay we are coming' before promptly hanging up.

The goal from their end, it appeared, was to minimise frustration,

---

1 foreigners

and thankfully, the system worked perfectly for us all. The next time the driver turned up, he placed the bottles on our front doorstep, took the cash we handed over, and gave us a quiet nod which we took as evidence that our water delivery agreement was settled and we could now get on with life.

13. Rugs, Knives and Possibly an Angel

Our new home was finally taking shape; only one feature was still missing, and in Turkey, it was a feature that could not be overlooked. The wooden floors in our apartment needed rugs. We had come across some rug stores, both in the centre of town and at the local mall, but the so-called 'Turkish' rugs on offer were mostly mass-produced in China; none of them seemed to be quite like what we had admired on our neighbours' floors.

We did find *the perfect rug*, in a hardware store, of all places. It was large enough to place in the lounge, had a beautiful mix of subtle colours and delicate patterns, and a quality to it that meant the appearance changed depending on the way the light shone on it. The sticker on the back confirmed that this was, indeed, a hand-knotted original silk rug from the East, and here it was, on sale for two thousand lira. Now I love good quality, but I like a bargain too, and anyway, our budget for rugs certainly didn't extend to two thousand lira. Nevertheless, we'd seen what we liked and went away heartened. Something would turn up.

And sure enough, it did. Jeff was walking home from the city one day when he came across a small out-of-the-way shop with an assortment of rugs displayed on the sidewalk and in the windows. '*Worth a try,*' thought Jeff, but when he ventured in, it seemed that this shop was like all the others—full of cheap mass-produced replicas and a couple of highly-priced genuine Turkish rugs.

Perhaps the store owner noticed the fleeting look of disappointment on Jeff's face, or maybe Jeff's attempt to convey in Turkish what we were looking for actually worked, but what happened next turned into a memory we will always enjoy. Pulling back an enormous rug that hung on the back wall, the manager gave a little smile and gestured to Jeff to follow him through a low doorway concealed in the back wall. It was like entering Aladdin's cave. *Oh!* exclaimed Jeff. So *this* was where Turks bought their secondhand rugs! There, in great piles on the floor and hanging from ceiling beams, were hundreds of truly magnificent rugs—genuine, hand-made, old Turkish rugs, passed down through generations, stunning in their variety and colour, each with their own minor imperfections that only added to their authenticity. 'Ne kadar?'[1] Jeff ventured to ask, and when the shopkeeper started pointing to one rug after the other and told him the various prices, Jeff could hardly keep from laughing. 'Yes, these would suit us just fine,' he told the shop owner, 'I'll come back and bring my wife.'

That evening we spent an immensely satisfying hour or two, sipping tea in the back of a seemingly typical rug store, running our hands over rugs that were far from typical, revelling in the choices, the incredible workmanship, the beautiful way each rug had aged, and hearing the stories of how such a collection had made its way to this concealed back-room in the middle of a busy Bursa street.

Choosing which rugs to buy was pure delight—a large red one for the lounge, a fairly traditional blue pattern for under the dining table and a couple of smaller ones for the bathroom and kitchen. As we bundled them all into a taxi, we felt rather chuffed. Not only had we stumbled upon an intriguing part of Turkish culture, we now also had the rugs to show for it.

~

The rugs and furniture were sorted, the utilities were connected, curtains even hung on the windows, but you can't do much in the kitchen without a few good knives. We had made do with tearing chunks of bread from the fresh loaves each morning at breakfast, but I knew we needed to find a more civilised solution soon.

Determined to make the trip into the city on my own, I hailed the 6F, squeezed in between women in headscarves and shapeless trench coats, intent on preserving their modesty despite the sweltering heat, took a deep breath, and cast my eyes downwards, like everyone else. I tried to stay on my feet as the bus jerked to the right and left and regularly came to an abrupt halt.

I was keen to explore the Koza Han while I was in town. The Koza Han was once the ancient silk market in the centre of Bursa, the meeting

---

1 'how much?'

place of traders at the end of the Silk Road, the point where East and West converged. These days, the Koza Han was a sprawling covered bazaar. 'You can buy everything at the covered market,' I had been told, and so, when I disembarked on Ataturk Çaddesi[1], just across the road from the main entrance, I was full of hope. So far, so good, I told myself.

And then, with no warning at all, an unsettling feeling came over me. It was the men, the never-ending masses of men that were getting to me, along with, I suppose, the near-absence of women. That's when it dawned on me that everywhere we had been over the past three weeks, it had been men we had interacted with. Men did all the upfront work, it seemed, and here at the silk market, it was no different—men were selling wares, serving at cafes, quilting bedcovers—you name it, there was a good chance a man would be doing the job and suddenly, I was tired of all the men. Something inside me longed to see a gentle, feminine face. I wanted to be greeted by a smile, not by shouting. I wanted to discuss my needs, even if it was just the need to buy a bread knife, with a woman.

The truth was obvious, now that I was finally alone in this new country; my capacity both mentally and physically, had long been reached. I was tired to the bone. Silly things were getting on my nerves, and I'd barely begun my search. Besides, I hadn't thought to look up the word for 'knife' in the dictionary, and now I regretted it. I had no idea where to look. Middle Eastern covered markets are enough to disorientate the most seasoned of shoppers, with their underground levels, crisscrossing streets, and countless wares grouped according to type.

Eventually, I happened across a little bookstore—a quiet, dark place, but a sanctuary in the mass of noise and crowds, nevertheless. 'Perhaps they have English books,' I thought, but *no*. I was about to find out how scarce English books were in Turkey, particularly so in conservative Bursa, and they were certainly not stocked in this particular shop. Arabic books, yes. Religious and Ottoman books, plenty. But English books? The storekeeper shook his head. *No.*

I justified being in the store in the first place by buying a little jigsaw puzzle to take home for Liberty. The young man serving at the counter was obviously a devout Muslim—not once did he look me in the eye, but he did kindly slip some Islamic literature in with my purchase, and with

---

1 Ataturk Street

a gentle *Selamlar*[1], bid me goodbye.

Was it God, or was it fluke? As I stepped out of the store, right there at the entrance, was a man sitting on a low stool behind a crude wooden table, on which were laid all manner of knives! He hadn't been there when I walked in, I was sure of that, but there he was, and I felt my heart lift a little as the thought came to me that this task might turn out to be unexpectedly easy. I scanned the table. *Bursa knives.* I was later told that Bursa was the home of knife-making. So our earlier impressions hadn't been so far off after all. They liked knives here in Bursa.

A quick survey of the selection was all it took for me to realise that the man at the little table had every sort of knife but a bread knife. *Do you have a serrated knife?* I attempted to demonstrate. *Ekmek?* I tried. I guess I must have picked up one word anyway. *Bread. I need a bread knife.*

What happened next both humbled and delighted me all at once. The knife seller kindly insisted, with motions and gestures, that I come and sit on his stool. I promptly obeyed, wondering how this might look to passers-by, but happy to rest a minute. With a quick indication that he would be back, the man disappeared into the crowd, and out of sight.

Just then, another man appeared. To this day, I cannot picture where he came from, but there he was, coming towards me, carrying a silver tray, on which were six or eight full-to-the-brim tulip-shaped glasses of hot, Turkish tea. Each glass sat on a little saucer, with two neat sugar cubes and a silver teaspoon on the side. Barely slowing his pace, the man placed one little cup on the table in front of me and continued on his way.

I felt I had seen an angel. Maybe the Lord Himself visited me in the form of that man—I will never know for sure. But in that moment, something changed for me. Deep in my soul, I sensed that I had just been welcomed to Bursa.

I sipped my tea, aware that this was the craziest scene in the world—a mother-of-four from Australia, perched behind a knife-seller's table in the heart of the Capital of the Ottoman Empire. And yet, somehow it also felt quite normal.

The knife man arrived just a few minutes later with a

---

1 Peaceful greetings; regards

locally-handcrafted bread-knife wrapped in a piece of brown paper. He had obviously hurried—he was puffing a little—but he carried himself with a look of pleasure that he had been able to find exactly what I needed.

It was time to pay. 'Ten lira,' said the shop owner. He held up all his fingers so I could understand. Reaching into my purse, I handed him a twenty lira note. *Eight Australian dollars,* I calculated. Taking the note from my hands, the knife-man promptly turned and went into the bookstore I had just come from. A moment later he emerged, holding my change in his hand, which he passed to me before waving a cheery goodbye.

Does Turkey have one big shared purse? I wondered. I had noticed this everywhere—people helping each other out to provide the right change to customers, yet with hardly the exchange of a word between them. I suspected that somehow a careful track was kept of it all and that the system worked to everyone's satisfaction, but the one thing that struck me in that moment was that these people took the concept of 'brother' to a level I was entirely unfamiliar with.

14. Losing Liberty

Speaking of angels, it was soon clear that we needed some reinforcements of our own because we hadn't even made it to breakfast the next morning when Liberty went missing.

I was in the kitchen, taking fresh muffins out of the oven, cutting fruit and calling the children to come and eat, and because no one tends to dawdle when muffins are on offer, the whole family soon assembled downstairs. Except Liberty. That morning, Liberty didn't show up at breakfast.

We sat at the table unconcerned, because our two-year-old had taken to playing a game only she completely understood. It involved hiding away, quiet as a mouse, not even letting us know that she wanted to be found until someone happened upon her, and then she would squeal with delight as if we'd all been playing along with her the whole time.

And so, that morning, after a few minutes of everyone calling, 'Liberty, Liberty,' we got up from the table, walked back up the stairs and began searching playfully under beds and behind curtains. Only, she wasn't there, she wasn't *anywhere,* and by the time we'd searched all four levels, we noticed something that made our hearts skip a beat. The heavy front door of our house was slightly ajar, and Liberty's little slippers which had been in the entrance the night before, were gone.

Suddenly, I wondered if we would ever adjust to this new way of life. In Australia our doors were always open; the children could run out the back door, and up into the side entrance whenever they pleased, and Liberty was used to taking herself quietly out to the sandpit, where she would play happily until we came to fetch her. I never worried that she might wander off.

But that, it appeared, was exactly what she had done, only we weren't in Australia, we were in Turkey, for goodness sake, and as the whole family raced outside to search for our girl, the uppermost question on my mind was, *how long she had been gone?* I tried to calculate the minutes in my head and realised it must have been half an hour at least since anyone had seen her. Enough time to get kidnapped and be on some road to who-knows-where.

I'm sure the neighbours watching from their windows had no idea what to make of the scene; only that the crazy foreign family were now running barefooted in random directions, because *which way do you go when there are three gates leading out of the garden area, one of which opens onto a main road, and all three gates are unlatched?*

The things that come to mind at times like these are, I've concluded, ridiculous, but suddenly, my mother's parting words as we waved goodbye at the airport in Brisbane were ringing in my ears: *'Don't let that girl out of your sight. She'll be kidnapped and taken across the Syrian border before you know it.'*

At the time, I'd shrugged off the warning, only now the possibility was all too real; we could have been facing every expat parent's worst nightmare, and yet all I could think was, *'how am I going to call my mother back in Australia and tell her we've lost her baby granddaughter in Turkey, only a few weeks after we've arrived?'*

There was no time to formulate a plan. Jeff and the boys started for the park opposite the house and then turned to search the basketball courts and the bushes nearby. I had no idea which way to go; all of us were shouting, 'Liberty, Liberty!' and inside I was growing desperate.

And then, in an instant, the most inexplicable calm descended, and I remembered the promise that God had given us for Turkey. *Peace and safety*. It was more than a promise, in fact, it was a covenant God had made with us, and now, when we needed it most, those two words came powerfully to our hearts. Still, I kept crying, and calling and shouting my little girl's name, because the appropriate thing to do at times like these is, of course, to panic a little; a bit of hysteria is to be expected, isn't it? And yet deep down, we all knew that Liberty was safe and well.

Only, *where was she?* We called on angels to surround her, for Jesus to protect her, wherever she was, and before long the neighbourhood women came out to see what the matter was. *'My daughter...'* I gestured with my hand, *'... my little girl... missing!'*

In Australia, any woman who heard those words would spring into action and begin searching. But not in Bursa, and not that day. One by one, the women, all donned in headscarves, came out of their apartments and gathered around. We had not yet met—in fact, it turned out they had never even spoken to a foreigner before, but *'sit down,'* they said, and one younger woman put her arm around my shoulders as if to say, *'Don't worry, this is Turkey. She will be okay. We'll find her.'*

I smiled at the implication that, though a missing child might be a catastrophe in Australia, it was nothing to be concerned about here in the Middle East. *'You need to drink some tea and wait,'* they agreed. A hunched-over old lady had already arrived on the scene with a glass of water for me, but *drink tea?! While my not-even-two-year-old baby is missing?!* The women continued to exude calm. They, at least, had absolutely no doubt that no one would hurt the little foreign girl. *Oh please*, I thought. *Don't mess with my mind right now.*

But they were right. Someone had noticed a car parked in the middle of the road just up the hill from our house; its engine was still running, and the driver's door was open, but there was no one inside. Soon, we heard the rest of the story. The man had just got back in his car, apparently, but before he drove off, he had called out to a passer-by and pointed back down the road.

The women on the park bench quickly conveyed the situation to me—the man had been driving to work when he saw a little blonde toddler with her pyjama pants on backwards and her slippers on the wrong feet, happily crossing the street in front of him with not an adult in sight. And so, he had stopped his car right there in the middle of the road, picked her up, and carried our daughter down the hill to the police station. We would find her there, we were assured.

There she was alright, out on the footpath where a policeman stood with a machine gun at his side and Liberty, happily sucking on a lollipop in his arms. We had noticed that no Turkish child was ever allowed to cry for long—the moment any child came to the verge of tears, there would always be someone ready to offer a boiled sweet. Notwithstanding local sentiment, when Liberty saw us, she cried, I cried and the neighbours who had followed us down the street kindly turned away so as not to embarrass us in our emotional display of relief.

Later that morning we discovered a new dynamic in the community we had come to, when the neighbourhood women got together, discussed the whole thing and came to a quick conclusion: *Obviously, these Australians were out of their depth; four children were more than anyone could reasonably look after on their own, and so, they would make our children's safety their business.*

Word got around quickly, and soon it became normal to see the neighbours smiling at us kindly as they pinched Liberty's cheeks and tut-tutted her about staying inside the gate.

Our neighbours had seen us at our most vulnerable. What they had also seen was that the instinctive love we had for our children was as strong as theirs! They'd also noticed how much their gentleness and care had meant to us when we needed it most, and with that, we were granted a place in the hearts of the locals.

Now I loved them too. These women had seen my fear and they calmed it. They noticed my lack of dignity and redeemed it. They surrounded me just like the sweet-spirited matrons they were and took control of the whole fiasco in the most gentle and natural of ways.

I didn't have to make that fateful long-distance call after all. But that night after we tucked Liberty into bed, we stood in the doorway a moment or two longer than usual and thanked God she was safely home.

15. Banana Cake and Belly Dancing

By now we had met most of the neighbours, but my waking thought the following morning was of preventing trouble with the family next door who we had seen, but not yet spoken to. I suspected they didn't really know what to make of us; they didn't smile at us the way most others did, and I felt for them because they didn't understand a word of

English, and most of all, they never asked to share a wall of their duplex with a large foreign family. How could they have known that back in Australia we'd had at least ten metres of space between our home and the homes of our neighbours and that we never had to think about whether our voices would reach them, let alone bother them?

So, I made a banana cake. I wanted to introduce myself properly to the people next door and try to make up for what I was sure was a level of noise unheard of by these one-child families. It was the first thing I had baked in my new oven, and I hoped like crazy that it would turn out well. It did, and I was relieved; even so, I was nervous at the thought of knocking on her door and standing in front of my neighbour with no language but a smile.

Nothing could have prepared me for what that afternoon held. As it turned out, standing on the doorstep was the easy part.

I had set the freshly baked cake on a plate, carefully dusted it with icing sugar, and walked the ten or so steps to Esra's house, already feeling like I was making a peace offering. There was no way to avoid the fact that we had crashed and thumped and hollered a lot over the past few days. The kids had stomped through empty rooms, exclaiming loudly about everything, and the boys had somehow discovered that if they were to lean a long way out of our fourth-floor windows and twist their necks, they could see right into Esra and Sercan's bedroom. On top of all that, I had read the statistics—eighty-five per cent of Turks reported feeling very uncomfortable living next door to a foreigner. I needed to get off to a good start, to try, at least, to redeem the first few weeks . . .

It wasn't Esra who opened the door. Whoever it was, she was smiling, though, which I appreciated. She took the cake from my hands and with barely a glance, placed it in the kitchen. Then with gestures and words that completely bypassed my understanding, whoever-she-was led me downstairs.

We had figured that our basement would make a great playroom for the children, but now I realised the Turks thought very differently. This basement was clearly the most formal room of the house, and that day it was full of women—Esra's friends, someone tried to explain, who liked to eat and gossip and just be together. A *gün*, I had already been told, was a Turkish woman's close circle of friends; they met every week at one of their homes, and it would be rare for a foreigner to ever be included in their inner circle.

The girlfriends had already eaten, but before I had even sat down, a plate with five or six different pastries was brought out and placed on a little side table in front of me, along with a tidy little knife and fork. *How proper.* This was obviously not the time to mention my recently diagnosed celiac disease, and so, with a weak smile, I began to eat, feeling for all the world like a spectacle.

The women were clearly intrigued by me. Talking among themselves, they tried to recall their primary school English in order to ask a few questions. Finally, one spoke. 'Where are you from?'

'Australia,' I answered.

'Are you a Christian?'

I was momentarily stunned. *What?! I've just come to your door, and that's the first question you have for me? What ever happened to avoiding religion and politics?*

Inwardly I compared the scene to a similar situation back home where we'd meet someone for the first time, and ask about the children, their ages, their school. We might ask about a person's interests or their work. We'd be interested to know what brought someone to our suburb. But, *'Are you a Christian?'* This was getting very personal very quickly.

'Yes.' I replied, and I had no way of saying, 'But it's probably nothing like what you think . . .' And then came the follow-up question that confounds me still. 'Did you use pig fat in the cake?'

Pig fat?

A rush of thoughts filled my mind, not the least of which was, *where on earth would anyone even buy pig fat?* I wouldn't know how to find the stuff in Australia, let alone Muslim Turkey. Did they think we were *idiots?* Did they honestly think I would deliberately insult them? Or was that just the first thing they associated with Christians?

I stared for a minute.

'No.' I answered. 'Just butter.'

And then everything was alright. 'We're Muslims,' they said as if that explained everything, and then they laughed about how they had eaten so much and how they were all getting too fat, and now it was time to dance off all the weight. With that, one woman went over to the radio and turned up the music and that was their cue—all the girlfriends stood up, threw off their excess clothing, put on little finger castanets, and began belly-dancing.

A couple of women had lit cigarettes during our brief conversation, and as the room filled with smoke and laughter and music, my head began to feel light and my gluten-assaulted stomach tightened with pain. I smiled at the women and tried to imitate their moves, but there was nothing in my DNA or my experience that gave me the ability to dance like them.

I left soon after, feeling like I'd done okay. I hadn't offended anyone, and I'd managed to join in as best I could. I'd even managed to apologise for the noise we had made over the past few days. Everyone smiled. We had managed to redeem a bad start, I decided.

And then, as I was leaving, I glanced into the kitchen. An open waste bin sat on the floor beside the bench, and there, upside down at the bottom of it was my still-warm banana cake. I turned and walked home with tears in my eyes and an angry knot in my stomach. None of that awkward encounter mattered anyway, I realised. In the eyes of the women next door, I was an infidel, and one on which they were not about to take any chances.

16. Health and Wellbeing (of Sorts)

I was sure over time I would get over the cake incident, but there was a chance I might never recover from the humiliation that was to come later in the week. It started when two women knocked on our front door. Standing there, covered from head to toe in trench coats and headscarves and carrying clipboards in their hands, the women began gesturing, pointing at me, pointing to the children as they tumbled around me, and pointing to somewhere out on the street.

I had not the foggiest idea what they were talking about.

'Benim Anya,' I tried, but no, it appeared they were not concerned with who I was. The lanyards hanging around their necks with their identification photos displayed didn't offer many hints in my direction either. I took the brochures they gave me and closed the door.

It wasn't until midday, when Fatih came home for lunch, that I understood. 'This is a brochure from the family health nurse,' he said. 'You must take the children to the health clinic to have them screened.'

Really? I had seen no information indicating such a requirement on any immigration website we had researched, but Arzu, Fatih's mother, backed it up with nods and gestures and the few words of English she had determined to learn for our sake. *'Yes, you must take the children to see the health nurse.'*

And so I did just that. I walked the four children to the scantily-marked clinic in the run-down concrete building nearby and presented our health records from Australia.

Soon we were ushered into a consulting room, where one of the ladies, still covered from head to toe and still making no attempt to slow her words or cater in any way to my foreignness, took the children's record books, nodded and ticked a box in the file she had already opened for us. And then, she got to the real point of the visit.

'Contraception? You use contraception?

I was speechless.

Are you kidding me? You think I'm going to sit here, talking to who knows who from who knows which department and discuss contraceptives?

'I'm fine,' I replied, and the answer was clearly inadequate, because then she pulled out a laminated card with various examples of contraception illustrated for the benefit of illiterate women like me, and asked me to point to which one I was obviously *not* relying on.

'Having four children is quite normal in my country,' I tried to explain. 'I don't have to prevent children if I don't want to . . .'

In my incredulous state, I scanned the card before me. Where's the *guy-had-a-vasectomy* box? I decided not to ask because, *come on now, this was Turkey, and this was women's business, and we wouldn't expect a man to do such a thing now, would we?!*

But there was no getting out of it. She needed to tick a box, and the fastest way out of this now fully embarrassing situation was to select an option.

I'm not sure which I pointed to, but the health nurse was visibly relieved. The Australian family with the multitude of children were all sorted in the contraception department, she had a complete health record to sign off for her director, and finally, she could enjoy her tea-break knowing there would be no foreign babies on her watch.

17. One Month In
(from Anya's journal on what was, obviously, a much better day)

We've been here a month now and I love everything about the place. I love the grandmothers who pinch the children's cheeks, nearly bursting with affection for these four little kids they've never laid eyes on before. Where do they get affection like that?

I love the lady who brings her two daughters to the park outside our house. She's fully veiled, and she's slow to smile. I adore her. I especially adore the tiniest of her girls—the four-year-old who looks all of about eighteen months, with malformed legs that have never walked. And then there's the bursting-with-joy neighbour who is, I'm sure, going to become one of my dearest friends here. She's an accountant who has offered to come every evening after work to give me language lessons.

I love the young Turkish girl who took my children to the zoo. In Australia, I would never have handed my baby over to someone on the bus and waved them off to a place I'd never been to before, but it seems different here. She loves them like her own. And she plays the violin and piano. I wonder if I should ask her to give lessons to Joseph. Oh, and I love the Aussie family who have prayed for a whole year for friends for their son. I love how they came for dinner and stayed half the night. I love the thought-provoking discussions between the men, the fun of sharing a pavlova and Anzac biscuits, and the games we played together. I love how we share a vision for our families here in Bursa.

They know me at the market now. They call out my name and offer me samples of cheese because they know I have no idea which cheese is which—there's the white cheese, for example, that's twisted into ropes but, like at least ten other varieties, it is simply labelled, 'beyaz peynir'—white cheese. The other day, an elderly lady all in black, sided up to me as I stood in front of the artichoke stall. She was gesturing and whispering and trying to give me a lesson on how to prepare artichokes. It was obvious, I guess, that I had never eaten them before. I asked her to come to my place and show me what to do with them, but she didn't understand, so I told the man behind the stall I'd Google 'artichokes' and come back next week.

We gather as a family every night after dinner to pair off and pray our hearts out for this nation, for the friends we've met and already love, for the needs of one another, and for our precious team of friends back home.

It's not as idyllic as it sounds. The time is difficult. The girls are restless. The boys can't think of what to pray. We do our best, but I sense this is the one time we will need to guard carefully; after all, there's a good chance it will be during this hour each night that our most enduring work will be accomplished.

As the final call to prayer sounds out from the mosque above our house, usually somewhere around ten p.m., we brew our version of strong Turkish coffee—thick, warm cocoa—and sip it from tiny porcelain cups while we pull out the board games, light some candles, and try to cement this sweet family together in the midst of all the change.

18. Liberty and the Neighbour

Before long, Liberty disappearing on us had become a regular event, and one that we no longer worried about. She and the next-door neighbour had quickly formed a bond, and with it, an understanding that Liberty only had to toddle over to her front porch and Arzu Teyze[1] would appear within seconds ready to dish out as many tiny cellophane-wrapped sweets as our little girl might enjoy. It seemed that every time we looked, Liberty had a mouthful of candy; sometimes we'd watch her skip happily back home, other times she'd follow Arzu through the house, where they would take up residence on the balcony.

Looking across from our window, we often saw Liberty and Arzu sitting there on their plastic stackable chairs, the table covered with a cloth, and both of them sipping apple tea and eating from a bowl of summer cherries. I watched as Liberty daintily spat the pips into her little palm as she had seemingly been shown and Arzu teyze chatted away in Turkish, and it always astounded me to hear how effortlessly Liberty responded in the language we had hardly begun to understand.

We began using our two-year-old as our translator whenever we wanted to have a conversation with Arzu, and it seemed to work well, though there was every chance Liberty was speaking some kind of mangled Turkish, combined with a smattering of toddler-English—and it was likely that Arzu was indulging us all by pretending to understand her perfectly.

Like so many expat mothers before me, I was concerned about the

---

1 teyze: aunty

amount of candy my daughter was consuming, but I had noted the look of satisfaction on Arzu's face whenever Liberty made another one of her little visits, and, because there are few interactions more endearing than that of a little girl chatting away with a besotted older woman, I decided that the overload of sugar was best overlooked for the time being.

19. Evangeline and the Broken Arm

I could hardly believe it. We were right on the brink in terms of our budget when we left for Turkey, and one of the costs that we decided not to bother with was health insurance. I know that will sound outrageous to our American friends, but coming from Australia, where private health cover was optional and a visit to the doctor or Emergency Department was essentially free, and with the hefty promise from God of *peace and safety*, we had decided that if anything were to come up in terms of our health, we'd use whatever system the locals preferred, and pay our way at the time.

Sooner than we'd expected that plan was put to the test. We were simply walking down the hill from our house, past the taxi station, past the police station and the covered market, when Evangeline tripped, landing heavily on her arm. Clearly, this was the day we would get to experience the Turkish hospital system first-hand.

Our neighbours told us what to do. 'Take her to the university hospital,' they said—and three bus rides and a short walk later, we fronted up at a plain grey building, about four stories high, on the edge of the university medical school.

There's a good chance we were the first foreigners to ever show up at that particular hospital and the woman at the front desk didn't seem to know what to do with us. It all began when she asked for the patient's name. *Evangeline McKee*, we replied, and already it was clear from the look on her face that something was wrong. Had she heard the word *evangelon* from neighbouring Greece, perhaps, and worked out the Christian connotations? Whatever it was, we knew right away that it wouldn't do our daughter any favours in Turkey to be called Evangeline. *'You can call her, 'Vangie,'* we said, but now the woman looked even more confused, as if that didn't sound like a real name either.

It was time to start again. 'Evie,' we said, 'her name is Evie. E – V – I – E.' It appeared we would have to adjust our daughter's name if we were to make a go of raising her in Turkey, but *Evie* seemed to work because the woman behind the counter suddenly looked less tense and gestured to us to sit with everyone else in the waiting room.

I still don't know if we were given priority as foreigners or if there was a policy of bumping children to the front of the queue, but within half an hour or so, a nurse came out and told us that our daughter needed to be taken for X-rays, and could we come with her? I'm sure they never expected all six of us to come along, but without any way of ascertaining what going for X-rays in Turkey entailed or even where the radiology department was located, we figured we needed to stick together. As it turned out, it was only down the hallway, but we travelled as a pack anyway and crowded into the room together while the x-rays were taken.

From there, we were taken into an examining room, and within minutes, an orthopaedic doctor reviewed the films. 'Yes,' he said, 'I can see a fracture.' He wrote a list on a piece of paper. 'Take this to the pharmacy and bring all the supplies back here,' he told us. 'Then we'll set her arm.'

Jeff asked for directions, went in search of a pharmacy, and soon arrived back in the waiting room bearing a bandage, a roll of plaster of paris, safety pins and a sling. The doctor went to work applying the plaster, and then handed us a follow-up appointment time. We barely understood a word that was spoken, but thankfully, fractures are treated pretty much the same the world over, and soon we were ready to leave amidst very little fuss.

We stopped off at the reception desk on the way out. 'Just a moment,' said the woman at the accounts desk, 'and I will work out what you will have to pay.' She punched a few figures into her computer as we held our breath. This would be the moment of truth.

'Thirty lira,' the accounts manager wrote on a slip of paper. 'Including the x-ray?' we asked.

'Yes,' she said. 'In total, thirty lira.'

So the whole thing—x-rays, cast and doctor's consultation—had cost about ten Australian dollars! Not even a day's worth of medical insurance! Sure, we hadn't been treated at the German-owned hospital near our home with its lovely potted plants and staff who spoke multiple languages, but we'd achieved the same outcome, and for all the world we felt like winners.

20. The Dentist

And that was only the start. It was just days later that an old dental issue blew up. I had been to the dentist for a check-up before we left Australia, only to be told that, yes, in fact, I did need some work done—it was a root canal, and a complicated one at that. The dentist had referred me to an endodontist, saying the full procedure should take about three appointments over the course of a few months and would cost between two and three thousand dollars.

We never had a chance to follow through. By that stage, we were holding garage sales, packing boxes and starting our goodbyes. Fitting in a drawn-out procedure for a tooth that had stopped hurting anyway, had well and truly fallen by the wayside.

Until now. Now we were in Turkey and the old pain was flaring up again until it was nearly unbearable. I called my Australian friend. 'Do you know a dentist?' I asked, and *yes, there was a lady who worked out of the basement of a building, in fact, a wonderful dentist, and would I like her to phone and make an appointment for me?*

'Oh yes, please.' I was grateful, especially since the dentist probably didn't speak English, and over the phone, I certainly had no chance of understanding Turkish. A few minutes later, my friend called back. *'Yes, sure, she can fit you in this afternoon.'* Really?! This was a level of service I wasn't used to! Catching the bus over to my Australian friend's apartment, I found her waiting for me on the footpath.

There are times when the kindness of friends means as much as their help, and this was one of them. 'Are you okay?' she asked when I stepped off the bus. 'Here, I brought some painkillers for you.'

As we opened the door and entered the clinic, the dentist herself came and stood behind the counter. On the surface lay a mobile phone and an old-fashioned exercise book, neatly ruled with days and times and handwritten patient names. She smiled. 'Come in,' she said. 'I'll look at your teeth.'

I smiled at my friend. *'Thank you.'*

The dentist led me to the next room—it had no door, which I realised later was because there was no receptionist, and if the phone rang, the dentist would simply pause what she was doing and attend to the enquiry.

I sat in the chair as she introduced herself. 'I am Melis.'

I smiled. 'I am Anya.'

'*Let's just put this around your neck . . .*' she wasted no time as she clipped the usual bib in place.

'So far so good,' I thought. Her English was not strong, but it was enough to convey the basics. '*Let me see . . .*'

And with that, Melis the dentist tilted the lamp above the bed, pulled out two stainless steel implements, and began checking each tooth. I couldn't talk, of course, and I realised I hadn't yet told her which tooth was giving me trouble.

As it was, she didn't need my help.

'There is a problem with this tooth,' she said, tapping it lightly.

'Yes, that's the one,' I nodded.

'You need a root canal,' she told me. I was impressed. *Did she assess that without even seeing an X-ray?!*

'It's a very difficult root canal,' she went on. 'We will need to do it slowly.' Really? This dentist, with no receptionist, no assistant and from what I could see, no equipment other than a drill, was about to attempt an endodontist-level root canal?

'Today I will clean the tooth and pack it with antibiotics,' she explained, 'then for one week you will take the antibiotics, and then you can come back and we will finish it off.'

Okay then.

The first thing my new Turkish dentist did was to sterilise the drill bit she was about to use in my mouth by holding it for thirty seconds or so in the flickering flame of a cigarette lighter. I gasped inwardly and braced myself for a botched-up job.

Instead, she worked, thoroughly, carefully, gently. 'Here, this will be a little painful,' she said every now and then, but it wasn't, really, and within forty minutes I was on my way, biting on a piece of cotton wool, supplied with a week's worth of paracetamol and antibiotics, and hailing the bus home.

The following week I returned. 'That looks very good,' the dentist commented, looking pleased. 'Just relax and we will get started.'

For another hour or so, she quietly worked on my tooth, with only the occasional break to answer the phone or drink some water. 'Are you okay?' she asked. 'Yes,' I said, sitting up in the chair. 'It's all finished, then,' she said. 'Come back if you have any problems with that tooth again, but I think you'll be fine.'

Really? Two visits and we were done?

Yes, in fact—and before I left, I asked her how much I owed her for the treatment.

'Oh, let me see,' she added it up. 'That will be . . .' she looked embarrassed to ask so much, 'one hundred and twenty lira. I'm sorry. It was a long procedure.'

Seventy Australian dollars?!

At that moment, I loved everything about living in Turkey.

21. Unexpected Sermons

By now the call to prayer had become familiar to us; the sound was even soothing at times, the way it rose and fell throughout the day. It was the sound of the call to prayer that woke us in the early morning, and we would fall asleep hearing it again at the close of day.

We had heard that Bursa had the highest concentration of mosques of any city in Turkey; literally from our bedroom window we could see the spires of at least five minarets, and since the call to prayer is passed around the world according to the rising and setting of the sun, we could hear it echoing in the distance as it crossed the nation from East to West, one mosque after another joining the wave of prayer, until finally it resounded and reverberated across the entire city.

Sometimes, though, as the sound of the call to prayer closed in around us, it felt as if something in the atmosphere also closed in, leaving us gasping, a little, for spiritual air, but then it faded again, moved on towards Istanbul, and then into yet another cycle around the world.

I couldn't help but notice, however, that one day, the rhythm changed. It was too soon after the morning prayer and too early for the next, but it was definitely the voice of an imam that was now blaring from the speaker system in the local mosque, and rather than the lulling call to prayer, this voice sounded angry, persistent; this was something other than routine prayer.

'Oh yes,' Fatih explained when we asked him later that evening. 'That was the Friday sermon. If possible, Muslims must stop their work and go to the mosque on Friday. If they are not able to because, for example, they are teaching at a school or driving a bus or sick at home, they can still hear what the imam is teaching.'

'But it sounded very angry today,' I persisted. 'Yes,' said Fatih, 'there has been some trouble out East.' And by the look on his face, we figured it was best not to ask for details, and so we left it at that.

22. Liberty and the Call to Prayer

While we had been gaining insight into our new environment, it was our youngest child who had us absolutely bamboozled. *What's with two-year-olds?* We had never had a tantrum-prone child before—in fact, we had renamed the *terrible two's* the *terrific two's* in faith that ours might buck the trend, and so far, so good. Since coming to Turkey, however, Liberty had taken to randomly and violently screaming at the most inopportune moments.

There was no rhyme or reason to it. A complete stranger might reach out to pick her up and she would smile placidly in their arms as if they were a long-lost uncle or aunt. Other times, she would nearly claw herself away from some well-meaning local who only wanted to pinch her cheeks and tell her what an angel she was. Holding our hands, she would skip her way into some shops, while others she downright refused to enter. There were children she would play with for hours and others she ran and hid from.

And now she had begun waking up at a ridiculously early hour of the morning, screaming as if she were being tormented. *What was happening while she was simply asleep in bed?* we wondered. She didn't seem to be having a nightmare—at least, nothing she was able to tell us about, with her two-year-old vocabulary. But we were getting concerned. It was happening every morning now—Liberty would wake up screaming and we would run down the marble stairs to her bedroom, pick her up, and cuddle her until eventually, she drifted back off to sleep.

It was at four a.m. one morning, just as her cries began to subside, that we heard the call to prayer, and at that moment, Jeff and I turned to each other and with a burst of insight, wondered out loud, 'Is Liberty sensing *the call to prayer before she even hears it? Is it as if some fright or darkness is closing in around her five times a day in never-ceasing repetition?*

Our little girl, it seemed, was picking up on what we could not see. We knew that the spiritual atmosphere was a big deal in our new city, and now it crossed our minds that if there was any hint of evil or demonic activity, Liberty had been sensing it right away. As I mulled it over, I began to realise that I probably picked up on it too, only I didn't react with a tantrum, or wake up screaming—I just got out of sorts, or felt exhausted all of a sudden, or something in me just didn't want to do business with that person, or to shop in that particular store . . .

We decided to take Liberty seriously since she was functioning, in a way, like a spiritual barometer for us all. If she was troubled by something, best for us all to step back, or move on, or whatever the case may be. For now, however, it was time to safeguard our children as they slept. Together we made a simple declaration that whatever spirit was attaching itself to the call to prayer was not welcome in our home and that our children were now off-limits. From the next morning on, Liberty slept right through the first call to prayer.

23. The Simit Man
(from Anya's journal)

It's the funniest sight—every morning around ten o'clock, a lanky man walks down our street balancing a huge wooden tray, loaded with freshly baked simit, on his head.

A Simit is a ring of crusty bread, covered in sesame seeds, and we have seen kids eating them everywhere. As the simit man approaches our house, he calls out, 'bir lira, bir lira,'[1] and I must say, for one lira, a fresh simit with a little pot of cream cheese thrown in is a very good deal.

Joseph and Liberty think so too. I have taken to keeping a little stash of one-lira coins on the kitchen windowsill; as soon as they hear him coming, I hand them a coin each and Joseph runs to the front gate with Liberty trotting behind him. Usually they get there just as the simit-man passes in front of our house, and he stops, of course, when he sees the children, lowers the folded wooden stand from under his arm and sets it on the path. Then with two hands he reaches up and lowers the tray off his head and onto the stand, setting up a little pop-up shop right there at our front gate.

Liberty gets to choose her simit, which is always a tough choice considering they're all perfectly identical—but the simit-man is patient and he doesn't rush her. He wraps one for her and another for Joseph, and when they come back through the door, the smell of fresh bread wafts in too.

---

1 One lira, one lira (about the equivalent of thirty cents)

Speaking of bread, we keep finding it in plastic bags, tied to gates and fence posts along the streets which has intrigued me, until today I found out what it's all about. Bread here is subsidised by the government to ensure that every citizen can afford it. The loaves are blessed by the baker as they go into the oven, are generally sold within hours of being baked, and I have not yet been served a meal in Turkey that has not been accompanied by an overflowing basket of freshly baked bread.

But this is not the sort of bread you keep for the next day. It's not made to last—it's made to be eaten. And so, should a household have any leftover bread, they simply place it in a plastic bag and tie it to the front gate or a nearby fence, where anyone who is hungry or in need may take it and be filled.

It's a constant reminder to me that having what we need for just a day at a time is not a bad way to live. But for people like us, who come from countries where the most vulnerable tend to be looked after by the government, it's a whole new way of operating. Here, it's the neighbours and friends who, in the first instance, share their excess so that each other's fundamental needs are met. Maybe one day we will feel part of the community enough to put our own leftovers out for others or to allow our children to take the bread when we are out and they feel hungry, but for now, it's just another reminder of the kind of traditions that make this nation so strong.

24. Visiting a Hammam

For three months, Fatih, our next-door neighbour's son, had listened to our endless stream of cultural observations and questions, and for the most part, he seemed to enjoy sitting in our lounge room night after night, helping us make sense of the world we now lived in.

Now, it was time for Fatih to return to Austria to begin another term of studies at the university. Our whole family wished he wasn't leaving—not only would we have to get by without someone to translate for us, but Fatih had become like a kind big brother to our children. We already felt how much we were going to miss his company, and I guess he felt the same way too, because he wanted to share his last evening with us—or more accurately, with Jeff.

(Jeff writes) . . .

We were not looking forward to saying goodbye to Fatih even though he was planning to return later in the year with his fiancée, Anna. We were excited to meet her too. Though we'd only known Fatih a few months, this guy already felt like family. Even so, his last night in town took our friendship to a whole other level. As it turned out, Fatih wanted to visit the hammam, and he wanted me to go with him.

I had heard about these places but had avoided any hint of paying them a visit, simply because the very idea of stripping down in public was way outside my comfort zone. To put it mildly, as cultural experiences go, this was nowhere near the top of my bucket list. Still, somehow, when Fatih mentioned the idea, I managed to scrape together just enough inner conviction to say, 'Yes, I can do this. I can do all sorts of things that are uncomfortable,' and agreed to go along.

When Fatih knocked on our front door at nine p.m. that night, however, my courage nearly failed me. 'You don't need to bring anything,' my neighbour-friend said, and I reluctantly dropped my bath towel at the front door, feeling about as vulnerable as a man can get.

There was a lot to take in as we entered the historic hammam; just getting to stage one involved a fiasco of lockers and slippers, rubber mats and tea towels. I call them tea towels because that is what they appeared to be—same size and similar patterns. I'm sure they have a proper name. *But why was I fixated on the tea towels?* —and my answer is, simply because of the incredible relief I felt when I realised I got to *wear* a tea towel! Up to that point I had been under the impression that we'd all be there, buck naked; my mind had been full of suppressed apprehension, wondering how I would cope with this cultural challenge.

Fatih showed me around the hammam which was made up of a number of rooms. The first had an incredible marble lion's head mounted on the wall, and from the lion's mouth, a three-meter stream of hot water spewed out into a large hot pool in the centre. Everything was steam and marble, and the water drawn from the ancient underground source smelled of minerals. It was quite the atmosphere. Tea-towel-clad men were scattered around marble ledges that lined the room—one at a time they would bend down, turn on a copper tap in the wall, and fill a metal bowl. Then they would raise their bowl and unceremoniously pour hot water over their head and back.

Next, I observed, came the scrubbing, which Fatih thankfully went to the trouble of explaining to me. I want to say at this point that I think of myself as a fairly open-minded kind of guy, but it certainly felt like we'd crossed some kind of friendship line when Fatih told me, 'You can scrub yourself, but you can also scrub each other.'

Oh. Alright. 'You have to scrub all the dead skin off each other.' *Okay. Alright. I can do this.* And so, we did just that—we alternated between scrubbing and pouring water from the copper taps over our heads, and all I could think, was that I was not in Kansas anymore!

The next stage involved the big pool. 'You have to be clean to go in the pool,' Fatih said. *Fair enough. Understandable.* I got to wear my tea towel in the pool. *Good.* I tried to focus on the lion. I liked the lion; he was majestic, and if I stood in just the right spot, the stream of water from his mouth hit me right between my shoulder blades, where the efforts of the past month had taken their greatest toll. Now, I was starting to relax and enter the sort of state of mind that comes with knowing that the worst is over. My breath was easing. My mind was clearing. *Everything was going to be alright.*

Then Fatih suggested that because it was my first time at the hammam, I should have the full experience.

'*Oh. What do you mean?*' I asked.

'You need a massage,' he replied.

'*Oh, really, I'm fine with the lion and the copper taps and even scrubbing the back of someone I haven't known more than two months,*' I thought to myself, but Fatih gently insisted. 'No, no, you need a massage,' he said.

I looked at the masseuse, and what he was doing to his victim did not look comfortable. If you turned off all the lights this could be a dungeon and that room would be the torture chamber, but I kept up my self-talk. *Okay, alright, you can do this, Jeff.* 'Yes, what a good idea! I will have a massage,' I agreed.

As if I had a choice.

What happened in the next ten minutes is a blur in my memory. A wiry little fellow torsioned a soapy cloth above his head, frothing it beyond anything I would have thought possible. Then, like I was a car in some sort of car wash, that lathery layer was applied all over my body before I was pummelled and slapped and rolled over and beaten to within an inch of my life. It hurt, but the masseuse seemed unconcerned, as he jammed his elbows into my muscles and then dragged them down their length to relax them.

I still don't understand how applying pain is meant to relax someone, but on and on it went, and then it was suddenly over. I stood up and thanked the torturer. Fatih was smiling broadly, asking what I thought.

'Oh, he sure knows what he is doing,' I said with a grin. 'He is amazing. What an experience.' We had one more dip in the pool with the lion, and then it was time to be wrapped up in towels—that's right, multiple towels—and once we were wrapped, we sat down on reclining chairs to percolate or something. Even now, I am not sure what that part of the ritual was about. Some men were reading books while others sat staring at nothing in particular. I had that feeling of relief once again. *Phew. I've gotten through this hammam thing. Great!*

Only, that's when I realised that I was in deep trouble; a hazy sensation had come over me, as if I were about to enter a coma—only I wasn't home yet. You see, we had just moved six people to the other side of the world. We had been speaking another language all the time. We had been walking everywhere. We had set up a house from scratch, in another language. Buying everything had been a big deal. Haggling had been complicated. My head had been full of exchange rates and Turkish numbers and visas and electricity bill bonds, and after all that, the only thing keeping my exhausted body awake was stress and adrenalin.

The problem now was that the froth-wielding torturer had just eradicated every ounce of stress from my body, and in an instant, the last few months all caught up with me at once.

Fatih was expecting that our hammam visit would last a few more hours, but I looked at him pleadingly and said I didn't think I could make it, and reluctantly but mercifully, he took me home. As unconsciousness descended, I could no longer say, '*okay, alright. I can do this.*' In fact, I could not do another thing. I didn't surface from sleep until the following afternoon.

25. The Novel-Writing Professor

Now that summer was coming to an end, it was time to get on with some income-generating work. We'd had many conversations about our company, but the one thing we hadn't yet landed was an actual job in Turkey. I had been up at night, editing assignments and theses for clients in Taiwan and Jordan, of all places, but what we really wanted was to get work locally.

Then, out of the blue, I received an email, and with that, I picked up my jacket, made sure my business cards were in my folder, and headed out the door to meet with Dr Necmi[1] Gurkasal, a statistics professor at Uludağ University. I had no idea how he had heard of our company, and already I was intrigued by this appointment. It appeared, from a quick search, that my first potential client in Turkey was not only a university lecturer but also a key benefactor of the City Museum. 'I have an interest in the preservation of the city's heritage,' he had written. I was about to discover that he was also an avid writer, with a new manuscript that he hoped I might edit for him.

The first step, however, was to get my greetings straight. '*Çok memnun oldum.*' I practised the phrase all the way in on the bus. 'Çok memnun oldum. *Pleased to meet you.*' I would address my potential client as Professor Necmi since, as Fatih had advised me, last names are rarely used in Turkey.

~

We met at the Bursa Municipal Museum right on ten a.m. as planned, though I had arrived early so I could walk around the building and pray over the meeting beforehand. I sensed the significance of this job and was especially delighted that it had effectively come to me. I had presumed it would be difficult to generate work in Bursa, but, knowing that one job usually leads to another, I was excited at the idea that this first project had the potential to unlock a steady stream of work. If this was God's plan to prosper us here in Turkey, I was blown away. Here was a man who was obviously high up in the university system, well-connected into the city council, and a key influencer across the museums. Would this job open the door for our company to be supplied with work from across all three sectors?

I introduced myself to the curator at the front desk, who was evidently expecting me, and immediately led me, up an expansive marble staircase lined with glass display cabinets, to the first floor. Inside the cabinets were some of the most ornate dresses and richly embroidered fabric I

---

1 Pronouced: Nej-mi

had ever seen; I decided right then to come back soon to properly view this exhibition that obviously showcased Bursa's lavish fashion history.

⌒

Professor Necmi was an older man with greying hair and a comfortable manner. With an outstretched hand, he welcomed me into his office, offered me a place to hang my coat, and asked the curator to arrange for a tray of tea to be brought. I looked around—it was a simple room we were in, with a heavy wooden desk and ornate chair, solid bookcases lining one wall, and large windows that faced onto the main city square below. The square functioned as a sort of pedestrian hub, linking the old city with the new, business with tourism, retail with the manufacturing sector, and here I was, right in the centre of it all, with my first client! I couldn't have asked for a more incredible opportunity. 'Take a seat,' Professor Necmi offered.

It felt strange, for a moment, to be seated on chairs facing each other with nothing solid between us—no desk, or table, not even a coffee table in the middle of the room. In Turkey, I had been told, meeting in an open space spoke of trust and mutuality; with only a rug beneath our feet, I realised there was no hierarchy in this meeting. Professor Necmi was the author, I was the editor, and the moment he began talking, I could tell that this man was passionate about his story.

'It's called, *Carlo of Florence*,' he began, '. . . and it's a novella about the Bursa in its glory days.' Already I was slightly confused, but I listened intently. This was a time to respect the man and his story, and most importantly, to admire the evident love for his city which had led him to weave its history into a nostalgic novel in the hope that he might stir up memories of Ottoman splendour and awaken a desire in a new generation to hold onto a heritage that was fast diminishing.

I understood the heart of this man, but as he spoke, I sensed the resignation in his spirit. While Bursa still retained evidence of its impressive past, the now-sprawling industrial city would never return to the days of orchards and gardens, exotic insects and architecture and spices, of tales with two meanings told at inns along the Silk Road trading routes—and Professor Necmi knew it. Still, he wanted history preserved, and he had done it by writing a novel.

'Why Carlo of *Florence*?' I finally ventured to ask. 'You said the story is set in Bursa, but the title alludes to Italy.' 'Ah yes,' he replied, 'Florence is simply the Trojan horse out of which the heart and soul of Bursa and its bygone days will emerge.' And with that, it was obvious just how masterfully my client's mind worked.

Half an hour later, my questions had been answered, I had the details I required, and it was time to head back home, where I would take a thorough look at the manuscript and draw up a quote.

Not at all, as it turned out.

As I stood to leave, Professor Necmi went to a drawer in his desk and pulled out a wad of Turkish lira. *Five hundred*, he told me, placing my first payment into an envelope. *'When the book is fully edited, I will pay another seven hundred. One thousand, two hundred lira in total. Is this agreeable to you?'*

'Yes, thank you,' I replied, dumbfounded once again by the sheer lack of fuss that such business agreements entailed. I smiled, however, a little perplexed when I realised that my client had been the one to decide the cost of my services, but without giving it too much thought, I dropped the cash into my handbag and made my way home feeling for all the world that I had just been validated in this unlikely city.

26. After Weeks of Work . . .

I began getting up at four a.m. to work on Professor Necmi's book because, while he had written an excellent story with an intriguing plot and rich use of language, the English translation I was working with was atrocious; there was barely a coherent sentence in the manuscript. I now had to come to terms with the fact that I had a mountain of a job ahead of me if I were to turn it into a story that was anything close to readable, let alone enjoyable, for an English-speaking audience. Nevertheless, I was excited to get started, and I wanted to honour Professor Necmi by doing an incredible job, even if that meant effectively rewriting the entire book.

After a week of painstaking reading and note-taking, I had a fairly clear idea of the setting and main characters, and very little else. The story seemed to flit randomly from the gardens of Ottoman Bursa to a mist-covered island in the middle of a lake I couldn't identify, and then, somewhat randomly, to the streets of Italy in an unknown century. My European history was clearly not up to scratch for this job and neither was the translation. In my journal, I wrote,

I have been researching palaces and waterways, bazaars and trading routes, the names of little-known artists and the meaning of words like 'han.'[1] I love gleaning knowledge and insight and understanding as I work—and I love that the more research I bring to this project, the closer we will get to what Professor Necmi intended. But I am also aware that we are providing a level of service that is unsustainable. I must constantly resist the urge to convert my lump-sum payment into an hourly rate, because the reality is, it's shrinking by the minute.

27. The Search for an Office

Every week we were meeting new people and making friends. Without exception, everyone was welcoming, friendly, and very much interested in why we had come to Turkey. 'We wanted to bring our family to experience life in a Muslim country,' we said, 'and we are hoping to expand our business into the Middle Eastern market.'

Our business cards were now printed, our website was being translated into Turkish, and Jeff had begun scheduling meetings with university representatives. People were starting to make sense of us, of why we were here—except for one standout issue: the concept of working from home. Though operating out of a home office is something many Australians or New Zealanders might choose, in Turkey, the notion was unthinkable. *Work is work. Home is home. Why mix the two?* After noticing one confused reaction after another, we realised we would need to rethink our plan if we were to minimise the confusion—even suspicion—among our neighbours and friends.

I could get away with working from home, of course. As far as everyone else was concerned, I was a housewife and mother, and if I did a bit of work online as well, so be it. What no one seemed to be able to get their head around, was the idea of Jeff working from home too.

Our issue, though, was what to do about it. We had thoroughly investigated the legalities of working in Turkey, and so long as our company was registered in Australia and we were being paid into an Australian bank account, we were technically not 'working' in Turkey. Perception, however, was a whole other thing. To the authorities, taking

1 Han: inn; guesthouse

an office space in the community equalled working. On the other hand, to the locals, it didn't matter how hard Jeff worked at home—it wasn't legitimate if he didn't *go to work.*

Thankfully, we were not the only expats with the same issue. 'Surely two heads are better than one,' Jeff thought, and decided to visit one of his friends. That night, Jeff arrived home with a new spring in his step. 'I'm going to go out and find an office to rent,' Jeff announced. As they had been talking that day, Jeff's friend shared a little piece of advice that had suddenly motivated them both:

'Get out of bed and get dressed! Don't loiter and linger, waiting until the very last minute. Dress yourselves . . . and be up and about!'
Romans 13:14 MSG.

Now Jeff was primed. He'd get up each day, he decided, get out the front door, and go to work, like a regular Turk—or perhaps more importantly, like he had done every day of his life until coming to Turkey. All he needed was an office space.

'I'll head out this morning and see what's around,' Jeff told me as we made breakfast the next morning. 'And I'll drop into the computer repair store on the way to see if they have that replacement part I've been looking for,' he said. It was a small job that we'd been putting off, and I was thankful Jeff was going to take care of it.

In the end, thanks to that errand, Jeff never needed to look for an office space after all. As he stood at the counter, chatting to the owner, the subject turned to what Jeff was doing in Turkey. Jeff briefly explained our company. 'We're still getting established and making connections' he said, 'but right now I'm looking for an office where I can get set up.'

The computer fix-it guy pointed to a mezzanine level at the far end of the store. 'Would you like to work here?' he offered, 'I have a desk you can use.' With a brief discussion, his generous terms were set and accepted, and just like that we had an amazingly simple answer to our dilemma. Now Jeff would be able to go to work like everyone else.

~

Jeff began walking down to the computer store each morning, and once he sat behind a desk, no one seemed to care what he actually did. In fact, it soon became apparent that productivity was not a priority for anyone in the office. Between regular tea breaks, Jeff could do some marketing, arrange to meet with customers, tend to our affairs back in Australia or do some personal study—it didn't matter. What counted was that Jeff had somewhere to go each day. Everything was good.

Good, that is, until the police decided to park their car out the front of the computer store. For three days in a row, they simply sat there, doing nothing, saying nothing. They never even entered the store, but their presence was enough. Now the locals had another issue to deal with. *Why were the police watching the foreigner?* After three days it was time for a difficult discussion. The intimidation had worked, both Jeff and the store owner were getting uncomfortable with the situation, and fewer people were coming into the store. With a feeling of defeat, Jeff packed up his things, thanked his new friend for the use of the office space, and said it might be best if he found a new arrangement.

It was Ishan who helped Jeff make sense of the situation. Ishan was a businessman who owned a tiny grocery store nearby and loved nothing better than for Jeff to show up for a chat any time of the day or night. With a bright smile, Ishan greeted Jeff, pulled up a second chair behind the counter, and, in between serving customers, devoted the rest of the afternoon to explaining the problem.

'It is simple,' Ishan explained. 'The police in Turkey do not understand online companies. They think that if you go to an office and work at a desk, you must be employed by the shop owner. Your friend at the computer store could be fined a lot of money if it looks like he is employing you.'

So once again, perception was everything. We were grateful for the insight, but without being able to work from home or sub-let an office without creating a stir, it seemed there was nothing left for Jeff to do but to get out and about during working hours, set up his laptop and work wherever he could and hope that, over time, we might learn to live with this irreconcilable feature of life in Bursa.

28. Jeff's Mountain

Being watched by the police was one thing but being stared at and noticed everywhere we went simply because we were foreigners, was another. *'Haven't these people ever seen a foreigner?'* we often wondered, but even if they had, they'd almost certainly never seen an Australian family with four blond children!

The constant scrutiny was especially getting to Jeff, who had begun taking long walks on his own just to get away from it all. He was tired of everyone wanting to know his business. 'Lord, would you give me my own *Mount of Olives*?' he prayed. 'I need a place of solitude where I can think and pray in peace.'

The next time Jeff set out for a walk, he decided to go in a different direction. Behind our house was a road we had not yet explored. And with no idea where it would lead, Jeff headed up the hill rather than down, figuring he'd just keep going straight ahead as far as he could. An hour or two later, his idea was well and truly rewarded.

Once Jeff had crossed the ridge at the top of the road, the landscape changed from well-kept properties like our own, to streets where the houses were more like shacks and nasty-looking dogs skulked about. It was obvious that people in this part of the city were doing it tough. Coming to the end of the road, Jeff scanned the fields of farmland on the other side. If his plan was to walk straight ahead, it seemed he had gone as far as he could only to be disappointed.

And then, he caught a glimpse of a small dirt track, running between two farms. With renewed intent, Jeff crossed the road, every step taking him mercifully further away from the never-ending city crowds.

(Jeff writes) . . .

For half an hour I walked between the farms, up another hill and then another where the trees on either side grew thicker. And then, just as I made it to the top of the hill, I saw a man sitting in a tiny wooden booth beside a metal archway, and in the arch were the words: *Atatürk Kent Ormanı. Ataturk City Forest.*

I nodded to the guard and headed into the park. There it was—just a pine forest with the odd clearing here and there, a couple of little gazebos and burned-out patches of ground where people had obviously lit fires or enjoyed a barbeque—but it was my own personal sanctuary! This was what my soul had been craving! Now I had a terrific place to escape to whenever I needed a little time out with God.

29. God Loves the City Council

It was on his way home from the forest one day that something caught Jeff's eye in a compelling, lightbulb-moment kind of way. 'Anya!' he said when he arrived home, 'I've got to tell you something!' The sparkle in Jeff's eye had me intrigued. 'When I was out walking,' he began, 'I wandered into an area I've never been to before. I went over the ridge as usual, and down past the river. I walked along the riverbank for a while, came across a little bridge, and crossed over to the other side.'

I was used to Jeff's detailed descriptions but still couldn't figure out where this story was going.

'You wouldn't believe how filthy it was on the other side,' Jeff continued. 'It looked like a city dump or something, but there was no sign of it being controlled or managed at all. It's absolutely feral over there.'

As someone who loves nature and beauty, it had obviously bothered Jeff to see rubbish strewn around so recklessly. 'And then,' he went on, 'I kept walking. Everything was in such a broken-down state of disrepair. I don't know if it's lack of money or lack of care and I'm not judging, but there was a complete absence of care and effort—even the grassy verge on the edge of the river which could be so lovely, was overrun with weeds. All I could think was, "*Oh dear! Just look at this place!*"'

'And then,' said Jeff, 'I came across a huge new development. It looked like it was still just some fields, but there were some large pieces of machinery sitting over in one corner, and a temporary wall had been built all around it. Then I saw this amazing mural on the wall! Right along the length of the wall were huge picture boards with architectural designs and concept drawings on them, and Anya! . . .' Jeff exclaimed, 'the pictures were amazing! It's going to be the most incredible transformation project you can imagine!'

But Jeff had noticed something more. 'I looked closely and saw that the Bursa City Council logo was on every picture. I'd say the city council here has come up with an incredible design for a huge new public park. Really—the pictures look stunning!' Jeff said. 'All I could think was that someone in the city council must really love this city!'

I smiled at my husband's enthusiasm. The contrast was vivid; green grass and sculptured gardens were being created to replace acres of rubbish and weeds and dereliction. Someone clearly had a dream to transform a space that reeked of ruin and neglect into a wonderful parkland where every detail had been carefully considered, and everything was in its place. Someone was intent on beautifying the city of Bursa.

'It was the beauty of it that captured me,' Jeff said quietly, 'it felt as if this project was somehow a reflection of the heart of God—like, He loves beauty and the City Council does too. Anyway, it just got me thinking,' he said, 'that someone in the city council really loves this city.'

(Jeff writes) . . .

Trying to convey the feeling in my spirit wasn't easy. When you live in a cross-cultural situation everything can seem unusually vivid and moving. The rational side of me was thinking about the rubbish and the lack of care and was telling myself to calm down and give the poor guys a break! 'Come on, Jeff,' I said to myself. 'You're in a new city. It's early days. Don't criticise when you hardly know what they're up against!' Still, I knew I was perceiving something incredibly important, and though the contrast felt overwhelming, I decided not to fight it.

And that's when the thought struck me. What if it wasn't just me who felt pleasure at what the city council was doing here in Bursa? What if God was feeling the same way?

~

When Jeff finally spoke again, there was conviction in his voice as well as enthusiasm. 'Anya! I really believe the Lord is excited about this city. He loves the city council!'

As I sat there taking it all in, my own spirit jumped within me. You see, while Jeff had been out walking, I had received a message from a woman I had only recently met. It read:

> Hi Anya! There is a meeting for foreigners at the City Council tonight. 7.30 pm. I can pick you up! Elizabeth.

30. First Working Group Meeting

Elizabeth swung by as promised and with a great smile and a quick 'hello,' proceeded to talk non-stop in an accent that sounded half-American, half-French. I liked her right away, and even more so when I heard her story. Elizabeth had arrived in Bursa one year earlier, along with her French husband who was now working in Bursa, and their four children who were around the same age as ours.

As we drove together to the city council meeting, I was in awe of what this woman had accomplished in just one year. Not only had she become quite fluent in Turkish, but she had also founded the Bursa International Women's Association, a small yet vibrant group whose mission was to connect expat women in Bursa through social activities and community projects, Elizabeth told me, gesturing with her hands as she drove.

I had already heard great things about BIWA's fundraising work to support local causes and was looking forward to attending some of their upcoming social events. In the meantime, I was delighted to meet the woman whose idea and passion it was.

I could already see why Elizabeth was so good at what she did. Not only was she focussed and capable—she clearly possessed the energy and personality that would carry her vision forward. And, she was a connector. At exactly five p.m. I had received her text message, and just two hours later, here I was, riding in her car to a meeting at a city council I knew nothing about.

Thankfully, on the way to the council headquarters, Elizabeth filled me in. 'The city council here is made up of working groups,' she explained. 'There are over twenty of them—one for the preservation of the city's heritage, one for the arts, there's a health services working group, a tourism working group, even a photography working group. There are also larger working groups, called assemblies. They are the ones with the largest impact. There is a Children's Assembly, a Women's Assembly, a Disability Assembly *et cetera*.'

Elizabeth's words came in rapid succession. 'Anyway,' she was saying, 'the president of the city council got this crazy idea a few months back. He decided he wanted to start a foreigner's working group. It's never been done in Turkey before, so this is very important to the city council. It is like a pilot group. The officials in Ankara will be watching closely, because, who knows, maybe other city councils will try the same thing. Or,' she said, 'most probably they just want to know who the foreigners are so they can keep an eye on us.'

I asked what Elizabeth thought of the idea. 'It's a good idea,' she said with hesitation, 'I guess we'll have to wait and see.' And then she said the lines I was to hear so often over the course of the years to come. 'This is Turkey, after all.'

I didn't get a chance to ask what she meant, or why she seemed to have reservations about the formation of this group, because Elizabeth had stopped her car at the gates to a place she called, *Merinos*. 'It is a large park precinct,' my new acquaintance explained, 'it's very nice in the daytime. There are lakes and cafes and a cultural centre. They have concerts here, and the Mayor's office and all the municipality buildings and city council offices are in that building there . . .' Elizabeth was pointing with one hand and turning the steering wheel with the other as she guided the vehicle into a carpark. By the time we arrived, I felt I had gotten a comprehensive history of the city as well as a rundown of what the evening would entail.

'It will be mostly a lot of official talk,' she said, 'but they're good people. I'll introduce you.' And she did—there were handshakes and hellos and a few minutes of chitchat as we made our way into a modern-looking boardroom with transparent glass walls and tables arranged in a U-shape. I took a seat. A woman with a professional manner and a warm, ready smile opened the meeting. 'My name is Ayşe,[1]' she said. 'I am the assistant to the Secretary-General.' She gestured to the woman on her right. 'This is Başak.[2] Başak will be the council representative for this group. And over here . . .' she said, turning to the woman seated to her left, 'is Duygu, the temporary president of this group.'

With the friendly introductions over, it was time to get down to business and right away, the atmosphere shifted as tensions between the foreigners surfaced and spilled out. I hadn't expected this. Nevertheless, I leaned in, keen to understand what motivated these expats to be present at a city council meeting, what they were concerned about, what mattered to them, and more importantly, why they seemed so threatened by one another.

As it turned out, there was a strong French and German contingent from the women's association; they outnumbered any other interest groups in the room, and whether it was their manner or the respect they

---

1 Pronounced Ay-sha

2 Pronounced Bash-ak

already had with the City Council, I'm not sure, but they dominated the discussion for most of the evening and seemed adamant that any initiatives the City Council had in mind for foreigners were already covered by their organisation.

Across the room from me was a British woman who took obvious pride in telling us that she had lived in Turkey longer than all of us (twenty years, in fact), that she was a private English tutor for the big companies, and—she looked at me to make her point—she was the one everyone in Bursa came to if they needed help with their English publications.

This woman was openly sceptical about the President's agenda. 'The Foreigner's Working Group initiative is a sham,' she said, 'it is only a ploy for the city council to look progressive.' Her unashamed take on the whole thing rang in my ears later that night, causing a burst of desire to rise within me. 'You'll get nowhere trying to work with them,' she warned. 'They'll say yes to your requests, and smile to your face, but you'll achieve nothing.'

Ayşe and Başak helped the meeting proceed with dignity, but I felt embarrassed by the response of these fellow expats I had never met before. It was the president's idea to form a working group to represent the needs of foreigners in Bursa and to undertake projects that would ultimately benefit those who came from other countries, and yet it was the foreigners themselves who seemed to object to the proposal.

I sat there, listening. Was the city council's agenda as simple as it sounded? And were the BIWA women worried that this fledgling working group might impinge on their territory—or were they wanting to take the leadership of both groups? I couldn't be sure.

What was clear, was that no one held high hopes for the success of the working group, and no one trusted the reason behind its formation.

Except me.

As I sat there taking it all in, Jeff's words from earlier in the day still rang fresh in my mind, and I was overwhelmed by the desire in God's heart for this city. The President of the City Council was a man of peace with a kind heart for the foreigners in Bursa—whoever they were—and if God had brought us here to facilitate His desire for this city to prosper, I was up for that. I kept quiet throughout the meeting, but I could barely contain the bombardment of initiatives and ideas bouncing around in my spirit.

Ayşe spoke calmly and clearly, attempting to bring reason to an unexpectedly opinionated roomful of foreigners; and as she explained the unique opportunity we had to make a difference and to work together with the leaders of the city, I caught a fleeting memory of a moment six months earlier. . .

We were still back in Australia, praying through the decisions about going to Turkey, and if there was one thing that had come clearly to our hearts, it was that we should get there by the end of May. And we had. Just. Despite a myriad of legitimate last-minute reasons to delay, we had held onto that date, and by sheer determination alone, arrived at Istanbul airport on the thirtieth of May.

Now here I was, sitting in a foreigner's working group meeting that had been birthed in the mind of the president of the city council— probably at the exact time we were back home, deliberating. *Had this been God's plan the whole time? The whole time when we thought we were heading to Izmir? When we had to choose between taking another six months to raise more funds or to just come? The whole time we had been determined that we'd go anywhere but Bursa?!*

A sense of excitement filled me, and with it, the words that had shaped a previous season of our lives:

Seek the peace and prosperity of the city to which I have carried you into exile. Pray to the Lord for it, because if it prospers, you too will prosper.[1]

Sitting there at the conference table, part of the scene, yet strangely separate, I breathed my love for God, that He would go to such lengths to make sure He had one of his followers there in the mix, sharing his heart for the blessing and wellbeing of a city.

The room was full of negativity and cynicism. Jealousy was simmering, contempt was evident. And yet, my heart felt enlarged within me. The date of our arrival, which we'd tenaciously clung to despite a huge last-minute pushback, suddenly made perfect sense, and the fact that I had been invited to the meeting that night felt like a privilege I could not yet comprehend.

As the meeting ended, Duygu spoke. 'I've been standing in as a temporary president of this group,' she said, 'but I want to call a vote

---

1 Jeremiah 29:7

next fortnight. We need a new president to take the group forward.'

Eyes rolled, and sighs went out, and someone called for the group to simply be disbanded there and then, but, 'no,' Ayşe said, 'this is an official working group now, and that's not the way it works. We will have a vote at our next meeting.'

With that, the minutes were signed off, the meeting closed, and I'm not even sure what Elizabeth and I talked about all the way home. I only knew that resounding in my soul were those compelling words: *Seek the peace of the city.*

31. Visiting Tanca's Home

One woman I met at the Foreigners Working Group meeting was Tanca, and right away, we took to each other. Tanca was Turkish, spoke fantastic English—she was the head of a highschool English department—and as we made our way out of the working group meeting that night, she invited me to visit her at her home later that week. *'How would Tuesday afternoon suit you?'* Tanca asked in her perfect British accent.

'I'd love to,' I replied, which is how I found myself sitting at her kitchen table, asking about her family, her job, and how she had ended up at a working group meeting for foreigners. 'Oh, I just enjoy being with people from other countries,' she said. 'I've travelled a lot myself.'

Her apartment was lovely, with its combination of Turkish and English features. Ornate Ottoman-style lounge chairs were placed against the walls of the salon, and a chandelier filled the room from above. The kitchen was small, typical of Turkish apartments, but there was a table for two, where we sat while Tanca opened one cake box after another. She'd stopped in at her favourite patisserie, she explained, because she wanted me to taste a range of wonderful local pastries, cakes and biscuits. 'I got some baklava, too,' she said, 'it's very sweet, but I know you will love it. It's the best baklava in Bursa!'

I braced myself for an onslaught of gluten. This was clearly no time to explain my celiac disease—I decided instead to enjoy the kind hospitality of a new and generous friend. Tanca reached up to a country-style plate rack on the wall above the table where two rows of Spode willow-patterned plates had already caught my eye.

We talked at length, she, obviously delighted to have a native English-speaker to converse with, and I, honoured at the chance to be in her home. We were only twenty minutes into the conversation, however, before the gluten I had consumed hit the lining of my stomach, and pain took over. Tanca was still talking, but now I was struggling to pay attention. Sweat formed under my arms and on my forehead as my entire gut, it seemed, formed a taut, twisted mass inside me. I excused myself and closed the bathroom door behind me.

Breathe, Anya. Breathe. I washed my face, took a deep breath and smiled as I stepped back into the kitchen. '*It's been wonderful to visit,*' I remarked. '*Thank you so much—the tea, the food, getting to know you . . .*'

I went home and cried. It was two full days before I could get out of bed. My arms, it seemed, were paralysed, but the reality was I had no strength to lift them off the bed. How I would navigate the years ahead, I had no idea. Steering clear of gluten in Turkey was going to be every bit as difficult as avoiding rice in China. Jeff and I had been praying I would be healed, but in the meantime, I kept finding myself in situations where all I could do was to eat what was served to me with a smile, say a quick prayer of protection over my stomach, and factor in whatever the next few days might bring.

32. An Issue with Confidence

It wasn't just the gluten that was getting to me though. Something else had been niggling at me, and with Jeff in Izmir for a day and the children playing across the road at the park, I decided to brew a pot of tea and talk to God about it.

I like it when God talks too. I'd barely sat down when I heard him say, 'You've thrown away your confidence.'

I knew where those words came from, but still, I was surprised to hear them spoken so personally to me. I wasn't a shy person, was I? I didn't *feel* particularly lacking in confidence—surely it had taken some level of courage to bring four children and come to live in Turkey. I'd thought I was making a fairly good go of things. I was meeting people and getting around and generally feeling confident about life.

And then clarity arrived, and it touched on an issue I did not expect. A number of instances suddenly came to my mind—situations where deep down I had known what to do, and yet I had held back, unwilling to take responsibility. In a moment of revelation, I understood. *I had thrown away my confidence.* I thought of the times when I knew, in my spirit, that I needed to visit someone or act on an idea or change my course a little, and yet I had become sluggish at following through. Despite having a finely honed sense of intuition, I had started deferring more and more to Jeff. I was doubting myself, becoming double-minded. *Was that really God speaking into my spirit? Or was it 'just me?'* I had become paralysed and unsure.

I picked up my Bible and turned to the Book of Hebrews. *'Do not throw away your confidence; it will be richly rewarded.'*[1] It was kind of God to link the problem with something to hope for. But what kind of reward could he have in mind? I had no idea.

33. The Working Group Elections

It didn't take long, however, to find out that the reward I was being set up to receive was beyond anything I could have imagined, and suddenly I would need every ounce of confidence I possessed.

The night the Foreigner's Working Group was scheduled to meet again was approaching, and even as the reminder came through on my phone, the confidence I had been urged not to throw away, was tested.

Should I bother going along, or not?

In my heart, I knew that this council group presented an opportunity to contribute to the wellbeing of this city and its people. I could also see the potential for incredible influence, and I believed the city council was in God's heart. The problem was, this group could also turn into a tremendous timewaster. Turning up a second time would only make it more awkward if I decided the group wasn't for me.

Sometimes it's the little decisions that feel the most difficult.

Eventually, I resolved to take my confidence in both hands, go with what my gut was saying, attend the meeting, and trust that something about the night would reap a reward. 'Who knows?' I thought, 'Perhaps there are people in this group who will connect us to customers for our company.'

I often wonder at the way life can be shaped by one simple decision.

I wasn't sure what I expected that night; some sort of variation on the last meeting, I supposed.

Only I missed the whole point. That night there was only one item

---

1 Hebrews 10:35

on the formal agenda—the vote for the new working group president.

Most of the seats at the table were filled by the time I arrived, and I was surprised to see a slightly different mix of people in the room. Perhaps some had given up after the previous meeting and decided to call it quits. Maybe others had heard there would be a vote and turned up, determined to have their say.

The one sense that permeated the room was that this whole initiative was futile, that trying to work with the city council on their terms, as foreigners, was doomed from the start.

Nevertheless, the vote would take place, and before that, Ayşe said, we would go around the table, introduce ourselves, share our vision for the foreigners in Bursa and the working group, and anyone who would like to be nominated to replace the interim president could simply indicate their interest. 'This is a volunteer position,' Ayşe reminded us, and the looks on the faces around the room suggested that it wouldn't have made any difference if there was a salary on the table or not. It seemed no one was enthused about the job or the group or the city council's aspirations.

One by one, we heard from our fellow expats. 'I think it's a good idea,' said one, 'but I don't think we can actually do anything. We don't even know who the foreigners are in Bursa.'

'That may be true,' said another. 'But we do know that there are immigrants from Iran here, there are businesspeople from China, we have the major European companies, plus the students from Europe and Africa, and there are English teachers who come and go. Everyone has different needs and besides, we don't even speak the same language.'

A few people brought fresh ideas to the mix, 'Well, one thing the city should do is make it easier for foreigners when they arrive at the otogar[1],' one said. 'You get there, and you think you're in Bursa, but then you find you're nowhere near the city centre and there's no information to tell you how to get into town. It's not a very good start.'

I nodded. He had that right. My mind went back to our arrival in Bursa. What a help it would have been to find an information desk where someone spoke English, or at least offer us a map or brochure in our language. 'Yeah,' one of the students piped up, 'it's the same at the

---

1 Otogar: bus terminal

yabanci polis[1]. No one has a clue what to expect, and they make it nearly impossible for us to get visas to stay here anyway. The procedure keeps changing and no one informs us. The city council say they want to work with us, but there's no way the police will agree to that.'

So far, no one had offered themselves for nomination, but we were going around the room and now it was Janine's turn to speak. I was surprised to see her there; the only explanation, I presumed, was that she wanted to lead the group. I waited for her to share her ideas. Perhaps after a week of reflection, she felt more positive about the group's potential, but if anything, her angst seemed to have increased. It was foolish, she said, even deceitful, for this group to continue. The whole thing was a farce, and nothing would come of it, except to make things more difficult for expats. Janine spoke like a woman who had lived her expat life with very little joy.

The next person to speak up was the same friend who had encouraged Jeff to lease some office space. Kerry was an avid photographer who had moved to Bursa with his wife and children seven years earlier, and though his words were few, they brought a kind tone to the room. 'Bursa is a special place to live,' he said. 'It feels like a privilege to be here, and I do believe it is possible for this group to make a difference.'

It was my turn to speak, and suddenly I felt strong again.

'I like what the city council is doing here in Bursa,' I said, 'and I believe that the people who came up with the idea of this group really love their city.' I talked about the new park that was being built, the wonderful potential to even make tourists feel at home in Bursa, and how it seemed an honour to be invited to work with the city leaders.

'I don't think it's an accident that so many of us have ended up in Bursa,' I said. 'I agree that one person alone cannot change much, but if we all work together with the city council, maybe we could leave a sort of legacy that makes life better for those who follow us.'

Tanca, the Turkish schoolteacher, leaned over and nudged me. 'You should offer to be president,' she whispered, 'you'd be good at it!'—and in the moment, her words gave me the gentle endorsement I needed.

'It would be an honour to lead the group,' I said.

From there, it was all formality. No one else wanted the job, my

---

1 Yabanci polis: foreigner's police

name was the only one put forward, and with a show of hands, the vote was tabled in the minutes. Duygu visibly relaxed for the first time that evening. 'That's great,' she beamed, clearly thankful to be relieved of the role.

It took all of about two minutes for reality to set in. Making my way to the metro station, I boarded the train and eventually began the now-familiar walk up the hill to our home. 'Jeff,' I said, as I walked through the front door. 'You're not going to believe it! I put my name forward and they voted me in! I'm the new president of the foreigners working group.'

34. A Little Matter of Beauty

In preparation for my unforeseen step into the wider world, I decided it was time to perk up my looks. Back in Australia, I had splurged on a brow wax and tint every month or so, but since coming to Turkey, I'd put it off. Now, it was time to muster my courage once again. And so, the following morning I slipped into a little corner salon I had noticed near our house—a salon, meaning a bare room except for two sinks, two chairs, two mirrors, and two women in headscarves who possessed not a word of English between them.

'Brows.' I pointed to my face and mimicked peeling wax, but they showed no hint of comprehension. '*Boya?*' I tried. I had looked up the Turkish word for *dye*, and predictably, it was the same as the word for 'paint.' Yes, that triggered a response. '*Iyi, iyi,*' they said, 'good, good,' and pointed me to one of the chairs.

'*Kapat.*'

That word I had seen above the door on buses. *Kapat.* Close. I closed my eyes. I had no idea what these women had in mind, but neither was I in any position to question or give directions. I had picked up enough Turkish to talk for a minute or two about family or work or food, but absolutely none to describe beauty services. Now I was, very literally in their hands.

For a while, I was fine. Applying dye works pretty much the same way in any country, and I decided to relax and let the women get to work. What I wasn't prepared for, was the threading. As it happens, Turkish women don't use wax to shape their eyebrows. *They thread.*

With my hands pressed at strange angles, apparently to keep my eyelids taut, the younger of the two women set to work, one strand of cotton tensioned, for some reason, between her teeth, and the rest flicking across my skin like a little razor, making me desperate to sneeze.

It's tricky, trying to stretch your eyelids just right, keep your eyes closed, and hold in a sneeze when tiny bits of brow hair are flying up your nostrils. By the time she was finished, I had tears happening as well, and could only imagine what I might look like by the time this would all be over.

When the flicking was done, the tweezers had plucked what felt like a myriad of hairs, and my brows had been powdered and preened, it was time to open my eyes.

I looked in the mirror and gasped at the result—perfectly shaped brows, perfect colour, not a stray hair to be seen, and all without a drop of wax or a word of English. These women knew their trade, that's for sure. I had just had my first introduction to Middle Eastern beauty treatments, and I was sold. Turkish women, I decided, were the global experts in personal grooming; I would from that day on, put aside my Western ways and gladly submit to whatever methods they should choose.

35. Meeting the City Officials

A few days later, Ayşe, from the city council, called me. 'Are you able to come to the office this week?' she asked. 'President Semih Pala would like to meet you. When you come, we will discuss protocol and talk more about your role.'

As I squeezed into a crowded train once again, my mind's eye flashed to the many new situations I had navigated across my lifetime. If there was one gift my parents had given me, it was the capacity to walk into any environment and pull off a conversation with ease and confidence. The meetings ahead of me would not come without effort, of course, but the environment I was about to step into felt completely natural, and, in a wonderful moment as I entered the council buildings and followed the signs to the first floor, my overwhelming response was, *I was made for this.*

Ayşe was waiting for me, and as I accepted her offer of coffee and took a seat, our conversation flowed as if we were long-time friends. We spoke for a while about our families and about our university studies.

Then I listened as Ayşe explained the history of the City Council, how the working groups functioned, and how the President had a special interest in helping our group succeed. 'It was his idea,' Ayşe reiterated. 'Remember, no one has done this in Turkey before.'

When we had sipped the last of our coffee and set the tiny silver cups back on their saucers, Ayşe made a brief phone call to the office next door. 'Now I will introduce you to the Secretary-General,' she said.

The Secretary-General was a man in his fifties, short and slight, and when I met him, I was glad I had decided not to wear high heels. His face lit up, however, as I shook his hand and spoke the only Turkish greeting I knew. '*Merhaba. Benim Anya. Tanıştığımıza memnun oldum.*' *Pleased to meet you.*

It came out garbled. We were a good few weeks into our life in Turkey and still I was finding even basic greetings extraordinarily difficult. The Secretary-General, however, had even less of my language. 'Hello,' he managed, and that was the two of us at our capacity. Ayşe would clearly be the glue that held us all together.

We kept it pleasant and short. I answered a few questions, and then, with a nod and a signature, I was officially installed as the representative of the Foreigner's Working Group. 'You will not need to speak with the Secretary-General very often,' Ayşe explained as we left the room. 'The man you will work directly under is the President. We call him *Başkani*. It means *'the head, the leader.'* His name is Semih Pala.

The door to the President's office was open, and as Ayşe and I entered, a grey-haired man with a kind face and a gentle smile stood up to greet me. 'Very pleased to meet you,' he said, extending his hand. 'I heard you are from Australia?'

'*Yes,*' I replied. We conversed for a few minutes about his son in America, how many children I had, and how the new foreigners working group was very important to him. 'Let me know any needs you have,' he said as our introduction drew to a close, 'and give my regards to your husband and children.'

Thanking President Semih Pala, Ayşe and I made our way back out to the corridor. 'He's a good man,' I commented. Ayşe nodded. 'Yes, and he really loves this city.'

Ayşe went on to tell me about the procedures involved in working for the City Council—but for a moment I had mentally paused. Did she just say, '*He really loves this city?*' My mind went back to the words Jeff had spoken when he first came home from his walk across town. 'Someone really loves this city,' he had said, and suddenly it was as if I could hear the echo of God's heart in her words. The astounding confluence of events that had led to this moment dawned on me just as strongly, and at that moment I had no doubt that our prayers had been answered. *We were being caught up in a God-story!*

For now, though, I needed to focus. 'When your group has ideas for projects or collaborations,' Ayşe was saying, 'you need to make a formal submission on this form.' I looked at the paper in front of me and registered the fact that not only was every word in Turkish but that I would need to write my project submissions in Turkish too. Still, this was no time to flinch. 'We need you to show us the scope of the project, including all your requests, and a description about how the project will benefit the foreigners and the city.' Mercifully she added, 'I can help with the translation and I can take your proposals to Semih Pala. He is the person who decides, *yes or no*, whether they will happen.'

As Ayşe stood to say goodbye, she added, 'Please come to my office any time. I am here to help you.'

With a spring in my step, I left the council building and walked the perimeter of the park surrounding it. I had no idea what being the leader of this unlikely group of expats would look like, but deep within I knew I had been given an incredible honour. '*Thank you, God, thank you, God,*' I found myself whispering.

I remembered holding my first daughter in my arms when she was just a newborn baby. With a heart too full of love to even know what to pray, I had resorted to saying the same words over and over, '*O God, I love her so much. O God, I love her so much.*'

Now it was the same, only it wasn't a baby that had my heart. It was the city God had brought us to.

36. Stand in the Sun

The following week, I stopped in to visit Tanca at the school where she headed up the English department. 'Come at two p.m.,' she had said. 'I want you to meet the other foreign language teachers.'

I had not yet seen inside a Turkish high school and was surprised when I was stopped at the front gate by a guard. Later we would realise that every private school was guarded—a gentle reminder that we were living in a country which, just below its peaceful surface, could quickly turn volatile. The guard picked up a phone, called Tanca, and then arranged for me to be escorted to her office.

'Hoş geldiniz!' Tanca greeted me with a big smile, '*Welcome!*' And then she introduced me to her staff. It seemed strange to me that all the staff were wearing white lab coats over their clothing—*so unlike our schools back home,* I thought, as we walked the corridors of Tanca's school, poking our heads into classrooms.

'Here is where we teach English,' she said as she pointed to the classrooms, 'Oh, and meet . . .' she motioned to a young man over in the corner. I didn't catch his name, but we smiled, said 'Pleased to meet you,' and without missing a beat, he fell in beside us as we continued our tour.

The three of us turned out to have plenty in common. The young teacher had written a full-length novel—*in English,* he said. 'He wants to make it into a movie,' Tanca explained, her eyes lighting up. 'I have talked to some people at the university and we are hoping to produce it together.' And then, as if we'd all come up with the same vision at the same time, we burst out on top of each other: 'You could edit the script!' and 'You could direct the movie!' and 'Let's get all the English students involved!' and . . . 'What if we got the foreigners to be part of this too?! Let's put all our skills together!'

Tanca and her teacher-friend laughed and grabbed my hands. 'Quick!' they said, pulling me along with them, 'let's stand in the sun!'

The three of us ran out of the shadows to the middle of the courtyard, where we stood with bubbling hearts in a ray of sunlight as it beamed down between the buildings. 'It's what we do whenever we realise that we've all been inspired by the same idea,' explained Tanca.

By now the bell had rung and crowds of students were crisscrossing the pavement around us, making their way back into class. I waved goodbye to my two new friends and smiled, I believe, all the way home.

37. Professor Necmi's Book

I had spent a few hours each day working on Professor Necmi's manuscript and by now the words flowed naturally and beautifully, and even readers who may not have been familiar with the Ottoman-era setting, would be able to follow along with what had turned out to be a rather intriguing plot. In just one week, however, I was due to lead my first working group meeting, and I wanted to have the job finished before then.

I was thankful for a deadline that forced me to be content, not with perfection, but that I had done the best I could. I had started with a nearly indecipherable translation and worked hard to turn it into a richly nuanced story that any native English-speaking reader could enjoy.

Nevertheless, the readers were not my clients—professor Necmi was, and I was confident that he would be delighted with the result. And so, later that week, in the quietness of the early morning, I saved a final version of my work, wrote a brief email, attached an invoice, and with a simple 'send,' delivered my first editing job into the Turkish market, with the hope it would be the first of many.

38. The Foreigners Working Group

I went into my first meeting as president of the working group with no idea who might show up; in fact, as yet, there was no way to tell whether I even had a group to work with. The evening, however, got off to a surprisingly sturdy start. The cynical crowd stayed home, but a fantastic group of university exchange students came, all brimming with issues they wanted us to address and ideas for initiatives we could tackle together. A few long-term expats turned up too, keen to contribute in any way they could, and I was excited that four or five newcomers to the city had also heard of our group and came along looking for meaningful ways to integrate.

Everyone in the room was focused and willing, and that was exactly what I had been hoping for; the one thing we needed to do was to get runs on the board as quickly and as easily as possible. So, after a few minutes of reiterating the city council's agenda and affirming what a privilege it was to work together, I opened the rest of the meeting up for brainstorming and discussion.

Our first decision was that we needed a logo—right now we were the only working group not featured on the city council website, and if we were to have legitimacy going forward, we would need to be openly identified and recognisable as a formal working group. One of the men who came was a photographer with skills in graphic design, and I was delighted when he offered to do up some logo concepts to present at our next meeting.

We decided that our first public event should be an informal foreigners' picnic hosted jointly by the city council and our group. Partly this was to give foreigners the chance to meet other expats, but it would also allow council staff to meet foreigners face-to-face, rather than simply through our representation.

As the discussion around the picnic proceeded, someone raised an important point—how could we get foreigners to come together when many of them deliberately went out of their way to avoid one other?! I decided to address the issue head-on. We had felt a tangible sense of jealousy and distrust, even among the few foreigners Jeff and I had already met. It seemed that most expats held each other in as much suspicion as the locals did; everyone was guarded, personal backstories were only shared in part, and even common difficulties such as obtaining visas and work permits were discussed, so to speak, at arm's length. I needed to respect the feelings of the people we were attempting to represent, but at the same time, to inspire our fellow expats to have confidence in one another.

'Here in Bursa, it is tough for foreigners,' I acknowledged to the people around the meeting table that night. 'Finding legitimate work, obtaining visas—it's difficult, and, of course, everyone wonders why we would all come to live in such a conservative city when we could be in Istanbul or Izmir or have stayed in our home countries. Most expats have opted to keep to themselves, they don't want to tread on any toes, and so they basically make a go of life here independently of one another.'

My fledgling group nodded tentatively. 'The picnic will test how deep these issues run,' I went on. 'It's not easy, after all, to front up to someone new, answer the *What brought you here?* question, and then have to skirt around the fact you haven't been able to obtain a work permit.'

The people in the room agreed. Although I trusted the city council, many were still concerned that the council staff might pass on information to the authorities that could jeopardise their situation.

We dealt with the tensions as best we could, and as I closed the meeting an hour or so later, I shared a thought that had been on my mind throughout the day—a kind of catchphrase that I hoped might find traction.

'I've had an idea,' I said, 'about launching a campaign of some sort, to change the way our city thinks about foreigners. Right now, Bursa is known as one of the most difficult cities in Turkey for foreigners. What if instead we were known as a city that loves foreigners? The phrase I've had in my heart is something like, 'Bursa: where foreigners become family.'

If we could ever get to the point where that statement was true for the city of Bursa, we would have pulled off nothing short of a miracle. But that was exactly what we needed to hope for. The familiar words, 'You are no longer foreigners and strangers, but . . . also members of God's family' were at the forefront of my mind. What if that same spirit could permeate and transform a city?

We were all aware, however, that such a shift could not be achieved merely by events and projects. If we were to transition from the distrust and distance that came with being foreigners, to the closeness and confidence of belonging as family, something would need to fundamentally change in the minds and hearts of the people—and now that I had grasped the paradigm, the best thing I could do was to start praying into it.

The other thing I hoped would come from our first meeting, was the beginning of a core team. I knew by now that, potentially, I might be representing thousands of people across the city of Bursa, and our working group, with its open invitation, would likely fluctuate from week to week. What I needed was a core team of people who would be committed to working with me for the long term. What I really needed in all this, I realised, was friends. Looking around the room, I could already see a few people who might be a good fit, and I took the time to speak with them individually as we made our way out of the building that night.

My heart was full, and as I made my way home on the train that night, I pulled out my journal and wrote:

By the end of this week, I will have gathered my team. Iza, Anna-Sophie and Eliza will form my core group. We will meet weekly, run all our ideas through each other, and contribute our individual strengths into the mix. We have two other guys who are also fully committed and who I have chosen to trust completely. One is Baris, from Greece. His name means 'peace,' and that was enough for me! I'm glad to have him onboard. The other is Ilir—the Albanian guy Jeff and I first met at the bus terminal *when we visited last year. I could hardly believe it when I called him and found he was still in Bursa, and yes, he said, it would be his privilege to join the working group. Seeing him at the meeting tonight felt something like serendipity.*

Perhaps I am overstating it, but when I look at my core team, I see family. How this has come together so quickly, I can't say. But I do believe we represent, in a way, a picture of what is to come on a larger scale as our city and its foreigners begin to embrace one another and put our hands to the plough together. If the days ahead are anything like the past week, one thing is for sure: we will need to run hard together if we are to keep up with the dynamic that seems to have already been set in motion.

39. Promoting a Picnic

A core team was all it took for our ideas to swing into motion. Within a week we had submitted our first proposal to President Semih Pala and I had got my first taste of working with the marketing team, the council's media liaison person, and of course, with Ayşe. I could tell that my approach to the job was rather novel, but we all got on well together, and soon I was picking up on the sort of details that were non-negotiable, and those that I could suggest or influence.

Watching our ideas blend with Semih Pala's vision gave my team a great sense of satisfaction. Before long, both the president and I were compromising quickly and easily, and I was happy to default to his wishes if it meant we could go ahead and sign off on a plan. Although I was getting more perspective on the foreigner situation in Bursa, President Semih Pala was the one who knew his city and his people best—and he could factor in the wider perceptions, including those of the officials in Ankara.

It had been a hectic few weeks, but now, after all our planning, our attempts at understanding what the city council could or could not provide, after watching the marketing team swing into action to produce advertising for the event . . . our banners were up!

We had featured the city's trademark green colour, along with a picture of bright yellow tulips, and the words, 'Bursa Foreigner's Picnic.' The banners had been suspended high over the main streets of Bursa, right where the ancient Silk Road had once been, and as buses and cars and domus' and pedestrians streamed underneath them day and night, it had got people talking.

There had never been a publicly-held event specially for foreigners in the city of Bursa—in fact, any such gathering, if it had not been formally approved, might have ordinarily been shut down. But now, with our fledgling working group's new logo and the well-recognised city council logo side by side on our banners, it was official. A foreigner's picnic was soon to be held in the very heart of the city of Bursa!

It was the speculative talk of the town. No one knew what to expect. No one knew who the other foreigners might be. How many foreigners were there in Bursa anyway? A whole bunch of people who had been keeping their heads down or keeping to themselves had now been publicly invited to show up and, truth be told, I had no idea how this was going to turn out.

~

The day itself started out tenuous. Grey skies hung over the entire city, there was every chance our picnic would be rained out, and lurking in my mind was the knowledge that people in this part of the world would rather stay home than risk catching a cold. But this was no time to waver, and so, after preparing a stack of sandwiches, I folded the picnic rug into a carry bag and posted optimistically on Facebook: *Sandwiches made. Kids excited. It's a good day for a picnic!* Then, after sharing our advertisement one last time, Jeff and I and our four excited children set off down the hill, and onto the city-bound bus.

We arrived to find Semih Pala pacing nervously inside an area of grass that had been cordoned off especially for us, a detail I had not foreseen. 'You must picnic within this particular area,' a staff member explained when I enquired. 'It makes it official.' We had discussed the issue of media in advance, but there was no getting out of it. The official photographer was already there with his camera and crew. 'After all,' he explained, 'the people want to know what their council is doing for them.'

I was worried, then, because it doesn't feel very friendly to sit in an area cordoned off with plastic tape like a bunch of suspects in an investigation zone; besides, I was well aware of the lengths many foreigners went to, to ensure their photographs were never taken, let alone splashed across newspapers and television. But this was protocol, and there was no budging on it. Besides, I was not about to cast any hint of dissatisfaction on the city council's operations. They were taking a huge risk on us too. I just had to hope the foreigners wouldn't take one look from a distance and keep on walking.

The council staff had erected two white gazebos, as we had requested, and set up tables so that any other foreigner's interest groups could advertise openly and engage with people. But between the drops of rain, the cordoned area and the complete lack of welcoming vibe, the mood was anxious. If no one turned up, President Semih Pala would be left shamefaced. He'd gone out on a limb, advertising so publicly, and at this point, there was no way to know if anyone other than my little band of friends would even come.

Still, I figured there were a few things we could do to change the atmosphere. With a quick word to my team, we found some upbeat music, which drew a few people in, got our children playing soccer, and over the next hour or so, people started arriving. Some recognised a familiar face or two, but most, I quickly realised, had very few foreign friends. I needed to go to work, introducing people, facilitating the initial conversations, and then moving on and leaving them to it.

Thank God for students.

They couldn't care less about cordons or protocol or whether they were on expired visas or not. And, they brought their skateboards. One guy, as it turned out, was once a professional skateboarder in Afghanistan—he'd started a skateboarding school in Kabul, in fact—and before we knew it, he had the kids practising tricks on the footpath and having a whole heap of fun.

Another guy came with a top-of-the-range Yo-Yo, of all things, and when word got around that he would be competing in the international Yo-Yo championships in Bursa the following week, a crowd gathered around him as well, to see his moves and give it a shot themselves.

And then, one of the women who had been so critical of our group at the beginning turned up. I hadn't expected her to come, but she did and was clearly surprised at the easy way everyone mingled together—surprised at the turnout, too, I guess—and it struck me how few people she seemed to know, despite having lived in Bursa for nearly two decades. I found myself longing for her to feel included, for her to believe, despite her cynicism, that she was part of a bigger, brighter story than she realised.

By the end of the day, the sun was shining, about a hundred people had come and gone, the reputation of the city council was mercifully still intact, and our fledgling working group had just pulled off its first event.

My core team and I stayed to help the council workers as they dismantled the gazebos and cleaned up the area—despite their protests, we smiled, insisted, and hopefully communicated that we were not only there to be served but that we also wanted to serve, to show the council that we were not above them, that we didn't take them for granted. Still, none of the Turkish staff seem to know what to make of an eight-year-old Australian boy helping lug chairs across a park, or a Polish intern dismantling trestle tables. But then, Semih Pala himself joined in, and everything changed.

Now, there we were, all pitching in together like family, and once again, I was so very proud of us all. We had put on this event together, established our solidarity with both the city officials and the wider community of foreigners, and been publicly validated in our city. In the end, we all agreed, it had been a perfect day.

40. Working with the Police

While I had been focusing on the picnic, Ilir, another of our subgroup leaders had managed to arrange an initial meeting with the foreigner's police. As a working group, we knew that this was the one partnership that affected every foreigner living in Bursa, and we had two projects to propose.

The first was that newly arrived foreigners who did not speak Turkish should have access to a police-approved translator. Our plan was to provide a list of people from the expat community who were fluent in Turkish and another language; the idea was that they could be on call in case translation help was needed during the visa application process.

The second proposal was that we should create a standardised checklist for resident visa applications so that everyone could conform to the same requirements. Through Ayşe, we arranged an appointment with the Chief of Police, who eventually but reluctantly agreed to meet—though more out of deference to the city council, I'm sure, than any regard for our working group.

We assembled at the designated meeting time, excited by the thought that our show of goodwill toward the police in Bursa could potentially pave the way for a more welcoming process in other parts of the country too. I was especially thankful that Ilir was in the mix. For a start, he was fluent in Turkish, but more importantly, he had a way with officials that came, I presumed, from having grown up in a similar culture. I hoped that once this initial meeting had taken place, Ilir would take over the whole project.

As it happened, the meeting was polite and not much else. I sensed right away that the police chief would rather not take suggestions from a woman, and that my role as president of the working group meant nothing to him. Although he listened when I spoke, he directed all his answers to Ilir or Başak, our council representative.

We did away with the usual pleasantries—they seemed superfluous given the attitude of the police representatives, who got right to the point, making it clear that they would be calling the shots. Yes, we could give them a list of expats who could possibly be called on to translate, but no, they could not commit to doing anything with it. 'No, a permit checklist is not possible,' the police chief brushed my next request aside as well. 'The ministry in Ankara decides what is required for visas, and they reserve the right to change it for different nationalities and situations.' *That's an understatement,* I thought. *We've been through the process three times already and every time there's been a new requirement that no one has yet heard of.*

'What about giving foreigners more than three month's permission to reside?' I asked. 'After all, in Istanbul and Antalya, foreigners often get a two-year permit. Why, in Bursa, do so many of us have to go through this process every three months?'

The question was answered with a polite, 'Everyone has a different situation,' which I interpreted to mean, 'We get hundreds of lira every time you reapply, so that's one reason. And besides, we get to keep tighter tabs on everyone if they have to explain their reasons for being here every three months.' It was time to change tack.

'Well,' I ventured, 'let's suggest another idea for a partnership. The foreigner's police station is very difficult to find for people who do not know Bursa well; there are no signs to help foreigners know where to go. Is it possible we could arrange some street signs to direct people from the train station perhaps?' The question was answered with a noncommittal nod.

I glanced at Ilir and decided to pull out the idea that had been mulling in my mind ever since the meeting began. The yabanci police station had to be one of the most unappealing, out-of-the-way, run-down places in town, yet most foreigners spent at least three or four hours there at a time, waiting for their requests to be processed.

'What if the police and the working group joined together for a volunteer workday at the station?' I ventured. 'We could clean and paint and generally brighten things up so it feels welcoming. It would be a way to show there is a good relationship between the yabanci police and the foreigners,' I said. 'We could talk with some local businesses to see if they would like to donate chairs for people to sit on, or a water dispenser, or . . .' But with that, I had stepped on the landmine called offense, and with a *'Pleasure to meet you'*, the meeting came to an end.

Ilir was realistic as usual. *'The only reason they agreed to come in the first place was so they could know what this group is doing,'* he said as he tossed his satchel over his shoulder. Maybe coming from Albania helps, I thought. From my experience, working with the police there was also an exercise in futile niceties. The problem was, now it was me who had begun to feel cynical.

But Ilir knew exactly how these things worked. Taking some initiative of his own, I saw him quicken his step to catch up with the police chief just as he left the building. For the next minute or so, I watched from a distance as they chatted quietly and unofficially, like old friends, and by the time they parted, Ilir had got what he had hoped for. The head of the foreigner's police department had agreed to ongoing discussions. We would continue to meet with representatives of the yabanci police once a month. Who knew whether we would be able to achieve anything tangible, but for now, it was a start.

41. Permission to Stay

Interacting with the foreigner's police was not only a working group project—it had become an ongoing personal saga for our family. We had started out in Turkey on a standard ninety-day tourist visa, but now that we had settled in Bursa, permission to stay needed to be granted by the foreigner's police department. This meant applying for resident permits for each of us, and while just a few hundred kilometres away, in Istanbul, this was largely an online process and most permits were granted for one or two years, this was not the case in Bursa.

Getting our first round of resident permits had been difficult, they too, had only been granted for three months, and already it was time to reapply—from scratch, it seemed—only Jeff was hoping that this time, things would go much more smoothly.

The first time we had applied for resident permits, we were well prepared—or so we thought. Jeff had set off with a folder full of passports, birth certificates, marriage certificate and business details, and, having been warned that hardly anyone in the police station spoke English, even took a friend along to translate for him. When they arrived, the clerk at the front counter had handed Jeff six forms to fill in. 'One for every person,' he said.

Filling them in had been a slow task, particularly with nowhere to sit, no bench to write at, and a crowd of Arabic-speaking people shouting all around him. He had hardly even gotten started when he was unexpectedly summoned by a police officer. 'Come with me,' the officer said, ushering Jeff and his friend up a couple of flights of stairs, 'You must speak with the director of the police.'

Jeff had noticed with some concern that no one else was being escorted up or down that particular staircase, but, with his translator in tow, and having done our research into the laws around living and working in Turkey, he figured we should be fine. The reality was, there *was* no law about online companies, and this, we figured, should stand us in good stead.

The police director, however, had wasted no time getting to the point. 'Are you working in Turkey?' he asked. 'No, technically, we're not,' Jeff explained. 'Our company is an Australian company and our payments go into an Australian bank account. All our work is done online, so effectively, we could be working anywhere in the world. Here in Turkey we simply promote our services.'

'But why are you living in Bursa?' the director had asked. 'Oh, because from Bursa it is easy for us to visit universities in Istanbul, Izmir and Ankara,' Jeff had said. For good measure he even decided to throw in a little compliment . . . 'and because this is a pleasant city for our family.'

Legally, we should have been fine, only we weren't, because the more

Jeff had talked, the more tensions rose, not between Jeff and the police chief, but between the police chief and our translator-friend. Jeff had been unable to follow their discussion, but clearly, it was not going well. 'There will be no visa,' his friend had eventually said. 'You will need to come back and talk another day.'

With no small amount of uncertainty in his spirit, Jeff had left the police station to begin the hour-and-a-half trip home. 'What happened?' he asked his friend as they parted ways. 'I do not know,' was the reply, 'I helped you as much as I could. I didn't tell him what you said, because I know the system better than you. So, I answered in my own way, and I'm not sure why, but now the manager is mad.' Jeff was horrified. 'But that's not translating is it?' he remarked in exasperation.

The following day Jeff had gone back to the police station with a different friend; this time, he made it clear that everything he said must be translated word for word. Thankfully, our first resident visas had been approved that afternoon, and the first thing Jeff had done when he got back home, was to sit down and make a list of every document he had been asked to produce. Next time, we were determined, getting a permit would be a breeze.

~

Ninety days had passed already, and this time we were confident our permits would be renewed. By now we had been in the country for six months, people knew us a little better, and our hope was that this time we might be granted permission to stay for a year. With our wad of documents assembled, Jeff decided he would brave the language barrier alone, rather than take a translator. *How difficult could it be the second time around?*

Quite difficult, as it turned out. 'Incorrect,' were the first words the clerk spoke when Jeff handed his stash of papers across the counter. 'You must follow the process. Go to the man at the back of the building. He will prepare your documents properly.'

The new 'process,' which the officer scrawled on a small slip of paper, bore no resemblance to any list Jeff had seen before; nevertheless, he made his way around the back of the police station where, sure enough, a middle-aged man sat behind an ancient manual typewriter set on a makeshift desk. The windowless space resembled more of a shack than an office, and the only sign on display was a square of cardboard taped to the back wall that read, '40 TL for one page.'

Well that's one way to make a killing, Jeff thought. With still no clarity about the service he was paying for, Jeff began mentally calculating the sum he was about to hand over. Four hundred and eighty lira! Jeff reluctantly placed the notes onto the desk in front of him, and, suddenly helpful, the man began typing. Half an hour later, with newly translated 'original' documents, Jeff headed back to the visa office. 'Very good,' said the clerk with enough enthusiasm to make Jeff wonder just how many people were getting a cut out of this newly introduced step in 'the process.'

But the clerk wasn't finished yet. 'You still need to fix one thing,' he said, writing some directions down on a piece of paper, 'you need to have the translations notarised.' A look of disbelief crossed Jeff's face. 'Don't worry,' the officer reassured him, 'it is easy. My friend can help you.' Jeff looked at the address. It would take at least an hour to catch a train to that side of town and back, plus however long the notary took to complete the job.

As Jeff thought of his meticulous preparation, something clicked. Maybe the seemingly random additions to the application process were not just a way to make extra money out of foreigners. Maybe the police didn't *want* anyone to get it right the first time. With their professional pride at stake, one way to ensure that we foreigners always knew who was boss, was to make it clear that they could turn us away whenever they pleased.

Compliance brought results, however. It wasn't quite the victory we had hoped for, but we celebrated nevertheless when Jeff arrived home with resident permits. For the next three months, we could continue to live in Turkey.

42. Saturday Soccer

On the home front, we had by this time become keenly aware that we needed to get out more, to integrate into the community and especially, to find some activities for our children. We had hoped to find social soccer clubs in Bursa, much as we had back home in Australia, but joining a sports team had not been as easy as we expected. It appeared we would need to give up our concept of Saturday sport, so prevalent in

Australia and New Zealand, where parents coach teams or cheer from the sidelines while their children play in friendly matches or practice their ball skills, because 'in Turkey,' as our Kiwi[1] friend explained, 'sport is either deadly serious or non-existent.'

It was as Jeff and his friend talked that their momentary frustration turned quickly into a workable idea. What if they started their own team? A team for any kids who wanted to join in? A team for all ages, so even adults could play with their kids? We had six children between our two families—that would be a start. *Why not just do something?*

Immediately their minds went to a nearby park with Astroturf to play on and football goals at either end. We had never seen anyone use the park, but it was perfect for a friendly game of soccer, and by the end of the conversation, a plan was made. The dads would simply turn up with our kids every Saturday morning, start kicking a soccer ball among themselves, and we all hoped the local children would soon join in too.

And they did.

On the first day, Jeff, Eric, Joseph and Vangie walked from our house, our friend and his two kids came from theirs, and at ten o'clock sharp, the game kicked off, bringing Saturday morning football to Bursa. It didn't take long for one or two local boys to meander onto the field. They came in pairs, linking arms in solidarity as they strolled towards the game, but our children were quick to welcome them in, and so long as the Turkish kids were evenly allocated across both teams, the games were a lot of fun. Every week the numbers grew until we had a regular football team!

Sometimes the boys just wanted to kick a ball around, other days it all got very competitive. And then there was the morning when one little kid came along with his 'uncles' in tow. Jeff suspected something was out of the ordinary when, just as the game was getting underway, the young Turks on our team turned to see their friend sauntering towards them, flanked by two athletic-looking youths. Suddenly the kids went wild with excitement!

It only took a few opening passes to figure out why—as it turned out, our little Saturday soccer club had been joined by semi-professional footballers. For the next sixty minutes, Jeff and his friend kept their focus

---

1 Colloquial for 'New Zealander'

simple: stay alive and do whatever they could to prevent humiliation.

The on-field dynamics of the soccer team were always interesting; it was a wonderful thing to watch Turkish boys play football because, like the rest of the nation, they were fanatical about the game. They all learnt to play early in life, mostly on the streets and by watching live games, and for young kids, they played incredibly well. For our children, Saturdays had now become the highlight of the week. If nothing else, it gave them a chance to play sport in a setting where they were respected by the locals.

So, with sport sorted, we turned our thoughts to education. It had been summer holidays since we had arrived, but with the new school year about to commence, and with no idea what might be involved, we began to make enquiries about enrolling our children in a local Turkish school.

43. Slaughtering for Bayram

Bayram[1] came right at the end of the summer break. It had been a full year since Jeff and I had first encountered the sacrifice festival, but the slaughter

we had witnessed on the road to Istanbul was still vivid in our minds.

Now, however, the scene was about to be replayed just down the road from our house, and let's just say that while there are many aspects of Islamic life that I appreciate, there are others that, to this day, I can barely stomach.

Earlier that week, the covered market had been cleared of its usual stalls and in their place, truckloads of sheep, goats, lambs and cows had been brought in, along with deliveries of knives, ropes and buckets of sawdust to spread over the ground. By the end of the day, the imams[2] and butchers had begun the work of blessing and killing, while the squeals and cries of helplessly tethered animals rang through the neighbourhood.

Our neighbour, Elif had visited our home the night before the sacrifice. Her father had died a few years earlier, and her brother was not able to come home that year for Bayram, so I wondered how she and

---

1 Bayram: nationally celebrated holiday or festival

2 Islamic worship leaders

her mother would perform the sacrifice. Her answer surprised me. 'Oh, my family bought a sheep last week and had it delivered to the Islamic college,' she explained. 'The young men who live there are students at the university, but they are also training to be religious leaders. They will say the prayers and slaughter the animal for us. Tomorrow, my mother and I will go there to listen to the prayers, and then we will bring the meat home to cook and share among friends.'

As a family, we had done our best to fall in with local customs, but with this being the holiest occasion on the Islamic calendar and us being neither Muslim nor Turkish, it seemed best to lie low for a few days while our local friends dressed in their lovely new clothes and came together as families to share in a joy-filled Eid[1].

And then, just as the days of feasting were coming to an end, there was a knock on the door, and there stood Omer Bey, our neighbour, holding a heavy dish covered in plastic. 'For you,' he simply said, and smiled as he waved goodbye.

On the plate was a huge piece of freshly slaughtered meat.

It's a lovely thing, the way the sacrifice works. Every family purchases an animal—usually a cow, but often a goat or sheep, depending on their means—and once it is blessed and killed, the meat is divided into three portions. The first third is reserved for the family; some of that will be frozen for later use, but most is cooked slowly and eaten as part of the Eid celebrations. The second portion is for sharing among neighbours and friends, and the third is gifted to charity or to those who may not have had the means to participate in the sacrifice.

As we accepted the gift, we were humbled. Not only was this a particularly generous portion, but we realised that despite the fact we were Christians and foreigners, we had just been treated not just as neighbours and friends, but most endearingly of all, as family.

44. Starting School

With Bayram behind us, the day had arrived for our children to commence school. I woke the girls early, brushed and tied their hair, fastened their shoes, and lifted the new backpacks onto their tiny shoulders, trying all the while to stay strong, to not let on how conflicted I felt about the

---

1 Eid: festive holiday

whole sending-them-off-to-school situation.

I made sure there was a change of clothes in each of the girl's bags—it was the only instruction I had managed to pick up during the ten minutes we had spent with the preschool principal the previous week before it became obvious that none of us had enough of each other's language to communicate any further details. The only other piece of information we had was that a school bus would stop outside our house at seven-thirty every morning to pick up the girls.

The lump in my heart grew heavier by the minute. I looked at the clock. *Seven twenty-five, seven twenty-six*, and right then, before we'd had a chance to hug our girls and whisper strength into their little hearts, we heard the short honk of a horn outside, and now there was no time for anything but to send them on their way.

Isn't it always the way, that in any given moment we can be both strong and weak, sure and uncertain, confident and fragile?

Jeff and I grasped our little girl's hands in ours and headed for the front gate. And it was then, when we saw the van that would take our girls off to a world we knew nothing about, that we lost our nerve. This was nothing like the sort of bus we had expected. In fact, it wasn't a bus at all. The vehicle waiting outside our front gate was a shiny, black, unmarked van with dark-tinted windows.

Our minds were trying to function. Was *this* the bus for our girl's school? Were there any other kids inside? And who on earth was this woman all shrouded in a headscarf and black ankle-length trench coat, who had opened the sliding side door and was impatiently calling to our girls to get inside?

Jeff had bought a special gift for Vangie which he had given her that morning as she woke—a little pink iPod, all loaded up with songs and audiobooks in English for her to listen to as she made her way to her new school; now she held it in her hand and I saw her clutch it tight, the only familiar thing she could carry into the day ahead.

Liberty, on the other hand, clung to me, crying and screaming and pleading and trying for all the world to lock her arms around my neck. The bus lady looked annoyed. We got the distinct impression that her job was to open and close the door of the van and fasten the children's seatbelts, and that what was going on with these foreign children in front of her was an anomaly she should not have to deal with.

It didn't help that I was crying too.

Who were these people, and why were we sending our not-yet-two and not-yet-four-year-old girls to a foreign preschool anyway?

The driver gave another honk of the horn, and with little choice, we whispered hasty words of reassurance in the ears of our girls.

'Jesus loves you,' 'Mummy and Daddy love you.'

With tears streaming down at least three of our faces, we pried Liberty's arms from my neck, and, thankful for Vangie's sisterly care, we watched as the door slammed back into place and the van took off down the street carrying two bewildered children from the other side of the world.

There wasn't time to sit and sob. Eric and Joseph were next—they needed to be walked down the hill and taken by taxi to their new school. From the look on their faces and the concern on Jeff's, we realised that once again, nothing but sheer willpower was going to get us on our way.

The boys, usually animated and ready to take on the world, were subdued as they sat in the back seat. For all the turmoil of sending the girls to school, we knew that the fact they were so little and angelic and fair-skinned would endear them to their teachers and that they would quickly adjust to their new environment. With the boys, we were under no such illusions. Starting Turkish school at their stage, we knew, would be anything but easy.

That day was the longest we had spent in Turkey yet. By mid-morning, Jeff and I felt as if we had run a marathon with a finish line that kept on moving. We pottered around, trying to attend to our work, but our thoughts were with our children. The first day would be the hardest, we told ourselves. Once day one was done and dusted, and we all knew what to expect, we'd be able to settle down.

If only.

The children did come home, of course; they entered the house with a mixture of shell shock and relief on their faces, but we hugged them, told them how proud we were of them all, and pulled out a dump box full of Lego, hoping that a few hours of playing together would keep their minds, at least for now, off the reality that the next day, and every day after that, we would have to do this all again.

It wasn't until we put Liberty and Vangie to bed that night that it dawned on us that having our children in school might not be the simple educational option Jeff and I had hoped for.

'The teacher told me off,' said Evangeline. 'She said I needed to bring another singlet tomorrow.' I heard the tweak of a Turkish accent in her voice and ignored the little tremble in my heart. 'A singlet?' I wondered. Taking a change of play clothes, I understood. But a fresh singlet too? I looked over at Arzu's house. Her lights were still on, and if ever I needed some mothering of my own, it was now.

Arzu was gracious as ever. 'Oh yes,' my neighbour assured me, using Turkish words just simple enough for me to understand. 'Maybe you do not know this, but sweating is very harmful for children. Children can get sick if they sweat.' We sipped our coffee through sticky pieces of Turkish delight, but my thoughts were back at home in Australia, where the temperature hovered in the sweat-zone for most of the year and children ran around barefooted and often bare-chested in the heat all day long.

Arzu must have been amazed at my ignorance. 'After the children play outside,' she explained, 'they must change into clean clothes. The girls must put on a fresh singlet every time they come back in from play, so they can stay healthy.'

Jeff was sitting on the couch when I came back home. He'd put the boys to bed, and he too was beginning to realise the magnitude of what we were doing. Sitting on the edge of their beds, the boys had finally shared some of the details of their day. 'We didn't understand a word the teachers were saying, Dad,' they said, 'They even set out the maths problems differently here.' Well, surely, we could work with that, we decided. But what they went on to say about how the teachers and children interacted with one another, concerned us. There were clearly going to be issues with Turkish schooling that we had not foreseen. Right now, though, we hoped that much of what the boys had experienced was simply first-day culture-shock, something that would ease off over time.

Jeff and I sat together awhile and then began emptying the schoolbags, ready for the next day. And that's when we found *the papers*—take-home notices, printed forms, little memos—between the four children we soon had a sizeable stack sitting in front of us which we now needed to read. Only we couldn't. We had no idea what any of the papers were saying, or asking, or meant to remind us of. With weary brains, we pulled out our Turkish dictionary and began translating one notice after another, one word at a time, as best we could. Health forms, stationary supply lists, permission forms for an excursion—we couldn't work out where that child was going, but we signed it anyway.

The pile slowly waned but we were waning faster.

If this was the effort it would require just to send our kids to school, we were already having second thoughts. But for now, we had to focus on the upside. Our four children were successfully enrolled in the Turkish system, all four had got to their schools and into their correct classrooms, and, more importantly, had arrived safely home at the end of the day. Now there was nothing for it but to move forward one day at a time.

45. A Turkish Website

With the children settling into school, Jeff and I were able to turn our attention to our business. Fatih, our friend from next door, had translated our website into Turkish, and now we were ready to go live. YouNeedAnEditor.com was up and running—and though we had no idea whether it would generate the steady flow of work we hoped for, it did lend significant credibility to our presence in Turkey. Hopefully, having a website in Turkish would also give us an edge over our competitors that were outside the country.

Still, we needed some breakthrough in terms of actual jobs. Though we had met many potential customers and Jeff had visited universities in Izmir and Istanbul several times, it had not yielded much in the way of paid work. We had come to Turkey with a sturdy business plan; now we were grappling with the realities of *doing* business in Turkey. On the upside, every meeting opened doors of friendship, something we valued as highly as the work itself.

Our local friends were generous with their advice. They understood that doing business in Turkey was difficult enough for Turks, let alone foreigners, and the one thing they all agreed on was that if we were to succeed, we would need to employ a local representative for the company. 'Turks won't buy from non-Turks,' they said apologetically. 'It is okay for you to *do* the work, but the person representing the company needs to be Turkish.'

The other issue we were up against was how few people even owned a credit card. Here we were in a predominantly pay-by-cash society, only we had built our business plan around online payments. Even using bank accounts, we had found out, was not as common as we might expect. We kept hearing about how people might be very wealthy, yet look for all the world like they had nothing; certainly there were many who had no record of savings in any bank, anywhere. What they did have, was gold—gold that had been passed down and added to from generation to generation, mostly kept in their homes, under their mattresses.

But a bigger issue was coming to light, and for this, there seemed no solution. Providing editing for academics assumed that there were people out there who had something original to publish; that they had undertaken research that was journal-worthy and would therefore, need to be polished in order to be accepted into foreign journals. The reality we were now facing, however, was that the majority of university students in Turkey were not particularly interested in doing their own research; surprisingly few even aspired to publish their work in English. Besides, most of our potential clients had no way of telling whether their translations were perfect—or riddled with errors. In their minds there was little distinction between translation and editing, so why pay for both? The result was that our company was attracting plenty of interest, but very few clients.

We were still grappling with ideas when the dearest thing happened. Jeff had spent the morning with Ishan, his friend who owned the tiny store at the bottom of the hill and loved nothing better than to talk about business. Perched on upturned crates behind a counter lined with cigarettes and packets of Nescafé and the best handmade Turkish delight Jeff had ever tasted, they spoke together about the difficulties we were up against. 'There's one more thing you should know,' said Ishan. 'We have a saying that money goes from foreigners to Turks, not from Turks to foreigners.'

Later that day, Jeff came home, smiling. 'It's going to be good,' he said with a laugh. 'Ishan is very worried about our company, but he doesn't want us to have to leave Turkey, so he told me he is going to pray for our company every time he goes to the mosque—which means at least once a day!'

If nothing else, Ishan was fervent in his faith. It was a kind gesture indeed, and amid all our attempts to make a go of life in Bursa, we were genuinely touched.

46. The Meaning of a Necklace

We took Ishan's advice to employ a Turkish representative for our company seriously, and it came as a pleasant surprise when the perfect person for the job appeared to be a twenty-year-old woman who I met one night as we were both leaving the city council building. I had just led a meeting of the foreigners working group, while Nurcan[1] had been translating for the disability group meeting, she told me. 'Translating?' I asked. 'Yes,' she replied, 'I am a sign language translator for the deaf people who attend.'

I warmed to Nurcan the moment we met. Here was a girl with a happy heart and a bright mind, *and* she showed a keen interest in our business. After a couple of meetups, I floated the idea to Jeff. 'Yes,' he agreed, 'Let's ask if she would like to be our company representative.'

The following week I met with Nurcan at the local mall, where we pulled up chairs at a table near the window. As usual, we began by enquiring politely about each other's families, but as we waited for our coffee to be served, my eye was drawn to the necklace Nurcan was wearing. It appeared to be a thin silver coin embossed with an Ottoman-style script, suspended on a delicate chain, and I rather liked it.

She smiled, obviously glad I had noticed. 'Yes, it's lovely, isn't it?' she said. 'It was a gift.'

'Oh really?' I asked. 'From someone special, perhaps?'

'Actually, no,' Nurcan replied, 'I was given this necklace when I lived in a dormitory in Istanbul.'

Nurcan had studied the Ottoman language at university, and during her years there, had lived, as did many other students, in a heavily subsidised Islamic dormitory. Hers, of course, was a women's dormitory. The men had their own—we had already seen one close to our house here in Bursa. These dormitories, we had been told, were owned by an Islamic foundation, and students who were lucky enough to be offered a place were not only housed, but fed, provided with tutorials, and transported to and from their lectures, all for a fraction of the usual cost to their families.

'In my dormitory, there were incentives for good behaviour,' Nurcan explained. I wondered where this story was leading.

---

1 Pronounced: Nur-jan

Nurcan touched her fingers gently to the coin. 'I received this as a prize for memorising the Koran,' she said. 'In my dormitory, if we performed our prayers five times a day, we were rewarded with money. But there was another prize—this necklace—and I wanted it mostly because I liked it, but . . .' she paused for a moment, 'but also because everyone knows what it means. It was a reward for students who memorised large parts of the Koran.' She looked at me meekly. 'I know that's not a proper motivation . . .'

And right then, I loved that girl, not only for her honesty but for her diligence and determination. Whatever environment she was in, I had noticed that Nurcan dedicated herself heart, soul and strength— and the years at her religious dormitory had been no exception. In fact, she had managed to earn two necklaces during her time there, a rare achievement.

'Some girls would sneak out in the evenings,' she said with a laugh, 'and then they would ask if they could buy one of my necklaces from me so that everyone would think they were a good Muslim girl!' I laughed with her. 'And the letters?' I asked, 'The script? What does it say?'

'It's one of the names of Allah,' she said simply. 'The script is Arabic.'

And with that, we moved on to the topic of business, but my mind was still on the conversation about the necklace because I had been hearing snippets like this more and more—gifts or bonuses that seemed at first glance to be gestures of appreciation or reward, but to those in the know, which was everyone in Turkey, they made a strong statement about where a person sat on the religious spectrum.

And suddenly I found myself thinking back to my own high school graduation, my name being called out, a gold tassel draped around my neck and the applause of the audience—*The Timothy Award for Diligence. The Christian Character Award. The Barnabus Award for Encouragement*—and for all my us-and-them thinking, it struck me that perhaps we were not from such different worlds after all.

47. Protestants and Catholics

And that was only the start. A day or two later, Iza came to spend the evening with our family. After the meal was finished and the table cleared, we stacked the dishes on the kitchen bench, made a pot of tea, and headed into the lounge room to relax.

It was not often that I had one-on-one time with the people in my core team, but as Jeff and the children headed outdoors for a game of backyard cricket before bed, Iza and I seized the opportunity to put our work discussions aside and talk instead about our personal lives.

Iza had come to Bursa on a year-long exchange program with the plan to return to her home in Poland when it was over. But, like so many others, she had fallen in love; now the road ahead was filled with decisions, none of which were easy.

Her boyfriend was a handsome young Turk with a ready smile and great aspirations for the future, who Jeff and I had met, and liked immediately. 'Last weekend we visited his family home,' Iza told me as we waited for the tea to steep. 'I finally got to meet his parents and grandparents for the first time.'

'How did it go?' I was keen to hear.

They were lovely, of course. Hospitality covers a multitude of underlying issues, and the village welcome had been genuinely warm. But it was never going to be easy for an older generation of Turks to get their head around the idea that their only son might end up marrying a foreign woman—my mind flitted to Fiddler on the Roof and then back to Iza, as she mingled the account of her visit with the emotion of it all.

They were not worlds apart, these two young lovers. He'd left the village a few years earlier and was very much a city boy now, educated, and with a future, he hoped, in the Turkish navy. All he needed to do, Iza explained, was to please his superiors, keep his political allegiances carefully aligned, and pass the gruelling navigation exams that lay ahead. Her eyes sparkled. Her boyfriend had asked her to marry him, she said, and she'd agreed.

I looked at the young woman sitting across from me with a mixture of love and admiration. I thought of her aging parents back home, how she couldn't wait to visit them again, how she'd mastered Turkish in the time it took most of us to learn a few greetings. She'd been at every one of our working group meetings, analysing, assessing, putting her sharp mind to use, and being straight-up with the troublemakers. If determination could measure the success of a relationship, Iza and her fiancé might just have what it takes, I thought to myself, hoping that this would be the sort of happy, meet-you-in-the-middle, lets-show-them-it-can-be-done love story I was longing to witness.

But then our conversation turned to the one subject that everyone wished was not the clincher—*religion*. Religion was the topic that had a horrible way of trumping everything—affection, social standing, hopes and dreams—everything. No one had mentioned it during the visit to her fiancé's home, of course, but it was the foremost issue on everyone's mind.

What would the young couple do about religion? Would they have an Islamic wedding? Would the children be brought up Muslim or Christian? Would his family come to a ceremony in a church? Iza and her fiancé respected each other's heritage—he was rather secular anyway—but it only took one generational step backwards, or forwards, for things to get suddenly complicated.

I noticed the expression on her face, but then, suddenly, the conversation pivoted, until somehow, we found ourselves grappling, not with the disconnect between her religion and *his,* but between her religion and *mine.* 'The difference between us,' she said simply, 'is that Catholics glorify suffering whereas Protestants glorify hard work.'

And with that, it was as if an invisible wall of water crashed straight into me, because, oh my goodness, I, who had been working day and night, called meetings when others were relaxing, written up proposals and speeches and reports when everyone else went home—I, who decided we're not just going to talk, we're going to deliver—I fit the protestant expectation perfectly.

Through my mind flashed Mother Teresa, embracing suffering and the contrast was vivid. I pictured icons, with Jesus on the cross, the epitome of suffering—suspended, in fact, in his moment of most extreme suffering. I thought of the concept of penance, and how Catholics saw self-imposed suffering as a suitable payment for sins . . .

And then my mind rang with the little phrase so ingrained in the culture I knew best: *Protestant work ethic. Hard-working Protestant.*

How on earth did we go from being all about salvation by faith alone, not of works, to what was essentially a love relationship with work?! But Iza had just summed up what I had never seen before. If suffering well is the pinnacle of the Catholic faith, working hard had become the pinnacle of the Protestant faith.

Lord, forgive us all.

I felt a surge of sorrow for all the generations who had lived with such a distorted message, but I needed to hear it too. There, in my lounge room in Turkey, Iza had opened my eyes.

I was not about to propagate the stereotype a minute longer. Something like deep remorse welled within me and I couldn't hold back. It was time to reject the whole premise out loud, for a centuries-old distortion of the Gospel to begin to crumble. It was time to dismantle some deeply entrenched lies—lies that effectively rendered half the Christian world weak, and the other half, tired.

In the next sacred moments, Iza and I found common ground. Jesus had undertaken the ultimate work of suffering. He submitted to it. He embraced it, and . . . he triumphed over it!

He suffered to the point of death *and* he finished the work God gave him to do!

So, there we sat, two foreign women in a Turkish duplex, both of us catching a fresh glimpse of the Gospel, and as we talked awhile about Jesus, suddenly he seemed a little closer, a little dearer, a little more precious to us both.

48. Alperen

One of the more regular visitors to our home was Alperen. Alperen annoyed me and amused me all at once. He was only in his twenties but was completely stuck in his ways, and I had worked out that it was better to pander to his idiosyncrasies than to try to reason with him. Having lived most of his life in Bursa, Alperen came from a family of quiet, conservative people who lived simply and worked together in a typical family-owned grocery store near their apartment.

But our family loved Alperen. Every time he walked into our home, we greeted him by pouring a few drops of lemon cologne into his hands—a traditional ritual in Turkey that our more modern friends didn't care for, but one that Alperen considered an essential part of a proper Turkish welcome.

Within minutes, he expected to be served tea. I had learned to prepare it in a double teapot, just like the locals—the bottom pot being for the boiling water, and the pot that sat on top, holding the tea.

Alperen smiled politely the first few times he came to our house, but soon abandoned his pretence and made it clear that my tea was not up to scratch. From that point on, he had taken it upon himself to come into the kitchen and oversee the process from start to finish.

I admired Alperen for that. It's not every Turkish male who would even step foot into a domestic kitchen, let alone take over in a foreign woman's home, but he did, because for Alperen, the most important thing about serving tea was to *get it right*.

'Same with the salad,' he told me one night. I had randomly diced tomatoes and cucumber and tossed in some chopped parsley. When Alperen sat at the table, however, and looked at his plate in confusion, I invited him to tell me the problem. Looking at me as if he couldn't believe my ignorance, he explained, 'The ingredients must all be chopped to the same size for the olive oil and lemon juice to properly infuse. You must cut the vegetables like this, you see . . .' He made a space about a centimetre wide with his thumb and forefinger. 'Every piece needs to be the same size and shape for the dish to be correct.'

Now realistically, if anyone in Australia had commented on my salad as Alperen did, they would be considered rather presumptuous—even by Turkish standards, this young man was unusually frank. But I also realised there was something more to his comments. Like every Turk, Alperen appreciated the fact that the very reason that traditional foods had been preserved through the centuries was that the little details mattered. The Ottomans treated meals and food with great care; the mark of a great modern cook was therefore in their willingness to faithfully reproduce what generations before them had served.

In my culture, where the opposite was true, chefs were awarded for their innovation, for coming up with new ways of working with ingredients. In my country, the value of simple recipes passed down unaltered, not just across generations, but from one empire or dynasty to another, barely came into consideration. And so, with context in mind, I smiled generously and took extra care to serve Alperen the kind of meals he was used to. Still, no matter how I rationalised our cultural differences, Alperen had a way of getting on my nerves . . .

. . . that is, until after dinner, when I got to hear his story and felt thoroughly rebuked for my frustration with our dinner guest because *who cares if a man is a bit pedantic when he's been somewhere out on the border of Iran and seen Jesus?*

We had left the table and settled on the couch with the whole family gathered around, when Jeff asked Alperen, 'How did you become a follower of Jesus?' In that moment, Alperen's face lit up. 'Lean in,' I whispered to the children, because already it was clear that this was no ordinary coming-to-faith story we were about to hear . . .

49. Alperen's Story (as told by him)

When I turned nineteen, I started military service. There was a big send-off when we all left on the bus. Straight away I was paired up with a Greek man who was a Christian. That was very interesting to me because I had decided that while I was on my military service I wanted to think about God, and now the first person I met was this man.

We spoke, but I never saw him again after those initial days. When the second phase of military service commenced, I was sent to Ankara, where I would spend two months at a naval base. I was very happy that I had been allocated to Ankara—it was a good posting and my family was pleased because I was in a proper city, and not too far away. Whenever I got leave, I was able to return home to Bursa. It was a very good situation.

Then I made a mistake. I had been home on leave, but instead of returning to my post on time, I went to visit my grandparents, because I desperately missed them. After a few days, I woke up to myself, but now I was worried. The punishment for returning late could be severe.

As soon as I could, I booked my ticket to Ankara. In the meantime, however, word came to me that my commanding officer was very angry. He said I would go to jail for what I had done and had sent soldiers to arrest me. Now I was too scared to return; I was paralysed with fear, in fact. In the end, my uncle came to pick me up and take me back to Ankara. He spoke to the commanding officer on my behalf, but still, the officer was determined that I was going to jail.

I began praying for a miracle, praying they wouldn't take me away. Finally, the officer said to me, 'Alperen, I am not going to send you to jail, but you will be punished. You are being posted to a military base near the Syrian border.' This base was thousands of miles away from my family, but still, it was better than jail. I was just glad that I had escaped that punishment.

One day I was on patrol near the Eastern border when I saw an old Catholic church. My Greek friend had given me a Turkish Bible, but I had not brought it with me because if anyone saw me reading it, I could be in a lot of trouble. But then I had an idea—maybe I could get away with reading an English Bible!'

I entered the church and found a priest inside who gave me a Bible written in English. I kept it in a cupboard in the barracks, hidden in a stack of other books, but every night, I read it. When the other soldiers asked me what I was reading, I simply replied, 'It's a book about history.' If another soldier asked me to translate it into Turkish, I would find an interesting story and share it with them. And then, one day, a fellow soldier called me aside and asked, 'Can I look at your book?' What I didn't realise was that this soldier also spoke English! With one look, he said, 'That's a New Testament!'

Now I was terrified. If the soldier told a superior, I would be in more trouble than ever. But to my surprise, the soldier said, 'I want to read the Bible too. Let's read it together.'

The barracks were surrounded by wide open fields and forests, so in our free time, we went outside to study the Bible and pray together. The other soldier finished his stint in the military before me, and I didn't hear from him again.

Then, two years later, when my own term of service was over and I had returned to Bursa, the phone rang. It was my old military friend! 'Something very interesting has happened to me, Alperen,' he said. 'I have become a believer in Jesus! I'm going to be a pastor in a church!'

Alperen's face was full of joy as he told us that his friend was now a pastor in Istanbul.

'That was God's plan for me,' said Alperen. God uses our choices and things that happen to us for His purposes. God will even use bad things for good. If anyone asks that guy about how he came to faith, he would say that I was the first believer he met! This is a wonderful thing to me.'

Alperen went on to explain the situation in Turkey.

'A lot of people here want to know about the Christian faith,' he told us, 'but there is a lot of prejudice. My friends are afraid of reality—I see that in my own family. I mostly try to introduce people to Jesus through my life, especially when there are films about Jesus on television. If a café is very crowded and there is a film about Jesus on television, I say to the

manager, "There's a really interesting film on a certain channel tonight. Can you change the channel so I can watch it?" Hopefully he will put that channel on all the TV screens in his café. It is an opportunity for people to hear about Jesus.'

We were intrigued about all Alperen had told us, but we were also confused. How had our friend come to faith in the first place?

'Oh,' he replied, as if it were an afterthought. It was three years before I went into the military. It was a very cold day. I remember the cold. I remember everything very clearly because it was such an important day. . .

That week I had a dream. In my dream, someone gave me a book. I got up in the morning and wondered, 'What is this book?' Then a few days passed, and I had another dream. This time I saw that exact book in a store near my house. I knew straight away that it was a New Testament, but how could it possibly be there?

When I woke up, I was afraid. I didn't know any Christians in Bursa. I said, 'God, I am a Muslim. Why are you showing me things connected with Christianity? You know that I read the Koran.'

A few nights later, I had another dream. This time a man on a white horse came to me. He said, 'I am Jesus. I am truth. Come to me. I am the one who is in this book.'

I woke up frightened and crying. Can you imagine? I didn't even know if there were any Christians in Turkey. How could I become a Christian? But that day, I went to the bookshop I had seen in my dream, and there, on the shelf, was the New Testament! When I reached out to pick it up, I was excited and nervous. There was a lot of fear from my past, but I didn't care. I was going to read the Gospel!

When I bought the book, the shop owner wrapped it in paper,' Alperen said, 'but I was in turmoil. When I got home, there were guests in the house. One of the guests said, 'Alperen, you look really bad' and I did! I felt physically sick and scared. I excused myself, went to my room and hid the New Testament. It was many hours before I got the courage to start reading, but when I started, I couldn't put it down! I read the whole book of Matthew, then Mark and Luke, and then I started reading the book of John.

As Alperen told his story, there were tears in his eyes.

'While I was reading John,' he said, 'something amazing happened. It was as if something came into me—something belonging to another world. Even then I understood that it was the Holy Spirit. At that moment I said to Jesus, 'I believe in you! 'and I started crying. I prayed until morning. That is how I came to faith. The interesting thing is,' he said, 'I had never met a Christian. I didn't know anything about Christianity. There was nothing anyone could do at that moment to bring me to faith. But I understood at that time that God really loves me. That's the thing I will never forget. Since then, I have had difficulty with friends, family, neighbours . . .'

We were intrigued. Had Alperen loved Jesus all these years without ever knowing another Christian?

'Not quite,' he replied. 'On the back of the Bible was a phone number. I called the number and some Christians in Istanbul answered. They didn't know if there was a church in Bursa, but they told me I could meet a man in a café. Eventually, we started meeting in a house here in Bursa, and soon after, I was baptised.'

Alperen downed a full glass of water before finishing the story.

'My family are peace-loving,' he went on. 'My uncle, especially, did all he could to establish our family, but before that, in past generations, the situation had been very difficult for us all. We had a long history of family troubles—sickness, financial difficulty, and so on. And then, when I was born,' Alperen said, 'my uncle decided this baby must be called Alperen. The meaning of Alperen is 'salvation.' He hoped my birth would change things, that I would bring salvation to our family.'

We sat quietly, letting the story sink in. A Muslim uncle gives a newborn baby a prophetic name . . . Jesus appears to the young man as 'the man in white' . . . a New Testament turns up on a particular shelf in a bookstore in Bursa, a store Alperen locates via a dream. He reads it and is filled with the Holy Spirit. Then a mistake during military service turns into a God-story, a salvation encounter for a soldier who would later become a pastor . . .

It was a humbling moment as we suddenly realised that his story had nothing to do with any 'Western' Christian. But I still had one more question. 'Alperen,' I asked, 'when Jesus came to you in your dream, what did He look like?' The question was beyond his comprehension. *'You have never seen Jesus?'* he asked with a look of utter disbelief, and before I could answer, he added with genuine concern, *'I will pray for you.'*

50. What to do about Schooling

In the weeks that followed, things on the school front deteriorated rapidly, particularly for the boys. Turkish immersion was not turning out to be of any use to Joseph—listening to a language he couldn't understand only caused him to tune out completely. Joseph's days now consisted primarily of gazing out the classroom window, biding the time until school was over, and he could head for home.

Things weren't going well for Eric either. The constant harassment from students who felt intimidated by the fact he was English-speaking and a foreigner, was getting to him, as was the level of Turkish nationalism among his classmates that apparently gave legitimacy to all manner of insults that were being hurled in his direction.

Every day started the same way with the entire school standing in military-style formation to sing the national anthem and recite their allegiance to (and willingness to fight for) the Republic of Turkey. This was neither a song nor a pledge that a foreigner could join in—after all, the premise of both was that anyone other than a Turk was, in fact, an enemy. It seemed that being from another country endeared our boys to no one except the principal, who was happy to receive the hefty school fees we were paying and found some level of pride in the fact that a foreign family had chosen his college for the education of their children.

Only, the education they were getting had its limitations. 'Your boys may take all the exams,' the principal told us one day, 'but we are sorry, they may not take the English exam.'

'Why is that?' we asked.

'Because your boys would naturally have an unfair advantage in an English exam,' he explained. 'This would upset the other parents. They will be angry if a foreign student is allowed to rob their child of the chance to top the class. Besides,' he said, 'they also pay for their children to have the best advantages. I'm sure you understand.'

And so, our boys were welcome to sit their exams—math, social studies, science, and religion—in Turkish. So long as they performed worse than their Turkish classmates, there would be no problem. I realised, at that point, that if I were Joseph, I would spend my days staring out the window too.

Crunch time came, though, when Eric arrived home one day, not upset, but (even more concerning for us as parents) absolutely deflated. 'Every morning our class has to run around the field,' he said, 'and today I was up the front with the faster boys when the teacher pulled me aside and told me to go to the back of the pack.' As he tried to finish the story, his voice started to break. 'When I asked why,' he finally said, 'the teacher told me it is because a foreigner never runs in front of a Turk.'

Hearing that, I must say, nearly tipped us over the edge too. Suddenly we were over the superior attitude of these people who cared so much about their own honour. By now, we had seen the other side of Turkish society—the brokenness and perversion, the porn kept in lockers and desks, the violence of the teachers as they physically lashed out at students. Quite frankly, we were at our wits' end. How on earth were we to educate our kids in Turkey without leaving them completely soul-destroyed?

The next morning Jeff decided that enough was enough. It was time to step up and fight for breakthrough in our children's education. And so, after dropping the boys at the school gate, he decided to prayer-walk the perimeter of the campus. The teachers and students were not our enemy, we knew that. If we were to release an outcome where everyone wins, we'd need to take the fight to the unseen realm.

For a solid hour or more, Jeff walked and prayed, declaring as he went that the future of our kids was not up for grabs, that neither were their hearts or their souls or their minds, and that in the name of Jesus, every violent or stifling or hostile nationalistic spirit must leave. 'I call for an outpouring of blessing over our children's school, over the principal and the teachers, and over every student,' Jeff prayed, 'including our sons!'

The transformation we witnessed only six hours later was profound. Eric walked through the front door after school that day holding up a piece of cardboard on which he had written, in bold lettering during his bus ride home:

I HAD A HUGE BREAKTHROUGH TODAY!

There was a look of relief and triumph on his face as the story came flooding out. The boy who had been most violent towards Eric, kicking and punching and ridiculing him ever since school began, had decided to become his friend!

With a chorus of *'hurrahs'* and *'thank you, Lords'*, we celebrated this amazing turnaround. Naturally speaking, there had been no way to fix the problem. One hour of prayer, however, had seen the whole situation begin to resolve. Eric's enthusiasm for life had returned, and that night, we went to bed relieved. Perhaps Turkish schooling would work out well for our boys after all.

~

The girls, though, were facing other sorts of problems. By now we were six months into the preschool experience. Evangeline and Liberty had done incredibly well adjusting to the new system and were now waving goodbye each morning and speaking the language with increasing ease.

But we were concerned. Our full-of-spunk daughters were becoming more subdued by the week; it seemed even the preschool children tended to be violent and aggressive. We decided to wait until the parent-teacher interviews, where we hoped we would get a clearer sense of the whole picture. To our amazement, however, it seemed the only thing the teacher was concerned about was how willingly the children ate their meals. On that topic, she was full of praise for our girls. 'They eat all their food!' she said, as if that made them star students.

We had already been told that this really was the number one issue most Turkish preschool parents cared about, so I was not surprised at the teacher's remarks. Apparently, if little Elif and Ahmet and Turkan were eating well, preschool was a success. For us, though, not so much. In addition to the classroom dynamics, it was the curriculum we were most interested in—and eventually the teacher conceded and pulled out a portfolio for each of our girls.

She started by proudly pointing out their artwork—identical cut-outs of shapes, all arranged perfectly on the page. No two children's artwork differed. If following instructions was the goal, this teacher had done a good job of educating her class. But it was not just the lack of creativity, the complete absence of individual expression, that troubled us. It was also the way nearly every activity involved some sort of reference to Atatürk[1]. Not only was his portrait displayed in every classroom, 'watching over the children,' we were told, but his image hung in every hallway, office, business or shop—even in the buses, for that matter.

And our girls were soaking it all in. Even Vangie had begun speaking in her quaint Turkish accent of 'our father, Atatürk'; his sayings were being etched into our girl's minds, and the political agenda that came along with the package of our kids' education, was beginning to cause us increasing concern.

51. Foreigner's Welcome Night

Our working group had significantly grown in the six months since we began; the success of the picnic had propelled us forward, and fresh projects were underway. We had already produced a brochure packed with information to assist newcomers to the city and had managed, eventually, to have copies available at the bus and ferry terminals. A subgroup had been meeting with school principals about how we might better cater to the needs of foreign children; and, we had begun hosting monthly activities and cultural experiences so that foreigners could meet each other and gain a better appreciation for our city. The project we hadn't been able to make much progress on, was our attempt to procure the work permits that were often promised but rarely eventuated for English language teachers from abroad. Being a complex issue, however, we took a long-term view of the situation and decided to simply persevere.

At this point, though, we were one month out from Christmas, and our last event for the year was coming up. Our first-ever 'Foreigner's Welcome Night', would be a large, public event that was dear to my heart. This night would give the city an opportunity to showcase its remarkable cultural heritage, to celebrate the incredible contributions of foreigners in Bursa, and, of course, to openly welcome and honour all those who had come from other countries.

The significance of the occasion felt weighty indeed. Following

---

1 Mustafa Kemal Atatürk, the founder of the Republic of Turkey

speeches from myself and our city officials, there would be performances from various sectors of the community, a video showing Bursa's global reach, and then, to finish the evening, a cocktail supper in the atrium of the convention centre. Taking a leap of faith, we advertised the evening as our 'Inaugural Foreigner's Night,' in the hope that the event would become an annual event, uniting the city of Bursa and its expats for years to come.

By now the preparations had turned into a hive of round-the-clock activity. Every detail—from the formal invitations being sent to every city official, to the interest groups that would be featured in the foyer as guests arrived, even the choice of finger food we would serve afterwards—needed signoff from me or my core team. Nothing must be left to chance.

I had already met with the director of the Children's Home and the result was excellent—a group of children would perform on the night, bringing with them their families and caregivers, along with a host of health and education professionals. A local drumming group had also responded favourably and were now included in the program. I was glad for these two groups—they were sure to bring a festive atmosphere and would, I was certain, receive a standing ovation.

That week, we placed posters in windows and advertisements in newspapers. Once again, our banners were strung across the streets. For our final event of the year, we wanted to make sure the whole city was invited.

52. Constructing a Speech

News of the foreigner's night spread quickly. This time we were not worried about whether people would come; instead, we were beginning to wonder if the concert hall we had booked for the occasion would be big enough to hold the crowd! Not only was this the first event of its kind in Bursa, it was the first for all of Turkey, and everyone from government officials to curious citizens was making plans to come. I wanted to arrive early so I could check in with President Semih Pala, look over the setup, make sure my team were feeling confident, and greet the guests as they arrived.

But first, I had a speech to write. With less than an hour before our taxi was scheduled to arrive, I brewed a pot of tea and sat down at the dining room table. 'Lord,' I began to pray—and straight away it hit me: this event was not merely an opportunity for *me* to speak; it was a chance for *Him* to speak! With fresh excitement, I finished my prayer. 'Lord, what would *you* like to say tonight?'

I barely got the question out before the windows of heaven seemed to fling right open and the words spoken by the prophet Jeremiah as he stood before the Babylonian exiles centuries earlier flooded my mind.

'Seek the peace and prosperity of the city to which I have carried you into exile. Pray to the Lord for it, because if it prospers, you too will prosper.'

I imagined those displaced people, figuring out how to establish a whole new life in a foreign land. How long would they even be there? Should they try to integrate, or hold onto their own identity at all costs?

As it turned out, those foreign exiles not only thrived, but as they adopted a posture of blessing towards the new culture they found themselves in, God saw to it that those around them thrived too. The whole picture fit perfectly. Quickly I ran my eyes over the biblical story, underlining key words and phrases. I hardly needed to write a speech at all—it was being given to me—and after ten minutes of scribbling, another ten for tweaking and refining, and a final read-through to ensure it would come across well both to Turks and to the expats who would be present, my final task was complete, and a wave of satisfaction and confidence washed over me.

My core team were waiting for me. Ann-Sophie from Belgium wore a lovely red dress, perfect for her role as MC of the evening. Ilir sported a jacket and his broad, relaxed smile. Ayşe had been appointed to translate the official speeches, including mine, but Ilir, we had decided, would take over the translation for the rest of the night. Iza and Eliza and Ben, a young Russian expat I had recently brought onto my core team, were checking over the venue, making sure that everything was in place. At that moment I couldn't have been prouder.

Who in the world gets to work with people like this? I wondered. And then, in their hundreds, the guests began to arrive. We shook hands with each of them and seated the officials in the front row. Already the room was alive with chatter and expectation.

I have to acknowledge that despite my high expectations for the evening, there were plenty of sceptics among the crowd; some were still unsure of our motives, others simply harboured deep dislike or were mindful of the difficulties that remained in this city despite my team's best efforts. But any cynicism in the room was soon pushed aside.

The concert hall was packed to standing room only, the crowd a wonderful conglomeration of women in headscarves sitting beside university students and foreign company executives, Turkish children, and directors of social services, all smiling and tapping their feet, waiting for the evening to begin. As we stood to our feet while the national anthem was played and turned to face the Turkish flag, I knew that we could already deem the night a success.

With a sheet of paper in my hand, I walked to the platform and turned to look into the faces of a multitude of people we had come to love and a city for which we would happily pour out our lives. Ayşe, my colleague, stood beside me, ready to translate every word.

I welcomed President Semih Pala, the Mayor of Bursa, the honorary consuls, and the foreigners and citizens of Bursa who had joined us in the spirit of friendship. Now, it was time to honour the city and its incredible history.

'Tonight,' I began, 'the city of Bursa has come together to welcome foreigners from many parts of the world. Bursa has a long history of this. The Silk Road, as you know, brought people from faraway regions to Bursa – travellers and merchants, scholars and dignitaries. They came from the East and from the West, and when they returned to their homes, they spoke of the glory and wonder of this city.

Others, when they received a hearty welcome and saw the potential to settle down in a city of great wealth and influence and beauty, chose to stay, making this green city at the base of Mount Uludağ their home. In those days, foreigners and locals alike intermingled.

Today, the situation is much the same, only we are the foreigners who have come—some seeking adventure or opportunity or inspiration, some to marry and raise families, some to rediscover the heritage of their parents and grandparents. Some of us simply seek a better life, a place to start again.

We may not have travelled the Silk Road to get here, but we each have come on a journey that has led us here. We bring a wonderful, yet diverse cultural heritage. In this, we, like many before us, contribute to the good image and reputation of Bursa.

To our city officials and our Turkish friends, we say this: Nations are *known for the way they treat foreigners. Thank you for your kindness to us. We hope we make you proud. You have offered us safety, and a warm welcome. We hope that you, in turn, benefit by having us here. We hope that Bursa continues to prosper. We hope that all her citizens continue to live in peace and safety.'*

The Mayor and President Semih Pala nodded their heads in agreement.

'*To my fellow expats,*' I continued. '*I want to leave you with some advice that was first given over three thousand years ago, to people who, like us, were living far from home. These are ancient words, but they are just as powerful for us today: 'Seek the peace and wellbeing of the city in which you live . . . because if the city prospers, you also will prosper.'*

I felt a weight lift off us all as I wrapped the ancient words of Jeremiah in the language of our day and declared the blessing every one of us yearned to hear.

'*May our years in Bursa be happy. May we enjoy peace and safety while we live here. I hope we can all continue to help and support each other. I hope many of us can settle here, establish our homes and careers here, and contribute to the prosperity of this city. We have all come for different reasons, from different backgrounds, and with different life experiences, but here tonight we have one thing in common. Though some of us are foreigners, we are all citizens of one world. I'm glad we all got the chance to meet each other here, in Bursa.'*

The room erupted. Some stood to their feet. My heart was warmed to see a friend who had previously been cautious about mixing with foreigners, sitting down the back, smiling. His support meant everything to me that night. On the other side of the room, however, was Janine, the British expat who had predicted the working group would come to nothing. As she leaned against the wall near the door with a seething look on her face, I braced myself for another round of angsty text messages.

But now was not the time to concern myself with that. The mayor of the city was speaking, sharing how he too had come from a migrant family, reminding us that, in a sense, everyone in the room was a foreigner of sorts. Some may have adopted Turkish nationality many generations ago, but each of us ultimately had origins elsewhere, and indeed this night was our chance to link arms and forever unite as brothers and sisters in this great city.

We could not have asked for more endearing words or a more welcoming tone from the leader of our city—he even suggested in jest that the word 'foreigner' had little meaning in a country so diverse and that the name of our group should be changed from 'foreigners working group' to something more to do with us all working together as family. Again, the audience responded with claps and cheers and shouts of agreement.

President Semih Pala took the microphone next, speaking well of the working group and of the cooperation between us all, and wrapping up the formal part of the evening with fatherly pride.

Now the main program could get underway. Ilir took the stage, welcoming one group of performers after another, and soon he had the whole room clapping along as musicians played and dancers twirled, and even a group of traditional Ottoman swordsmen showcased their astonishing skills. An hour or so later, amid a great buzz of satisfaction, the crowd made their way into the atrium where hors d'oeuvres were ready to be served.

I tend to judge the success of an event by how long people want to stay around afterwards to mingle and talk and draw the occasion out for as long as possible. That night, it seemed no one wanted to leave. I took myself off to the side of the room for a few minutes to quietly enjoy the scene before me. Expats who had never met each other before were laughing together, passing around platters of food, and exchanging phone numbers. The council staff were mingling among the crowd, effortlessly engaging with people of all ages and abilities and cultures. Expat and Turkish children sprawled on the steps together, making up games to pass the time.

I came home that night with a full heart . . . and yet something was troubling me, some little niggle I couldn't put my finger on.

It wasn't until close to midnight as I lay in bed that I realised what was bothering me. The chief of police, in his front-row seat, had not smiled once. I had invited him as a distinguished guest, but he had come reluctantly, as if on duty the entire night. Then I saw them—the row of vaguely familiar men who remained standing along the back wall throughout the evening. They weren't just latecomers who couldn't find a seat. I hadn't recognised them out of uniform. But suddenly I realised, it was *them*—the foreigner's police, in full force, scattered through the audience, positioned carefully near the doors, taking in every word, ready to act should there be any hint of an uprising. But why had I not been told?

I consoled myself with the thought that at least the police must be relieved. Surely after tonight they could see that the expats they were so reluctant to issue visas to posed no threat to national security after all.

What I didn't realise that night was that I was still missing the point. It wasn't until I started hearing little clicks at the end of my phone calls and saw that my file at the police station had tripled in size that I began to understand. It wasn't the foreigners in general they were worried about. It wasn't even the working group. It was *me*. The foreigners' night had only confirmed what they already knew. In leading the foreigners of the city, *I* had become a threat.

53. The Comfort of a Movie

With the weight of increasing police scrutiny heavy on our minds, we decided it was the perfect time to take refuge for a while in someone else's story. Our family loves a good movie, and 'The King's Speech' had just been released on DVD, so with plans to curl up on the couch for a night, Jeff and the boys made their way down the hill to see what was on offer at the local video store.

We'd noticed the store just down on the main road but had not yet ventured inside. The front windows were always plastered with posters, making it impossible to see who was inside or what anyone might be borrowing, but with the determination of a man on a mission, Jeff walked in confidently and smiled as he approached the counter.

Guneydin. Kings Speech adlı bir film izlemek isterim. 'I would like to watch a film called "The King's Speech."'

Sende var mı? 'Do you have it?'

'One moment,' the man behind the counter motioned as he began to scan the shelves.

If there's one thing about Turks, it's they never say 'no.' Whatever the need, no problem, a Turk will make it happen, and the video store owner was no exception.

'Please, if you will come back in half an hour, I will have it for you,' he said with a smile.

Thankfully, the blip on Jeff's Western morality radar had plenty of time to dissipate as he and the boys went outside, purchased three ice-creams from the cart nearby, and sat down on upturned crates to enjoy them.

In the end, half an hour wasn't necessary. Before the boys had even finished their ice-creams, the video-store owner emerged onto the sidewalk, handed a freshly cut DVD to Jeff and beamed with satisfaction at having yet again delivered exceptional customer service. The cover slip was printed in full colour, and apart from the title on the disc, which was written in black permanent marker, it could very well have been taken for a genuine copy.

In one final amusing moment, the store owner offered his parting assurance that although Jeff had rented the DVD, he need not worry about returning it. 'How's that for customer service?' thought Jeff, but he thanked his new friend and headed for home because normality counts, even for expats on the other side of the world. And so, later that night, we popped the disk into the DVD player, ignored the piracy warnings as they flashed across the screen, and snuggled together on the couch, happy to immerse ourselves for a few hours at least, in someone else's drama.

54. First Christmas in Turkey

By now it was mid-December, and though we expected Christmas would be low-key in such a strongly Islamic country, we were unprepared for the complete absence of anything to do with Christmas. For sure, there were artificial trees for sale, but they were advertised as New Year trees. Tinsel hung in shopping centres, but instead of 'Merry Christmas,' they read '*Mutlu Yıllar*', '*Happy New Year.*'

People seemed genuinely confused about Christmas. 'Isn't it the same as New Year?' they would ask. I knew that in some countries, people might not know when Eid falls, or when Ramadan begins, but that, I understood, was because those dates move with the cycles of the moon, whereas Christmas is fixed—the twenty-fifth of December, everywhere in the world.

Happy New Year indeed. There was no way we were going to let Christmas slip, regardless of the city we lived in; we bought a tree, strung it with lights, set a star on top, and placed it right in the middle of our front window for all the world to see. Day and night, it shone, baffling everyone who passed by. 'Why have you put up a tree before the New Year?' they asked, and over and over again we found ourselves telling the story of how the Saviour of the world has come.

The highlight of the season came a few days before Christmas, when Fatih and his fiancée, Anna, arrived from Vienna. It was Anna's first Christmas away from home, but to us, it felt like family had come to stay as we sat together under the twinkling lights of the tree and talked late into the night.

Over the next few days, joy filled the house as we lit candles and baked lebkuchen laden with cinnamon and gathered with friends; in fact, it seemed at times as though angels surrounded our home, singing as they did on the night of Jesus' birth, and as they still do wherever people welcome him today. 'If we worship Jesus, Jesus will come,' Liberty once said, and she was right. Jesus had come to our home that winter in Bursa.

~

The tiny historic French Catholic church in the old quarter of town opened its doors at six o'clock on Christmas Eve, where a priest from Istanbul had made his way by ferry across the Sea of Marmara, to conduct a Christmas service.

It was Anna who invited us to go along with her and Fatih. I knew this night was important to Anna—after all, she was German, and if anything, Christmas is even more lavish and moving and meaningful in her tradition than it is in ours. We got all dressed up with coats and scarves and hair slicked into place—and then, there was a knock on our front door. Anna stood there, anxious and apologetic, explaining that Fatih was still not back from his dentist appointment.

And that's how it was. In Turkey, Christmas day was another ordinary day; the school buses made their rounds, kids went to class as usual, factory workers produced the textiles our city was famous for, the city council was open for business, and Fatih had a dentist appointment. Only a handful of people in our city of four million had any clue that the twenty-fifth of December might be a holy, historic day. The rest of the world may have paused while families gathered and prepared and celebrated Christmas, but at that moment, we were just seven people on a doorstep, not even sure if we would be able to get to church on this one night of the year.

But Fatih knew what the night meant to Anna, and he did make it home in time; he had even prepared a car to take us there, and as he drove us all across to the old city, my heart was full of gratitude to God for placing this neighbour beside us. Perhaps he was the only Muslim driving a carload of Jesus-lovers to church that night, I don't know. But he came, and sat with Anna and our family, and the church filled quietly as foreigners and Turks converged amidst candles and songs and scripture readings, all in honour of Jesus' birth.

Afterwards, we shared Christmas dinner at our home. Anna baked her German apple pie, I had prepared a spread of meats and vegetables and gravy, and Omer Bey had graciously finished work early so he and Arzu could join us. I'm not sure Omer and Arzu had ever seen a meal quite like it but before long, we were all reaching across the table, passing plates, and serving up a hearty roast dinner.

Later we sat under the lights of the Christmas tree sipping Turkish coffee and eating the gooey-soft Turkish delight we had purchased from Ishan's shop. Everyone was tired. It had, after all, been another workday for our neighbours, but our hearts were happy. In a small but significant way, we felt we had brought a little bit of Christmas to Bursa.

55. Aşure Pudding

The elderly woman who lived across the grass courtyard came to our door the following week. I had watched her venture out of her home every now and then, always huddled over, her headscarf sitting just above her eyebrows. She always wore a dull grey trench coat, which got me wondering what it must be like to spend a lifetime hidden under layers of shapeless clothing, even if just to visit a neighbour.

But there was one thing she couldn't hide and that was her kindness and courage. It must have taken great determination along with a great heart, to make a special batch of aşure[1] pudding, divide it into six single serves each garnished with sparkly pomegranate seeds, then place them on a silver tray and walk across the lawn between our homes to bless a woman whose language and culture she could not begin to comprehend.

And yet, that's what she had done.

---

1 Pronounced: ash-ah-ray

Aşure pudding is traditional in Turkey, but until that day, I had never tasted it. The recipe harks back to the story of Noah landing his ark on Mount Ararat, presumably in Eastern Turkey, and as the story goes, he needed to use up all the leftover food while the floodwaters receded, and so he combined it all in a big pot and made a pudding.

Aşure is based on wheat, beans and rice, but is laden with sugar and dried fruits, and is delicately flavoured with rosewater—now the lady on my doorstep was holding a whole tray of it, the red pomegranate and green pistachio festively sprinkled on top! I smiled. Despite living so close, we'd not yet met. I suppose we both knew that we'd never get far in terms of conversation, me not able to string sentences together in Turkish yet, let alone in her dialect, and she, knowing not one word of English.

She handed me the tray and walked away.

Later that night I told Fatih what she had done and remarked how kind she was to think of us. 'Oh yes,' he said. 'She is very kind. But also, it is a sort of good deed. She wants to be blessed and find favour with Allah. That is also why she made you the pudding.'

I nodded. 'Okay, so what do I do? Do we return the tray and the little bowls?'

Fatih laughed. 'Oh, no!' he said, 'You kept them?'

'Of course,' I answered. 'What should I have done? Eaten it in front of her?'

Fatih explained. 'It's only a good deed if the recipient does not add anything to the gesture. You should have emptied the desserts into your own bowls, then returned hers so that you didn't have to wash the plates or even walk across the lawn to her home.'

That's why we loved and needed Fatih so much. Not only did he help us make sense of these small everyday occurrences, but he also knew the best way to patch things up or to minimise offence. We couldn't have asked for a better neighbour. 'Don't worry, he assured me. 'I will have a quiet word with the old lady across the garden and all will be well. You don't need to think of it again.'

56. Back to Austria

Soon, however, the weeks of holiday had passed and once again it was time to say goodbye to Fatih and Anna. This time, we would miss them more than ever. Anna had won our hearts the moment Fatih had introduced her, and when she came over to our house the day before they left with beautiful handmade cards for me and the girls. As we read the lovely words of thanks and encouragement she had written, I found myself fighting back tears. She too, had become like family to us.

The following morning, we stood outside on the grass together wishing we could draw out the minutes before Omer Bey would drive Fatih and Anna to Istanbul where they would board their flight to Europe. When the time came to say goodbye, there was no putting it off. Fatih pinched Liberty's cheeks one last time, twirled Vangie around and around, lifted the boys, one in each arm, up high, then setting them down, he put his big basketball-player hand on Joseph's shoulder. 'My man, Joseph,' he said, and our hearts melted as our youngest son beamed with pride.

Although Fatih's parents put in a huge effort to communicate with us, having Fatih in town had changed everything. Through him, we had learnt a lot more about their lives, their business, the kind hearts they had—and we had also become less of a mystery to them. With someone to translate, Omer and Arzu had been keen to discuss why we had come to Bursa and having now shared many an evening sitting around our lounge room with Faith bridging the language barrier for us, our friendship had flourished.

57. New Year's Visa

We had only two days before the nationwide New Year's holiday break to take care of our final concern for the year—renewing our visas. This time, Jeff decided, he would pander to the police. If they needed to feel they had the upper hand, he would make it easy for them. This time, when he assembled his stash of official documents in a folder, he deliberately kept one aside. That way, he reasoned, the police could shake their heads, demand further documentation, and Jeff would be able to respond with contrition before correcting his 'mistake.'

The tactic worked. Handing over the usual paperwork at the front desk, Jeff felt confident. 'You need one more document,' the clerk told

Jeff, exactly as predicted, and with an appropriately disgruntled look, Jeff left the police station, spent half an hour sipping coffee in a local café, and then returned with the missing document nicely included among the others. For once, everything was going smoothly, so Jeff took the chance. 'I would like to request a twelve-month resident permit this time.'

'That should be fine,' the clerk answered, 'you will just need to talk with the director'—which would have been the perfect time for Jeff to recall the word that had been on his heart all morning: *discretion.* Only, it skipped his mind in the moment, and after more than half an hour of frustration, Jeff was once again on the back foot with the chief of police, going around in circles as he talked again about our editing company.

This time, it was a friendly policewoman who had the job of translating.

'I think you are working here in Bursa,' said the director.

'Not officially,' Jeff replied, 'My income comes from Australia. I only visit universities here to greet the professors and promote our company.'

'That sounds like you are working,' the police chief argued.

'Yes, but technically it is not classified as work,' Jeff replied, and for the next ten minutes, attempted to explain the loopholes in Turkish law and how our company fit within the requirements. To finish, he reiterated our request: 'I am only asking if we can have permission to stay for twelve months instead of three.'

'No,' came the reply, and this time, it was said with finality. 'I will give you three more months only.'

'What a pain,' Jeff thought—and as they walked downstairs, his police interpreter turned to him and chided him. 'You shouldn't have told him the details of your company,' she said. The director wants to give you a longer permit and if you would only answer *yes* and *no,* he could give you what you want. But when you tell him all the details, you make it difficult for him. Now he has no choice. He has to say *no.*'

By that time Jeff was reeling, because the word he'd had in his heart all day was *discretion,* and while somehow a Turkish policewoman had picked up on the need for discretion, it was too late. As far as he could tell, he'd already blown it.

Then, as he made his way home, Jeff had an idea. Though the Turks had no understanding of Christmas, they certainly knew how to celebrate the new year, and as he passed a store window with *Yeni Yıllar* splashed across it and greeting cards on display, he decided this was not a moment for overthinking the crazy notion that had sprung to mind. Making his way into the store, Jeff purchased a card, wrote a short message of appreciation in Turkish, tucked it in its envelope and headed right back to the second floor of the foreigner's police station.

The director of police was gobsmacked. Clearly, this was the first time any foreigner had thanked him for doing his unenviable job.

And yet, all the way home, Jeff felt peeved with himself. *Why hadn't he picked up on the need to keep his mouth shut, to show particular discretion in that interview? And what a pity about the twelve months.*

But things looked to get worse. At three p.m. that afternoon, the phone rang. 'I am the son of the Muhtar[1]' said the voice on the other end. My father needs you to come to his office now to fix a problem. Your family does not appear on our register.'

Suddenly Jeff recalled an altercation with an elderly man who had angrily lectured him in the street a few months earlier. The gentleman had spoken in a dialect which, combined with his insistent, angry tone, had left Jeff unable to make out what on earth the man was trying to convey. Now he remembered the man had said the word *muhtar*, over and over again. Jeff had shrugged off the incident at the time, but it appeared the man had reported us directly, and now, to top this whole day off, Jeff was being summoned to the local official's office.

The Muhtar was unexpectedly pleasant, and thankfully his son was there to interpret, having returned home from the United States for his university holidays. 'Yes, you should have registered earlier, but it doesn't matter,' he said, 'we can do it now if you like.' And then he asked kindly, 'How do you like it here? Do you have any problems? Are people treating you well?'

Jeff talked for a few minutes about how our neighbours and friends had helped us in so many ways and how we enjoyed living in this particular locality. 'The one thing that is difficult for us is that we can only seem to get three-month visas,' he mentioned.' It makes it hard to settle in, plus it costs a lot of money every time we have to reapply.'

The Muhtar understood. 'Thank you for coming in,' he said.

---

1 Muhtar: elected head of a region; 'village chief'

New Year's Eve was the last day we expected anyone to be working, but the phone rang and once again it was the foreigners' police department. 'We need you to come to the office today please,' said the caller. Jeff's mind was whirling. These requests could go a number of ways, none of them reassuring. What was wrong now?

As it turned out, nothing was wrong. 'Oh Jeff, so good to see you,' said the clerk at the front counter with unusual friendliness. 'The director has instructed me to extend your visas. If you have your documents with you, we can change them now to twelve-month resident permits.'

The flourish of a few Arabic-looking signatures and the ka-thump of an approval stamp was all it took, and that afternoon Jeff walked home with a light heart and a spring in his step. The Lord had gone to work behind the scenes for us, and we couldn't have asked for a better way to end our first year in Bursa!

That night we set off with trays of food to celebrate New Year's Eve with some friends. Our hosts had given us plenty to anticipate—a round of tombola, dancing, fireworks for the kids—though they never mentioned the tradition where all the women retreat behind closed doors right before the stroke of midnight to don a fresh pair of lucky red knickers! But there you have it. Our hearts were full of hope for the future, and with fresh new visas in our passports, we felt we were up for anything! As we welcomed the new year in with gusto, everyone agreed life could not possibly get any better than this!

The Second Year

58. Jeff and the Dormitory

The first days of the new year were quiet—everyone was resting and recovering, and with some downtime on his hands, Jeff took the chance to catch up with Ishan. By now the two were completely at ease with talking in a mix of Turkish and English, and as they sat together in his little shop, Ishan began telling Jeff about his university days. 'I studied engineering,' he said, 'and, like so many others here, I have ended up working in a simple grocery store.'

'Did you enjoy university?' Jeff asked, and Ishan's eyes lit up. 'Oh yes,' he said, a mixture of pride and fondness in his voice. 'I especially liked living in my dormitory. 'It was a religious dormitory, where we could stay for very little cost. Everything was provided for us. Hundreds of young men stayed there. We were taught the Koran and practised our faith while we studied at university.'

When Jeff shared the conversation with me later that afternoon, I knew exactly the sort of dormitory he was referring to. Ishan's dormitory was simply a male version of what my friend, Nurcan, had described, only instead of being in Istanbul, his was only a few blocks from our house.

Jeff had noticed the ten-story building during his walks around the area, although it was shut off behind large iron gates. Ishan spoke as if it were still something of a second home to him. In fact, he told Jeff, following his divorce some years earlier, he had returned there to stay while he rebuilt his life. 'There is even a mosque on the top floor,' he told him. 'The dormitory is a place where young men become very good Muslims.'

Whether it was pre-meditated or not, we do not know, but right then, Ishan turned to Jeff and, catching him by surprise, asked, 'would you like to come and teach at my dormitory?

There are moments when you just know that an invitation comes, not only from the person asking, but from heaven itself, and this was one of them. Here was an opportunity to meet with university students in their own environment. 'They need to practice their English so they can run businesses and get jobs in Western countries,' Ishan explained. 'You can come once a week after the final prayer. There will be a group of young men for you to talk with in English about business.'

'Of course! I'd love to teach at your dorm!' was the immediate response in Jeff's heart, but for good reason, he held back. It had been less than a week since he'd sat in the police chief's office explaining that simply representing a foreign company didn't count as work in Turkey. This opportunity, however, whether paid or not, firmly crossed that line in anyone's books. As quickly as his excitement rose, Jeff's heart was sinking. There was simply no way to go ahead.

But why did it feel like God was so *in this thing*? Was there any way forward? 'I'll get back to you,' he eventually said, and for the next few weeks Jeff lived in a state of complete quandary, pacing around, tossing around the ethical dilemma in his mind.

'What if I offered to do it for free?'

'No, they wouldn't understand that.'

'What if I gave the money to Ishan?'

'No, they want to pay me.'

'What if I applied for a work permit?'

'No, there's no way an Islamic dormitory could legally employ me. Besides, God has been very clear that I should not apply for a work permit.'

Back and forth the reasoning went as Jeff grappled with the sense that God had brought this opportunity yet seemingly with no way to pull it off. Feeling defeated and more than a little confused, Jeff eventually made his way back down to Ishan's shop.

'I can't do it, Ishan,' he said.

'Why not?' his friend asked, looking confused.

'Because technically, it's working, Ishan,' Jeff replied, 'and there is no way for me to do work in Turkey without a permit.'

'Oh,' Ishan visibly relaxed in relief. 'That's no problem! You see, Jeff, you are not Muslim, so you cannot come to my dormitory during working hours anyway. You can only come after the last call to prayer. At that time of night, it doesn't count as working.'

The reasoning as to why certain hours might constitute legally working and others did not, was beyond Jeff. But Turkish law was clear that work permits were required to teach English, and there was no distinction in the law about the time of day.

The two men discussed the situation for some time until Ishan gave in. 'I understand,' he said, visibly disappointed. 'You are very good to think like this. You always want to do the right thing, my friend. You are a much better man than me.'

The words took hold of Jeff's gut and made it wrench. We hadn't relocated a family to Turkey to lay a guilt-trip on our friends. It was never our goal for our morality to outshine theirs. In any case, the whole conversation left Jeff feeling terrible.

I was glad we had booked a holiday. The next day we were due to leave for the coastal town of Kuşadası. Mid-winter or not, we needed a break, and so, with bags packed and bus tickets in hand, we set off the following morning. Hopefully, by the time we returned the following week, we'd have made peace with the whole unfortunate situation.

59. Kuşadası

We thoroughly enjoyed Kuşadası. For five days we explored ancient fortresses, clambered over rugged islands and strolled through olive groves, all rugged up because it really was freezing cold, and with pretty much everything in town closed for the winter, we could see why no one else was even attempting to holiday at that time of year.

For us, however, it was time to relax—if only Jeff had been able to shake off the feeling that he'd messed everything up with Ishan and the dormitory.

(Jeff writes) . . .

I was walking on the hills behind Kuşadası, thinking about the situation with Ishan and chatting to the Lord. 'So, it's over, God. But what on earth was that all about?' Bringing to Him my troubled and tangled thoughts, I told him I was resigned to the fact that I had messed things up, but I still wanted to make sense of it all. Ten minutes went by and no response. As the snow kept falling and my footsteps left their mark behind me, the barest inkling of a story came to mind—just the suggestion of it—but my reaction was like someone had set off fireworks inside my head. 'Of course! Why hadn't I thought of that before?!'

It was the story of Peter and the vision he received from heaven. Nearly running back to the hotel, I grabbed Anya and blurted out: 'Honey, tell me this: what is the one thing you think God would never ask us to do?' and without a moment's hesitation she responded, 'to break the law! He'd never ask us to do something illegal.'

And that was the point of what God had been showing me!

For the apostle Peter, eating food that was deemed unclean was the most unthinkable thing God could ask of him. It went against the very laws he respected and lived by. In fact, even the thought of eating unclean food was detestable to him.

The penny had dropped, but in a startling kind of way. That vision wasn't given because Peter was secretly craving freedom to eat bacon. Quite the contrary. Peter had nearly a visceral revulsion to those unclean foods. He didn't want to defile himself, nor did he want to be seen by others to be doing that either. That was exactly how I felt! For me, to work without a permit was effectively putting 'dirty' money into my wallet—it was no different to Peter being told he could put 'unclean' food in his mouth. My reaction had been the same as his. There was a bridge that, like him, I had been unwilling to cross.

The shift in my mind that day was as momentous for me as it must have been for Peter. My thoughts went to two pivotal occasions that had called for an unprecedented response in Peter.

The first took place on the day of Pentecost. If the Spirit of God was to be released upon the Jewish people that day, Peter would first need to stand up and make a bold declaration. Something new was taking place, and it called for a new level of boldness.

The second was when the Spirit was to come upon all men and women, Jews and Gentiles alike. For that to happen, Peter would need to sit down at a Roman Centurion's table, accept his hospitality, and share the news that the Gospel was good news for the whole wide world! Something new was taking place once again—and it called, not for a new level of boldness, but a new level of *freedom*!

Something momentous was going on—something more important than Peter's hang-ups! Peter's freedom plus the righteousness of Christ rather than his own, suddenly needed to meld together under the leading of the Holy Spirit so that a great big Kingdom door could be opened according to the will of God! And so, Peter managed to pull himself together, do the thing he most recoiled at, and open the way for a new, more glorious paradigm.

~

With his own scenario surprisingly resolved, Jeff spent the rest of the holiday with a much lighter heart, and, as soon as we returned home, made his way down the hill to visit Ishan once again. It was time to set things right.

'Ishan, my friend,' he said as he walked through the door and sat down, 'I need to apologise to you.' Jeff wasted no time in getting to the point. 'My friend, I am sorry. I realise now that you understood the will of God better than I did.' Now Ishan was the one looking confused. Jeff told him the whole story—how the one thing he never wanted to do was work without a permit. He told him the story of Peter and the vision, and how he also had a line he refused to cross. 'I realised that Peter also wanted to serve God and be a blessing to others, but his determination to keep the law held him back when God, in fact, was wanting to extend his love far and wide.'

Ishan was intrigued by the story of the early church, and, for the next hour, they talked it over like two brothers. 'Anyway,' Jeff finished up, 'if it can still be arranged, I would be honoured to come and teach at your dormitory.' Ishan's face lit up. 'Let me drive you home,' he said, 'I'll call the director of the dormitory to tell him you can come after all.'

They talked as they drove up the hill, but it wasn't until Jeff was about to get out of the car, that Ishan seemed to remember an all-important detail. 'Before you go,' he said, 'I have to tell you about my dream! One year ago, I had a dream, and in that dream, a man from Australia came and taught English in my dormitory. Tonight,' he said happily, 'my dream has come true!'

Just over a year ago? Jeff was gobsmacked. Just over a year ago we had been preparing to leave our home on the other side of the world, thinking we were on our way to Izmir, knowing little more than that God was at work in Turkey and that we were being invited to join him.

Jeff wished for a moment that Ishan had told him about his dream right at the start—that extra piece of information might have made the last few tumultuous weeks less confusing. But now we not only had complete peace of mind about Jeff teaching at the dormitory; we now had a heightened awareness that we had come to exactly the place God had intended for us all along. With that reassurance, we would step full swing into the year ahead. From that point on, our greatest challenge would be simply to keep up with what God was already doing.

60. Dealing with Death

But let's go back for a moment to our time in Kuşadası because another strange thing happened at the end of our week there. I couldn't explain it at the time, except that my friend Nurcan, from Bursa, was constantly on my mind one day, and I couldn't seem to shake the feeling that something was wrong, that she was, perhaps, in some kind of trouble.

On our final day, as we prepared to travel back home, I finally dialled her number. 'Nurcan?' I said, 'It's Anya. How are you? I've been . . .' and I had to stop right there because she began to reply and even with poor cell phone reception, I could hear the tremor in her voice.

'I'm okay. It's been a difficult few days,' then she burst into tears as she said, '. . . my father is dead.'

Oh, darling. This twenty-year-old who had been such a source of help and insight and friendship to me, had just lost her *dad*? I wanted to wrap my arms around her over the phone, but all I could do was let my heart feel the weight of what my friend was facing—Nurcan, who visited her grandmother twice a day, wrapping a towel around her aged shoulders and feeding her one spoonful at a time, the granddaughter who made sure she took her medicines on time, who went out into the streets when the old lady wandered, gently leading her back home; the woman born to two deaf parents, effectively becoming the link between them and the rest of the world. She was a pillar of strength, for sure, but now she was faltering, and—one thing I knew about Nurcan—she had adored her father.

Her dad had been so proud of her as she'd studied hard, learning sign language, then English, and now working for a degree in the Ottoman language, such was her love of her city and its heritage. . .

'Nurcan, what happened?' I asked, still not sure I had heard her correctly. But it was simple and stark and altogether too sad. 'He got sick,' she explained. 'A few days ago he couldn't speak, so we took him to the State Hospital . . . a stroke, they thought . . . not very severe . . . but it was the holidays, and all the doctors were away, so the nurses put him in a bed, but he couldn't eat or drink, and then he just . . .'

I tried to imagine the week my friend must have had—communicating between hospital staff and her distraught mother, the long waits for buses during the public holidays, preparing food to take to her father only to find he couldn't swallow, the lack of medical help, the dirty floors, changing his bedsheets, and then, at the end of it all, returning home to convey to an old lady in the grip of dementia that her son was gone forever, like her husband. Dead.

'Oh Nurcan, I'm so, so sorry,' I said. 'Are you alright?' But the call cut out, and as we made our way home, I faced the confronting reality that if a middle-aged man had experienced a stroke in our part of the world and made it to hospital, as Nurcan's father had, the outcome, in all likelihood, would have been different altogether.

Two feelings welled up within me over the next few hours. One was a new appreciation for the vulnerability that so many people in the world live with day after day. It's a level of vulnerability I must confess, I was not the least bit accustomed to. The other was the realisation that I could not have loved Nurcan more if she were my own sister.

~

The death of Nurcan's father allowed me great insight into local customs surrounding death in Turkey, as well as the fears and stress that accompany them. Nurcan was among the most educated, progressive of my Turkish friends, and yet, when it came to death, even her response took me by surprise. When I asked her, a few weeks later, how she was doing, I could hardly tell whether she was speaking literally or in some sort of symbolic way—and there was no way to clarify without seeming to insult her.

'I'm okay,' she said. 'We buried my father on the day he died, which is Islamic practice, and we offered all the correct prayers in the days and weeks that followed. But now we are grieving. Every Friday my mother and I visit his grave, but my mother worries that he might be getting cold with all the snow and rain we have had lately, and it makes her cry.' Nurcan had tried her best to explain in sign language to her mother, who had never even attended primary school, that he could not feel the cold now . . .

'Last week was very hard,' she said. 'My mother and I went to the grave to plant a tree. It was very difficult with all the snow, but it was important because summer will come soon enough and, in a few months, it will get very hot. We planted a tree by my father's head, and now we will water it and pray it grows large, because when summer comes, there must be shade for my father's head.'

'Nurcan,' I said, 'can you come over to my house for tea?' 'Yes,' she said, and so, with a clear idea in my mind and heart, I went outside to look for a stone. It needed to be smooth and clean, just the right size to fit in the palm of my friend's hand. It didn't take long—there were plenty at the edge of the footpath right by my front gate, and so, without any fuss, I picked one up and came back to the warmth of the house. Taking my finest brush and a little pot of ink, I painted on the stone the words that had jumped into my spirit that day: 'Jesus wept.'

As Nurcan and I talked that afternoon, I told her how Jesus also lost someone very dear to him. 'He visited the grave, just like you,' I said, 'and he wept.' Placing the stone in her hand, I looked into her eyes, shiny with tears. 'I made this for you, so that whenever the grief is too much to bear, you can hold it in your hand and remember that *Jesus knows how it feels . . .*'

We shared smiles and tears and hugs and another round of tea, and throughout the afternoon, the presence of God seemed nearly tangible; in fact, for a few hours, death seemed to have lost its sting, and a little glimmer of life on the other side of grief shone through.

61. Teaching at the Dormitory

Within a week, Jeff began visiting the dormitory and to say those young men quickly came to love Jeff is an understatement. They didn't care that it was ten or eleven o'clock at night before they even began their lessons—hospitality always came first.

Half an hour or so after the final call to prayer had sounded, his students would come to the front gates, where they greeted their 'teacher' and then led him up a richly carpeted staircase until they arrived on the sixth floor. There, in a simple classroom, they settled in for tea and biscuits, and after the usual enquiries about work and family, the conversation class would start.

(Jeff writes) . . .

I felt enormous joy every time I arrived at the Islamic dormitory—it was as if I only needed to walk through the front gates, and in so doing, Jesus got to enter there too. The Lord had assured me that my prayers for 'my boys' were like opening a door for him to bless and touch their lives. He told me some other things too—that others would follow me after I had gone, that I was part of a long game and that I should not enter into any discussion that debated or compared our faith. In fact, he went further than that and cautioned me not to even share my faith with these boys.

So, with my perspective further defined, I jumped enthusiastically into our conversation sessions. My students were keen and ready to participate, so our chats were vibrant and never dull. These young men didn't want grammar or formal lessons—they wanted to learn to talk and function in English, and so, after a few weeks of general conversation, we moved on to discuss business-related topics.

The boys were all commerce and economics students, and soon we were all enjoying the lessons on a whole other level. We talked through a lot of scenarios—applying for a job, what to do in meetings, how to negotiate buying and selling. We discussed why some businesses succeed and why others fail, and what business leadership means. Often our classes would run well past midnight, but it was fun, my students' ability to converse in English was improving noticeably and being with them was a great highlight in my week.

~

A few months into the arrangement, our friend, Rob, came for a short visit. Taking a side trip after some business meetings in the region, he had set aside time to come to Bursa before heading home. As soon as we heard, Jeff got an idea. What if Rob could come and meet his students at the dorm? Knowing he would first need to have the visit approved, Jeff went to see Ishan.

'Ishan,' Jeff said excitedly, 'I have an idea. My Australian friend, Rob is the CEO of a global company. It would be fantastic if the students at the dormitory could meet him.' Ishan was delighted. 'Leave it with me,' he said, 'I will pull some strings,' and with a quick word to the director of the dormitory, the evening was planned.

It was a rare privilege for the students to hear a man like Rob speak, and their respect that night was evident. For a few hours, they listened as Rob shared perspectives on business and leadership and answered their questions. To Jeff, it meant the world to share the dormitory experience with a friend from home.

Rob's visit lifted our spirits too, even beyond what we had anticipated.

For our kids especially, it was as if a much-loved uncle had come to town. And so, when Rob checked the weather forecast for his last day in town, saw we were set for a stunning winter's day, and suggested we all go skiing on Mount Uludağ, we jumped at the idea. What better way to spend a day than riding chairlifts and soaring down slopes of sparkling snow, best of all, with the company of a friend from home!

It felt as if we had not a care in the world. Soon we were all laughing again, especially little Vangie who took to the slopes with abandon. Nothing could contain her joy that day—even when she unwittingly plummeted into a deep snowbank, only to emerge, minus one ski and ski boot, but with a smile the breadth of her face.

62. Unwitting Advertisers

While a visitor from home gave us a fresh boost, I had a regular treat to keep me going, thanks to a young woman from home. Before we left for Turkey, she had messaged me: 'I can only afford five dollars a week,' she said, 'but I want you to think of it as coffee money. Have a nice coffee out each week and know that I'm cheering for you.'

It was enough to strengthen my spirits anytime they were flagging, and one morning a few weeks after Rob left, Jeff and I dipped into the designated coffee stash and headed to *Kahve Dünyası*[1]. I liked Kahve Dünyası because it was one of the few places in Turkey where we could get a very good flat white or latte, always served with a little dish of chocolate-coated coffee beans on the side. Kahve Dünyası stores were furnished with deep, plush armchairs for customers to sink into, which made me happy too. I particularly loved the Zafer Plaza store, because the whole mall was essentially a huge glass pyramid where natural light flooded in from every angle, and sitting there on the second floor, it felt like we were in a stunning atrium.

We took our time that particular morning, and with still another half hour to fill until the next bus home, I suggested we browse around another favourite store of mine—Tchibo. Tchibo is German, which meant we could count on the quality being superb, and their range of stock changed every few weeks, which meant there was always something new to admire.

---

1 *'Coffee world'*

Even I was not ready for the surprise, though, when we entered Tchibo that day only to find that there, in the front window, was a full-page Tchibo advertisement with a picture of our four children in the snow, bundled up in ski jackets and gloves and beaming with the fun of it all.

Jeff and I turned to each other. *You've got to be kidding!* While we were enjoying the mountain with Rob, there must have been a photographer snapping shots for Tchibo, and now, there were our kids, advertising their winter jackets! Obviously, the concept of asking permission hadn't come into consideration, but by all appearances, the ad seemed to be working because the store was packed with mums and dads trying ski pants and beanies and all manner of snow equipment on their kids.

'Well, if we can boost business for Tchibo, that's great,' we decided—and then laughed at the irony of it all. 'Yeah, and maybe one day our business will go well here too,' we joked as we rode the bus home.

63. Children's Day Speech

We couldn't have been prouder of the way our children were navigating the nuances and realities of life in Turkey, but right when we started wondering if we were asking altogether too much of any expat kid, Eric grabbed onto an opportunity that left us astounded. Arriving home from school one day he told us that he had agreed to give a speech in front of the whole school at the annual children's day celebration concert.

His teacher presumed that Eric would give his speech in English and offered to stand on the stage with him to translate as he spoke. But Eric loves a challenge, and with a quick 'thank-you anyway,' he let the teacher know he would rather give the speech in Turkish.

The following evening was devoted to crafting a speech—as we talked it over with Eric, we decided it must hit the right tone between formality and warmth, convey something distinctive about being both a foreigner and a youth, and that this was a chance to honour the historical ties between our countries.

The speech had to be approved in advance and so, the following day, Eric proudly handed his script to his teacher. 'Please can you translate this for me,' he asked, 'and then I will memorise it for Children's Day.' The teacher smiled, agreed, and took the speech.

Eric brought the translated speech home a few days later, and right away I was concerned because with even a casual glance, it was obvious the speech was noticeably shorter than the script Eric had handed in. But something else was amiss—we couldn't seem to make out many of the carefully chosen words we had used.

We decided to show the speech to Fatih. 'Astounding,' he responded. Not only had the teacher cut out any hint of emotion, but the speech had been culled so as not to appear original or even intelligent. 'And that,' Fatih said, 'is the problem.' The teachers were happy for a foreign boy to stand and stammer his way through a standard heard-it-all-before speech, but what they would never allow, was a foreign child to express a unique idea or personal opinion, or—particularly—to outshine the local children. In short, no one wanted Eric's speech to be a flop, but neither could it soar.

At that point, we decided to toss local insecurities out the window and deal with the fallout later. With Fatih as adamant as we were that Eric's speech should be preserved, he translated the script, word for word this time, then coached Eric until he pronounced every syllable correctly.

On the night of the concert, we sat among the fifteen-hundred-strong crowd with the Turkish national anthem still ringing in our ears, and suddenly there he was, our little boy, all of ten years of age, standing in the centre of a wide, empty stage, alone before his peers, his teachers and an auditorium full of Bursa's most influential families. He blinked as the spotlight fell on him and a look of momentary terror crossed his face. Jeff and I couldn't breathe, our hearts were racing for our son, hoping he hadn't stretched out too far this time, yet knowing that if any kid could pull this off, it was him.

And he did. Lifting his head, Eric fixed his eyes on the faceless crowd, raised the microphone to his lips, and gave a flawless speech in Turkish. *'Iyi akşamlar öğretmenlerim ve arkadaşlarım . . .'*

'Good evening teachers, friends and fellow students. One year ago, my family came to live in Turkey. I left my school, my friends, my grandparents and relatives, and my house with the kangaroos that came to our garden at dawn every morning.

We arrived in Turkey with great excitement and started to make a new life. It has been an adventure for me. In Australia, I hardly ever rode on a bus. Everywhere we went, we drove our car. Today, I know most of the bus drivers in Bursa! I have tasted new foods – lahmacun and köfte. I have camped on Mt Uludağ and explored an old fortress at Kuşadası. I have become used to hearing the call to prayer every day. I have tried to learn a new language. It is a privilege to experience these things.

It is also very different here, and I often feel like going back home. I still don't really feel like I belong here. Maybe that will change.

Australians love to come to Turkey because of our shared history. Most Australians want to visit Çanakkale[1] once in their lifetime. Turkey became a new nation after the battle of Çanakkale and in a way, so did Australia. This was the first time Australians had fought under their own flag. So Çanakkale was the birthplace of our nation also.

After the battle of Çanakkale, Ataturk spoke to Australian and New Zealand mothers whose sons had died in battle. He said: "Heroes who shed their blood and lost their lives! You are now lying in the soil of a friendly country . . . there is no difference between the Johnnies and Mehmet's where they lie side by side here in this country of ours . . . after having lost their lives on this land they have become our sons as well."

Australians think of Turks as our brothers and sisters. We fought with each other, but we respect each other. We welcome each other with hospitality. We laugh at the same things and fear the same things. We both love our freedom and our national identity. In Australia, I rode my bike, played soccer, surfed in the ocean, read many books, played on my computer.

Children are the same all over the world. Sometimes it doesn't feel like it. But everyone wants to be included and feel respected. All children want to learn and discover. Every child needs to be loved, to feel safe, and to enjoy their happy childhood days.

You have welcomed me and my family to your country, your community, and your school. Thank you. I have been in Turkey for one year. Someday, when I return home to Australia, I know I will take happy memories with me. Happy children's day!

There was no thunderous applause—we didn't expect that. The honour culture in Turkey doesn't extend easily to foreign children. But Eric knew, and we knew, that he had absolutely nailed it, and that night as Jeff and I stood in the doorway of our son's room we enjoyed

---

1 Turkish for 'Gallipoli'

a moment of parental pride. After all he had dealt with in the past six months, the speech he delivered that night had been extraordinary.

64. Looking for Volunteer Opportunities

The working group plunged into its second year full of enthusiasm; many newcomers had joined over the previous months, and I now had a huge group of foreigners who were keen to contribute. We were beginning to catch a vision, not just of our group pulling off projects together, but of many foreigners, hundreds of us, all adding to the wellbeing of our city. The best way to pull that off, I knew, was to find as many opportunities for expats to volunteer as possible.

Beyond our working group were the people we represented—many hundreds, possibly thousands, of foreigners, many of whom I had now met with personally. These people brought a valuable mix of experience, generally had plenty of spare hours in their week, and best of all, the desire to contribute was integral to who they were. These people had come to Turkey with a global village mindset, and now we had to find a way for that village to let them in.

Of course, there were varied motives behind the desire to volunteer. Some were simply bored and wanted a meaningful way to fill their days. Others were motivated by a specific cause or the desire to widen their circle of friends outside the expat community. Many, I suspected, hoped that volunteering might lead to paid work down the track.

I was excited. What if our working group could help create a culture where foreigners and locals worked side by side, sharing their skills and partnering together for the good of the city?

The obstacles sprung to mind as well, of course. We'd already come up against them numerous times, not the least being the fact that the authorities didn't differentiate between volunteering and working. We would need the foreigners police to create a new category for volunteers, perhaps even issue volunteer visas. Then we'd have the potentially more difficult task of convincing local charities and businesses that they would not be doing anything illegal or unpatriotic by hosting a foreign volunteer for a few hours a week.

But we never even got that far, because as it turned out, Bursa had a history with foreigners and charity work, and an incident that took place many years earlier had festered in the city's memory for over sixty years. Until the past was addressed, there would be no sustainable way for expats to volunteer. If we were to move forward, I would first need to unwrap an old wound.

The account went something like this: Apparently, a freelance journalist had come to Bursa many years earlier, requesting a visit to the city orphanage, where, at the time, expats and locals volunteered side by side; his aim was to write an article about the care of children in Turkey. The city of Bursa was justifiably proud of their orphanage at the time, and so the reporter was welcomed in under the presumption that the story would reflect well on the city.

The report that was published ended up doing quite the opposite; most embarrassingly for the orphanage directors, the journalist had secretly photographed his visit in a way that portrayed the children's home as a run-down place, implying substandard care and leaving the entire nation, and Bursa in particular, humiliated. In a blanket response, the government of Turkey denied all foreign volunteers further access to Turkish institutions on the spot.

Sixty years had passed, but the distrust of foreign volunteers was as strong as ever; moreover, the situation was not confined to Bursa— this was a national issue. It seemed the whole country was closed to any opportunities to formally lend a hand unless the context was *by foreigners for foreigners.*

Deep down, I felt it was time for the wrongs of the past to lose their grip, *and* I believed that the people of Bursa could pave the way for change, difficult though it might be. Though Bursa had been hurtfully misrepresented, I longed for the situation to be forgiven and for locals and expats to have the freedom once again to contribute side by side for the benefit of the city.

In fact, I wanted to go further than that—I wanted to establish a cutting-edge culture of volunteer tourism in Bursa. That, I could see, had the potential to bring great benefits for generations to come. In my heart, I could see a city where foreigners were trusted, valued and welcomed once again, and where Turks were honoured in return. I longed for the walls to be broken down and for history to be rewritten. But I also knew that forgiveness was not a normal part of the society we were in. In Turkey, it seemed there was no desire either to forgive *or* to forget.

My mind went back to the powerful moment when our Australian Prime Minister had stood on the grass outside Parliament House and apologised to the Aboriginal people for the devastation inflicted on them by white colonists in past generations.[1] The words may have come decades too late and may have seemed inadequate to some, yet I sensed the shift that happened as he uttered those words, like a heavy memory was lifted from our nation's shoulders and now there was a chance old wounds might finally heal.

I kept wondering if I could do the same. What if I were to make a similar public statement, owning the wrongs that had been done, apologising on behalf of us foreigners for the humiliation that was inflicted all those years ago . . .

But Turkey is not a nation of forgivers. Fear and the lengthy holding of grudges had given rise to a stark and robust form of nationalism—one that discriminated against non-Turks at every turn. If my working group were to be the means of opening the doors to foreign volunteers again in Turkey, a grand-scale shift would need to occur. For now, all I could do was wait.

65. Forgiveness in the Schoolyard

In the meantime, the forgiveness deficit in Turkey confronted us on a personal level when Eric ended up in a fight with a classmate from school. 'He was taunting me all day,' Eric explained. 'I couldn't take it anymore, so I hit him.'

It was as simple as that, but the whole class rose to the Turkish boy's defence, and, with Eric deciding to hold his own, the scene had turned into an outright brawl. In true Australian parenting style, we called the office and made an appointment to meet with the principal the following day. 'Sure,' he said. 'I can see you at ten a.m. tomorrow.'

As we stepped into his office the following day, it was Jeff and I who were about to get an education. 'We understand the boys got into a fight,' Jeff began, 'and it is clear they both stirred up trouble. Eric is here to apologise.'

Apologising is something our family has down pat, and so, as

---

1 www.australia.gov.au/about-australia/our-country/our-people/
apology-to-australias-indigenous-peoples

expected, Eric looked at the principal and said he was very sorry for fighting at school and for hurting his classmate. 'I lost my cool, and I'm sorry,' he said. 'Please forgive me.'

Thankfully, Mehmet Bey was a generous man; he had also travelled extensively and was educated abroad, and he understood foreign ways. With a smile, he kindly patted the head of the ten-year-old Aussie boy standing on the ornate rug in front of him and assured him that, yes, all was forgiven.

But we had one more request. 'Before we go, could Eric's classmate join us here so that the boys can apologise to each other properly? We want them to put things right, so this doesn't get any bigger.'

That was the moment we got some insight of our own. 'I'm sorry,' said the principal, 'we cannot do that. It is fine if Eric would like to apologise to his friend, but his friend is not able to apologise to Eric. You see, this boy's parents pay for him to come to this school and it would not be right for me to humiliate him by asking him to apologise to a foreigner.'

So there we had it—money, pride and a system that would rather let two boys remain hostile than restore a friendship. As we drove back home, I could almost feel the weight of a nation that would rather live with the burden of guilt than admit its wrongs and be free.

66. Liberty and the Paediatrician

There are moments when you feel like you've somehow failed to tick even the most basic of parenting boxes, and this time it was Liberty who fell through the gaps. For a while now, Liberty had been having episodes where she cried and told us her stomach was sore. We'd hugged her, rubbed her little tummy, popped her into bed at night, and not thought too much of it until the night when we met up with some friends and decided spontaneously to go out for dinner together.

It was one of those occasions when we all loved being in Turkey, like when the bus driver sat the kids on his knee and let them help drive the city bus through town—things that would be unheard of back home. This particular night at the restaurant, the kids got to help the chef knead the pizza dough, place it into the large wood-fired ovens, and pull out the long wooden paddles when the food was ready to serve. Priceless!

But we were only a bite or two into our meal when Liberty, clearly in excruciating pain, began, not just crying, but screaming. Right there at the table, she doubled over as if to vomit, all the while, fighting us off, unwilling to let us touch her or help her at all. *Let's get her out of here*, I figured, as I picked her up and carried her to the only private place I could think of—the Turkish toilet on the ground floor—where I closed the door, placed her down on the floor of the cramped little closet, and tried to make sense of what was going on as Liberty huddled in the corner looking terrified. Twenty minutes later, when her tears had subsided and our little girl had relaxed into my arms once again, we returned to the table.

'Is she okay?' my friend asked.

'I don't know,' I answered. 'It seems really strange, like she's in pain but she's also scared. She's not telling me anything except that her tummy hurts.'

My friend asked how long she had been having these episodes, but the truth is, I hadn't really thought about it. Three weeks, maybe four? I didn't know—perhaps it had been longer. The weeks were flying by, blurring into one another, we never knew what was coming next, and . . .

I should have known, though. Should have paid attention. 'Have you taken her to a doctor?'

'Ah . . . no.'

The look on my friend's face was a parenting wake-up call. How can a mother not notice her daughter is ill right in front of her eyes?

The next day I called a paediatrician, and within hours we were sitting in his office. He started with a few easy questions.

'*How old is she?*'

'She's three.'

'*Did she have a normal birth?*'

'Yes.'

'*How long has she had this pain?*'

It was time to get real. 'I don't know. It could be a few months.' I figured it was time to cover all our bases. Maybe it wasn't as long as we'd thought, but there was no point understating things now.

'*Is it getting worse?*'

'Well, yes. Last night was certainly the worst we've seen her.'

It was then that I realised how little time we'd actually spent with our girl—one hour before school, three hours after, and then she was in bed.

'*Is she drinking plenty of water?*'

I knew right there, when I didn't have a clue, that I'd dropped the ball big time. Truth is, we paid good money to send her off on a bus at eight a.m., and for the next seven hours, we figured she was being fed, watered, educated and socialised. I didn't give a minute's thought to how much water she was drinking.

The doctor lifted her up onto the examination table and opened her mouth. 'She's dehydrated,' he said. Gently, he pulled back her t-shirt and started pressing on her abdomen. 'She's constipated too. Severely. Has she been going to the toilet?'

His eyes held a level of concern I had not seen before and by now I was ready to put up my hand and own up to the fact that I was the world's most incompetent, negligent, ignorant mother, unfit for the basic task of raising a child. *What made us think we could handle bringing four children to a foreign country like this?* More to the point, *how did this happen?* I'd found Liberty crouched behind curtains, her little fists clutching at the folds, her face tense, and I hadn't put it together. I just figured she went to the toilet at preschool. Surely, they would have told me if there was a problem?

No, as it turns out.

The doctor went over to his phone and called the school. It didn't take a genius to work out he was worried—and angry. From the sound of the conversation, we had quite the situation on our hands.

It didn't take long to get the picture once the paediatrician set down the phone. 'This is the situation,' he said. 'The teachers are toilet-training the children at school. There is a set time each day when all the two and three-year-old children must sit on their potties, yes?' I nodded in response. 'The children are expected to learn,' he continued, 'but unfortunately, Liberty doesn't seem to be getting the hang of it and has sometimes been having 'accidents' later in the day.

My horror grew as the doctor relayed what had been happening. '. . . and so,' he went on, 'the teachers have been getting the cleaner to take her to a bathroom, where she runs a bath, and puts Liberty in there until she is clean.' I shuddered at the thought of my daughter being bathed by some stranger at school, but that wasn't all . . . 'The problem is,' he said, 'that the cleaner got tired of doing that job. She was getting upset with Liberty because she used to scream when she was in the bath, but the teacher has told me, "It's okay now. She doesn't seem to need to go to the toilet anymore.'" In fact, they had forgotten all about it because they hadn't had a problem with Liberty in a few weeks. 'Do you see what has happened?' he asked.

Oh .my. goodness. Yes!

Liberty always came home with her clothes cleaned and neatly folded in her schoolbag, yet I had never realised what was happening. Now, she wasn't eating, wasn't drinking, and her little bowels had simply stopped moving.

We didn't have long, the doctor was saying. Liberty would need around-the-clock care until her little body was working again.

I won't go into it. Suffice to say, for weeks, we massaged that little belly through the night, we spooned prune juice into her parched little mouth, we held her shaking little shoulders as she braved the bathroom, and we said 'we're so sorry, darling,' over and over and over again.

We humans aren't made to carry guilt, but Jeff and I had heard its taunts, and we knew that if we didn't silence its accusations right away, this feeling of parental failure could drive us back onto a plane and right on home. Then, of course, it wouldn't just be a little girl's gut that came to a standstill, but the whole Turkey gig, once and for all.

But we were annoyed too. What do you do with the awareness that the people you entrusted your child to had set her up for humiliation day after day? What do you do with the whole national mentality that no one questions a teacher, that parents of all people, must not question what goes on inside the walls of their own child's preschool?

We poured out forgiveness—for the teachers, the cleaners, the chef who heaped up endless platefuls of bread and rice day after day—we went wild with forgiveness. Mostly though, we took heaping amounts of forgiveness for ourselves as parents; we bathed in it, in fact, because if there's one thing we have learned, it's that once guilt gets a toe in the door, it is quick to consume us *and* destroy the ones we love.

We gave the school the required two weeks' notice, but we never sent her back. It would take the next six months for the damage to be fully reversed in Liberty's gut, the doctor had told us, and we would have to keep her off rice and bread, and give her a chance to play and run and move again.

The emotional damage was evident too—we often prayed over our littlest girl as we pleaded for her health to return, her smile to come back, and the trauma to soon be passed. In the meantime, though we had approached the whole schooling situation in Turkey with some serious grace, there was no question in our minds . . . it was time to home-school our kids.

67. Meeting Mildred

Soon after, I travelled to Istanbul to attend a conference for Christian women in Turkey. It was wonderful to be in a hotel, to have my days planned for me—that was a rest in itself—and to be with women who loved Jesus and were similarly navigating expat life in Turkey. But the huge God-moment of the weekend happened when about twelve of us were seated at a round table having dinner one night. Leaning over, a woman I had met only a few hours earlier casually asked, 'Your family lived in Albania when you were young, didn't they?' and though fifteen years had passed, I began to tell the incredible story of my parent's faith and perseverance, coupled with spiritual attacks and disappointments on so many levels.

As I spoke, it was evident that my family's story seemed to resonate with every woman at the table; I saw some wipe tears of understanding from their cheeks while others nodded because *they really got it.* Soon everyone at the table was listening in, hanging on every word, and in that moment, I could see once again how Jeff and I, in bringing our family to Turkey, were in many ways, living out a redemption story.

I finished speaking as dessert was being served and turned to the girl sitting on my right. She had a sweet face, looked no more than eighteen or so, and when she spoke it was with an accent from the American deep south. Her manner captivated me. Mildred was softly spoken, gracious, confident, she had come to Turkey straight out of home-school to teach in Istanbul, and her passion was science, she told me. For the past few months she had taught a small group of Turkish students in after-school classes, but her time was coming to a close, she was planning to head back home in the next month or so, and she was trusting God to show her what to do next.

I felt a familiar stirring in my spirit. 'Mildred,' I asked, 'would you consider coming to live in Bursa? We have two families of children who need to be home-schooled. Would you like to help us? We'd love you to be our science teacher.'

I could hardly believe I was saying it myself. We had talked with the other Australian family in Bursa about the idea of joint home-schooling, but without some support, neither of us felt we could do it adequately. 'Oh, I love Bursa!' said Mildred with rare enthusiasm. She even had friends there and *yes, of course, she would pray about it.*

I left the conference with a whole new outlook on the days ahead.

~

And she came.

Within the month, Mildred relocated to Bursa, enrolled in Turkish lessons, moved in with a group of Americans, and agreed to teach our children two afternoons a week. It was the breakthrough we had been waiting for. With six foreign children between us now removed from Turkish school, the other expat family and ours had gone about ordering curriculum, planning our teaching schedule, and best of all, sorting out a school room.

We decided to use the basement of our apartment because we could leave it set up as a dedicated area, the other family's children were old enough to catch the bus to our place, and because my connection with the city council meant we could probably get away with home-schooling even though there was no provision for it in Turkish law. We also had a lovely grassed area outside which would be perfect for lunch breaks.

My friend and I went to work, buying tables and cupboards and dividing up the teaching schedule. Between us, we would share the teaching of English, maths and history, and two afternoons a week, Mildred would come and teach science.

It was Mildred who offered to decorate the schoolroom. Oozing with passion and joy she set to work, and by the time she was finished, I was delighted. The room had come alive with colour and purpose. We were ready to educate our kids at home in Bursa!

68. Cadriye

With our children now at home through the day and Jeff and I juggling our editing company, city council meetings, the dormitory work and a multitude of visitors, it was Arzu, my neighbour, who told me in no uncertain terms that we needed a housekeeper. She couldn't believe a family with four children would even try to do it all themselves. The way we were living was decidedly un-Turkish, and she proposed a solution.

The following week, when Arzu's housekeeper came to clean, she brought her over to meet me. 'This is Cadriye,' Arzu said, 'and she is happy to clean your house. She is a very good cleaner.' I didn't doubt it for a minute, but even so, Arzu's recommendation didn't begin to do this woman justice. Not only was she a superb cleaner, she was honest, hardworking and a delight to have in the house.

Cadriye must have been in her late forties or early fifties—it was hard to tell. She wore the traditional trench coat and simple headscarf that told me she was devout in her faith and probably had her roots somewhere further East.

There was a system to her cleaning. Every Thursday morning at eight a.m. she arrived at our house and within fifteen minutes had stripped the linen off all the beds, put on a load of laundry and filled her bucket with fresh soapy water. Beginning at the top story of the house, she then worked her way down to the basement; in every room she wiped over the walls from ceiling to floor, moved the furniture, washed the floors by hand, and threw her leg over the window sills, balancing precariously until every pane sparkled before beating the Turkish rugs until barely a whiff of dust was left. To finish the day, she remade the beds, puffed the pillows and tidied the shoes at the front door.

Often Liberty would trot alongside Cadriye as she worked, chatting away in her toddler-style Turkish and every now and then the older woman would pause to take her little cheeks in the palms of her hands and squeeze with motherly affection.

Cadriye only took three breaks during the day, one for a brief cup of tea and two to perform her prayers right there in the middle of whatever room she happened to be in when the call to prayer sounded. She often worked until five o'clock in the evening, and, she insisted, she would only accept the going rate—forty dollars a day. *God bless her.* She was an angel, in every sense of the word.

69. Beauty and the Burqa

With the household now under control, we were able to get around to other things—like buying new shirts for Jeff. I had tried rummaging through the random stacks of clothing at our local covered market, but with all the original labels removed and not a changing room in sight, I'd had no success. What we needed was a proper menswear store.

Of course, traipsing four children into the city at nine o'clock at night was never going to end well. By quarter to eleven, though, with Liberty in the midst of an exhausted meltdown, it was clear that we'd pushed everyone too far. Jeff had finished trying on clothes, the boys had gone in search of a drink, and I sat on a leather seat with one daughter crying in my lap and the other fighting to keep her eyelids open as she rested her head against my arm.

We weren't the only ones out that late. Another family were lingering right on closing time—tourists from Saudi Arabia, I presumed. The men amused me as they popped in and out of the changing rooms, pedantically checking the fit of every garment they tried and openly admiring themselves in front of each other. In the meantime, the women, all in burkas, chatted among themselves, quietly tending to their own children as they waited.

There were two men and three women in this family; I wasn't sure if they were all wives, or wives and a daughter—their eyes were concealed behind a grid-like square, making it nearly impossible to determine any features at all.

Liberty had never adjusted to the sight of women wearing the burqa. In her three-year-old mind, they probably looked like strange black ghosts that every now and then walked past her on the street or sat beside her on the bus—only now, I noticed, one of the women was making her way over to us! I braced myself for an awkward scene. The moment Liberty caught sight of her, I felt her body recoil. Lifting her little head, I whispered in her ear '*It's alright, darling*' and, wiping the tear-soaked cheeks once again with my hand, I prayed for strength. It wasn't only Liberty who was exhausted—I was too. The last thing I needed was for Liberty to be upset all over again by this scary, black-robed woman.

But there are moments in a foreign culture that completely mess with your expectations, and this was to be one of them. I could only see her expression dimly through the veil, but it was that of a kindly mother-figure, only she appeared quite young. Whatever it was, there was a quiet confidence in the eyes behind the grid, as if this woman knew exactly what the situation called for.

What happened next will forever remind me that humanity is indeed wonderful and that people all the world over share an amazing capacity for kindness. Without a word, the woman reached into the folds of her burka and pulled out a bottle of bright red nail polish. Squatting down in front of us she gestured to Liberty to hold out her hands. Liberty, suddenly wide-eyed and compliant, did as she was shown. And then, the stranger in black took those little white hands in her own, wiped another tear from Liberty's cheek with all the tenderness of a much-loved aunty, unscrewed the lid of her nail polish, and began painting each tiny nail—slow, careful strokes, making sure the edges were covered just right—one, two, three, four, five . . . *little blow to help them dry . . .* next hand—six, seven, eight . . . her eyes smiled, and Liberty smiled too, like a child whose very soul had been soothed.

'How pretty!' I said, admiring her beautiful work. I looked through the gauze, wishing I could see who this woman was who had just ministered so sweetly to my girl, but it was impossible. By now, the men had finalised their purchases and the store was about to close. I reached out and placed my hand gently on the sleeve of the woman before she turned to leave. I had no words, of course, but I was close enough now to see her eyes, and they were smiling.

In that fleeting moment, it did not matter that we were from opposite worlds. My tiredness had lifted. Peace had been restored, and on the way home, with Liberty's sleeping head tucked under my chin, and her nails gleaming crimson, I entertained the recurring thought that perhaps she too had been an angel, a ministering spirit sent to help just when we needed it most.

70. Prayers for the Dead

Three months had passed since Nurcan's father died when I received an invitation. 'Would you like to come to pray with us?' Nurcan had asked. 'After three months we have special prayers.'

My dearest friend had lost her dad and she was asking me to come and pray? *Of course.* And so I turned up, oblivious to the series of embarrassments that were about to come my way. For a start, when Nurcan met me at the front door I didn't recognise her. My friend, usually sharp and on-trend, was dressed in a headscarf and coat, she wore no makeup, and she looked like she hadn't slept in weeks. Oh my. This was a Nurcan I had never seen before, and all I could do was reach out and hug her close.

Oh darling. How are you?

But that day, she was more interested in me. She was the only daughter, every room of the tiny apartment was filled with guests all concerned about food, and it was her job to make me feel at home. 'Eat,' she said, handing me a plate of salad and köfte, and with that she led me to her room where a few school friends sat cross-legged on a simple single bed, their heads covered with scarves as well. I felt rude at not having brought a plate of food and bare for not having worn a headscarf, but Nurcan seemed proud to introduce me to her friends. We'd all heard of each other, of course, and as I met these girlfriends she had spoken of many times, I could see they were all more like sisters to Nurcan than I had realised.

The young women switched to English, talking with ease about death and Nurcan and her dad and their own lives. I sat on a cushion on the floor, eating salad and trying to be chatty despite the ever-present reality that this was a wake.

An aunty came into the room, took one look at me, and a look of horror crossed her face, followed quickly by an understanding smile. 'Nurcan's friend?' she said, *'Evet.'* I replied. *'Yes. I'm her friend from Australia.'* This woman had no English, but she assured me that the cake she was handing out was the favourite of Nurcan's father, and we must all eat some now. Then she went to the cupboard and pulled out a scarf. Her gestures made it clear. *Put this on. Wear a scarf.*

'Thank you,' I whispered in Turkish. 'Thank you so much.'

I usually carried a scarf with me, but that day I hadn't, and I stood out terribly. Now, wrapping the scarf carefully and tucking the edges into a fold just as the local women did, my heart was conflicted. Thankfully I didn't stand out for all the wrong reasons—I couldn't bear the thought of dishonouring my friend's father. But neither was I comfortable with being all covered up. With no idea what was coming, I was simply grateful to be away from the lounge area and the older, more severe-looking women.

And then, the prayers began. I don't know what I had expected, but certainly, it was not fifty or more women squished cross-legged into a two-roomed apartment holding Arabic prayer books and rocking back and forth. I tried to pray but I couldn't. I tried to focus on the Arabic script in my hands but of course, it meant nothing to me. A female imam was leading the prayers in the lounge—I could hear her, but from my spot in the hallway, I could not see her.

Nurcan was with her mother, near the imam, and as I sat there, surrounded by women I didn't know, chanting prayers in a language I did not know, about a man I had never met, I suddenly wished I hadn't come. I placed the pages of prayers beside me on the floor and clasped my hands together.

That was my next mistake. Now, I had insulted the Koran.

A woman behind me clicked her tongue and tut-tutted as she picked up the booklet. Lifting it to her lips and then her forehead, she gave it back to me with a shake of her finger and the clear message that the booklet must not touch the ground. 'I didn't realise,' I wanted to say. 'I wouldn't have placed the Koran on the ground, but I didn't know a printed selection of prayers had the same rules.' But of course, I couldn't say all that, and anyway, it was too late. I had shown myself up as an infidel, the scarf was no cover for my complete lack of religion, and now I had disgraced my friend.

The prayers went on and on and on. I couldn't excuse myself—that would have been the ultimate taboo—but when the whole ritual finally came to an end more than an hour later, I lost no time in finding Nurcan, told her I loved her and her family and with a 'Thank you so much for letting me be part of these prayers'—and I meant it sincerely—I headed for the door, removed my headscarf and asked Jesus to comfort me. Because that wasn't just grief I experienced in there. It was fear and superstition and ignorance and embarrassment, and all I wanted to do was get as far away from it all as I possibly could.

71. Apologising to the Neighbours (again)

In the midst of home-schooling and housework and writing memos for my working group, the doorbell rang one afternoon. It was my friend Emek from the house across the garden, asking if our girls would like to come over for a playdate with her daughter. 'That sounds great,' I answered and, calling the girls to the door, asked them if they would like to go for a visit. It was presumptuous of me, I suppose, but still, why couldn't they just have smiled and said, *'Can you come too, Mummy?'* or, *'We'd love to come but we just need to finish our lunch first,'* or something of the sort?

No, they wouldn't look at my friend, wouldn't smile, just blurted out, *'we don't want to'* and hid their little faces as if Emek were some scary sort of stranger on our doorstep. As if to top off the insult, Liberty began screaming as if her world was about to end. I stood there, watching the disaster unfold. *Seriously?* Had these girls not learned *anything* about how to treat people in their combined six or so years of life?!

I smiled sheepishly and Emek turned around and walked back up the path to her house. Already I could imagine the fall-out from this whole unfortunate situation; in fact, with *so much* patching up of the relationship to do, familiar taunts started ringing in my ears: 'Maybe we should just pack up and go home. If we can't even hold down a decent friendship with our neighbours, what kind of cross-cultural failures must we be?'

My usual policy in such situations, however, is 'better sooner than later,' so that evening, I prepped the girls to give a proper apology, fixed their hair, traipsed them up the path and timidly knocked on Emek's door. My friend's mother opened it, told us her daughter was not at home, and we left, feeling like we'd only added further insult to the situation.

But I'd got it wrong. Around eight o'clock that evening, Emek came back over. *'We've made coffee,'* she said. *'Would you like to come and have supper with us?'*

'We'd love to,' I heartily replied, then quickly rounded up the children and joined our neighbours at their garden table where a few relatives were sitting together enjoying the warm mid-evening breeze. The girls were thrilled to come this time and happily ran on ahead—perhaps our quick refresher course in 'how to treat people with kindness and respect despite how you happen to feel' had hit the mark.

In any case, there we sat. Emek brought out fresh pastries from the oven, plums from the shared tree in the garden and wonderful Turkish ice cream with chocolate topping for all the children. I think I apologised about three times for what had happened earlier in the day, but Emek replied with a smile and said, 'Honestly, it really doesn't matter.' Talk about forgiving. Talk about repaying insult with kindness.

In the course of our conversation, my friend asked me the meaning of my name. 'It means *grace*,' I replied in English because I had no idea of the Turkish equivalent. 'Grace. Do you know that word? It's like kindness, only a lot deeper and more, well . . . ' She nodded and smiled and left me none the wiser as to whether she knew the meaning or not. As we were about to leave, however, I remembered that Liberty's birthday was coming up. 'Why don't you come over to our place next week,' I asked, 'and we can have a little party together?'

Emek looked at me as kindly as if she were my own sister. 'You have had a busy week, Anya. Why don't we have a party for Liberty here in our garden? My mother and I will make all the food and you can just come and relax. Would you like that?'

Truth is, I may not have had the words to explain the meaning of 'grace,' but neither were they needed. Emek had shown us what it looked like in real life, and I went to bed that night knowing that her response to us that day provided a better definition than I could have ever come up with.

72. Late-Night Coffee

By this stage, I was holding meetings at the City Council at least three times a week. Our working group was constantly growing, and to ensure everyone had a choice of what to engage in, we had recently established a number of subgroups. Though we were all volunteers, our approach was professional, our discussions productive, and the list of projects we were managing was impressive. My job had, by now, extended to building relationships with other organisations, and in so doing, to establish our group as an integral part of the city.

We estimated that the working group represented around ten thousand foreign residents, and with over forty different nationalities in the mix, I needed, more than ever, to keep my finger on the pulse, and focus on strengthening our connections for the long term.

There was no master plan. Although I had a team of strategic thinkers around me, I often defaulted to intuition, going with whatever current seemed strongest in the moment, and by and large, it worked. But as my core team took on more responsibility and newcomers were integrated into the mix, I felt a longing to know them all better. 'People are always more important than the project,' was something I often said, but getting one-on-one time with the people in my working group was becoming increasingly difficult. If we were to sustain our good start, we would need to interact not only as a working group, but as friends.

I began by inviting anyone who came to our meetings to join us for coffee together afterwards. Most people jumped at the opportunity—at least, most of the under-thirties. Together we would walk to the iconic café at the top of the old Bursa water tower. Packing ourselves into the elevator, we headed up to the rooftop lounge, where, for the next few hours, waiters took our coffee orders and left us to relax as we enjoyed the lights of the city and the friendship of one another.

I liked to sit back and listen to the conversations as they buzzed around me—it gave me a chance to pick up on each person's passions and skills, to understand what annoyed them or inspired them, and to hear how other parts of their lives were going. Inevitably they talked about their families back home, confiding to each other what they loved about being in Turkey, and what they desperately missed.

Watching my team bond together in that cosy environment soon became a highlight in my week. As I tuned into one conversation after another, it struck me that the mixing of cultures and opinions and perspectives never grows dull. And though I often felt like I didn't quite fit in such a youthful scene, something about it also felt perfectly natural, and when we all made our way back down to the ground floor after an hour or two of unwinding and everyone was kissing everyone else on one cheek and then the next as we bid each other goodnight, I knew we were building a community that superseded all our individual cultures and would unite us as friends long after our time together in Bursa had passed.

73. The Germans

When Ayşe asked me to come into the office to talk about some German university students who were coming to town, I had no idea what God was about to pull off. 'They are on an exchange program for one year,' she said. 'Their university has requested that we find some civil-society projects for them to participate in while they are here.' I leaned in to hear what exactly was on her mind. 'We think this is a great opportunity, and we have agreed to support them in this,' she said. 'The girls will attend a full schedule of lectures at the university here, but we would like them to work on some of the working group initiatives too.'

I jotted down notes as she spoke. 'Also,' she continued, 'they are training to be teachers and need to get practical experience, so perhaps we can arrange some way for them to teach children while they are here. I was wondering if you would be happy to mentor these students . . .'

And at that point, she didn't need to say any more, because already my spirit was saying *'yes, yes, yes'* and ideas began flooding my mind.

They could help tutor our children.

I bet they're Christians.

Christians? On the university campus? This is huge!

'Oh wow—Christian, German and female—what a crazy combination! And to get sent to Bursa, of all places. How will they ever survive? I can't wait to bring them home. We'll give them meals, hugs, whatever it takes. . .'

Of course, I was getting ahead of myself. But then came the thought that trumped them all.

Volunteering—teachers—children . . . I staggered inwardly as I realised the significance of this placement. *Had we just been given a way for the past to be rewritten? Was this the redemption story our city had been longing for? Was the door being opened for foreigners to volunteer once again?* Ayşe kept speaking, while I silently marvelled at all the unexpected directions life could take on any given day.

Sure enough, the girls arrived, and you could tell from one look at their faces that these young women were unaffected, confident, happy and not the least bit phased by their placement in this conservative, industrial, Muslim city.

I introduced myself. *'Hi, I'm Anya.'* I knew the name would sound familiar. *Don't you love it?* The name had made me feel so awkward as a child, and yet now, as I met these Germans, it was that same name that gave us common ground. Who would have thought that a Kiwi girl from Australia, living in Turkey, with a German name could now make perfect sense? I reached out my hand to greet them. 'What university are you from?' I asked.

Sure enough, it was a tiny college called *Evangelischen Hochschule Ludwigsburg*, and even a non-German speaker could pick up on the fact there was something decidedly Christian about that name. I asked how they'd ended up at a university in Bursa and their answer blew my mind. *'Oh, we asked to be placed here,'* they replied. *'We're going to study theology.'*

'Theology? As in, *Islamic* theology?' These girls clearly had spunk. They were unswerving in their love for Jesus, and yet here they were using their teacher training opportunity to further their understanding of Islam and study alongside Muslim students as peers.

I understood exactly where these girls were coming from: Live as followers of Jesus in a place where most people have never met a Christian, and just be yourself. Do whatever it is you do. Work, interact, share life with fellow human beings, only do it in a whole other setting. *Good on them.*

We covered the basics, and they were fine. *Accommodation?* Oh, we'll look for a student flat out near the university. *Transport?* Yeah, we bought bus passes. It's all good. *Safety?* They looked at me with not a hint of fear on their faces. *We're not worried. We're intelligent.*

And they were. Intelligent. Culture-wise. Passionate. Unashamed. Confident. I had yet to find out, however, the full extent of what the Germans were about to bring to Bursa.

74. Walking with Mildred

We got more than we bargained for in Mildred too. Not only was she a beautiful soul and the most earnest and engaging science teacher we could have asked for, but she absolutely threw herself into blessing our city. She was one of those people who seemed to wake to each new day in Turkey as if it were her very first—her eyes shining, still delighted by everyone and everything. Only God knew how much we all needed her joy-filled personality.

'Let's do some prayer-walking,' she said to me one day, and within minutes we had a plan. Once a week, we decided, we would meet at the main intersection near the local Islamic high school, and from there, we would set off together.

Mildred turned up on our first morning with nearly childlike enthusiasm. And, she'd come prepared. 'Let's read this before we set off,' she said, opening her pocket-sized bible to the book of Psalms. Her voice was almost breathless, more from sheer exuberance than physical exertion, and as I read along with her, it was as if the heavens parted above us and the street corner where we stood became holy ground. The ageless words seemed to pass from the page to her heart before they were even spoken, and I found myself experiencing the now-familiar feeling of having a foot in two worlds—one, the solid street on which we stood, and the other, the very presence of God.

For the next hour, we walked up and down the streets, perceiving the Lord's heart for our suburb. To Mildred, prayer-walking came naturally, and I found myself agreeing with her as she spoke.

'Lord, please visit that home with your love. . .'

'Lord, we bless that man as he heads off to work. . .'

'Father, we pray that this apartment block might be filled with the glory of the Lord. Drive away the darkness. Work miracles there, Jesus. . .'

Now and then, as we walked, we felt a strange heaviness come over us. In fact, some streets seemed oppressive the moment we stepped foot onto them. If I had been walking alone, I realised, I might have avoided them or called it quits for the day, but with two of us in the mix, we simply invited the Holy Spirit to join us, clearing the way, shifting the atmosphere. With a fresh measure of boldness and love, we pleaded the words that all creation longs to hear: 'Your kingdom come, your will be done.'

We worshipped as we walked, our quiet songs making a way for the Spirit of God to minister to the precious people of our neighbourhood, and I believe that if anyone had looked on from a heavenly perspective that day, they might have seen, not just two foreign women walking down a street, but a little posse of angels too, some hurrying to keep up, some lending a hand along the way, others beckoning us forward, and all of them adding their *amens* with every step we took.

75. Semra and Riada

My love for God was enriched, not only by other women who shared my faith but by two other women I was about to meet.

Riada turned up one night at a working group meeting, and the following day I took her out for coffee. 'Tell me about yourself,' I asked, 'what brought you to Bursa?' And though she told me a little of her life, it was her friend she was determined I should meet. 'You'd love her,' she informed me a number of times throughout our conversation. 'I really want you to meet my friend, Semra!'

The three of us finally got together at Zafer Plaza, where we looked forward to a long, unhurried chat. With the usual, 'kiss on one cheek, kiss on the other,' we greeted each other, and as we waited for coffee to be served the surrealness of life in Bursa hit me again. There we were, three women from vastly different backgrounds, breathing in a confusing mix of alpine air and diesel fumes in a state-of-the-art mall overlooking an ancient Caravanserai. In bygone years, I reflected, travelling merchants from East and West would have stopped right here to rest their animals, trade their wares, and catch up on news from other parts.

Different worlds had always collided in Bursa. Even as we introduced ourselves, I was aware of the call to prayer sounding out from the famous Green Mosque nearby with its twenty domes and impressive minarets, competing with pop music being played through the mall's speakers.

The waiter delivered our coffee in traditional Turkish style—each tiny cup was embossed with Arabic symbols and Ottoman-style flourishes and presented on its own silver tray. The cups themselves were covered with a silver dome-shaped lid, a quaint replica of the domes of the mosques, only with the more pragmatic purpose of keeping the coffee hot until everyone was served. A tiny piece of perfectly soft, rose-pink Turkish delight poked onto the end of a miniature skewer accompanied each cup—just enough sweet to balance the bitter richness of the coffee, I had been told.

Turks treat coffee drinking as a ritual, an opportunity to draw the finesse and style of a past era into the present. Having come from a country where two hundred years covers most of our European history, I found myself increasingly intrigued by this concept of building a dynasty. *How does one establish culture that generations far into the future will continue to own and celebrate?*

I sighed with happiness. The forty-minute bus ride, the dodging of the traffic, the wondering if this meeting represented more than just a chance to share a coffee-break—it all receded as we settled at the table. We couldn't have looked like a more unlikely group of friends. There I was, with my short blond hair, a mother of four who seemingly spent my days going from one coffee catch-up to another—and Riada, a woman in her early twenties, with a wealth of good breeding and education behind her. She was articulate, opinionated, poised and polished, wonderful in social situations and one of the few students in Bursa whose English was flawless. Then there was Semra, and right away I understood why Riada had insisted I meet her. *Semra was intriguing.*

She looked a little worn-out to me, and although at first I put that down to the effect created by wearing a black trench coat, no makeup, and a headscarf, I wondered later if it had more to do with the general tiredness of a life marked by fear . . . or of sheer effort. Despite all that, her eyes held a quiet look, as if she had made peace with herself, as if the opinions of others were inconsequential to her, as if her heart were incapable of being distracted by the world around her.

As Semra shared her story, I realised how vulnerable she was. She was studying at the university in Bursa, but was living in a local hostel for women. Without permission to work, however, money was tight. 'How do you make ends meet, then?' I asked gently.

'It's difficult,' she acknowledged, and then added, 'some people from a religious sect came to my hostel recently. They offered to give us fifty lira every week to attend discussions about the Koran . . .'

Riada candidly scorned the obvious buying of religious allegiance and it irked me too. Semra, however, seemed less perturbed. 'It's okay,' she concluded, 'these are genuine people. They care about our spiritual needs and they want to care for us practically as well.'

'Where do your family live?' I asked and was surprised at the answer. 'Bosnia,' she replied. 'I am from Bosnia.'

'*But Bosnia is in Europe,*' I thought. '*How then, did this young woman end up in one of the most conservative cities of Turkey, and what made her choose such an extreme version of Islamic dress?*'

But as her story unfolded, my heart went out to her and I began to understand . . .

'I have a younger brother who I love with all my heart,' she said. 'A few years ago, he became ill. I was desperate for him to live, but he was close to death. I told God that if he would heal my brother, I would devote my entire life to Him. I promised that I would show my gratitude to Allah by wearing the hijab for the rest of my life.'

It's humbling to sit across the table from a young woman who spoke of '*my dear God*' with such affection. 'God healed my brother,' Semra said confidently, and then her expression changed. 'The thing is, my family are not very religious; they could not understand why I chose to wear the hijab. But my brother is alive, thanks be to God. I will always be grateful to Him . . .'

Semra had my complete respect. Her deepest desire, she said, was to show other women how they too could love God fully. She wanted to speak, to write and to lead others by her example. 'I love God and I want to please Him forever,' she whispered, but I noticed how sad she looked, how burdened, like she had no idea how precious she was, and I longed for her to be filled with joy. Despite her devotion, Semra admitted, it was not easy to love God when she had no sense that He also loved her.

We sipped our coffee slowly as Riada shared her story. She too had grown up in Bosnia but had studied in America. Like Semra, her family were gently religious—not at all conservative, but Muslim, nonetheless.

Riada displayed none of the outward signs of religion. Her hair was long and sleek and free. She wore heels, enjoyed dancing, and carried designer handbags, but she too was ambitious to educate and encourage women. 'I want to articulate our faith in a way that all women can relate to,' she explained. 'I want to show them that Islam is a religion that modern women can be proud of.'

For the next hour, the three of us talked with caffeine-fuelled enthusiasm as we dreamed of all the ways we might change the world together. What if the three of us could somehow unite, even as women of different faiths, to equip and inspire others? Hours later my mind was still buzzing, and though nothing ever came of our audacious ideas, I remember that day fondly, when, as three unlikely friends, we met in the city of Bursa.

76. How to Speak a Blessing

Speaking of heart-warming, a small group of women in Bursa had begun getting together once a month to pray. It was an unusual dynamic; we came from different home countries, some had spent decades in Turkey while others were newly arrived or had come only for a short time, we spanned the age-groups, and our approach to life in Turkey differed markedly. But our love for Christ and our shared experience of coming to Bursa was enough to unite us. I loved those women and looked forward to our prayer-nights.

It was my dear friend Shari, though, who took the whole thing to another level. We had carried our mugs of tea into the living room one night, prayed our hearts out for each other, our families and our loved ones back home. Then, as we all congregated at the door of her apartment to say our goodbyes, Shari stopped us for a moment. Quietly moving from one woman to the next, she took our hands in her own and began blessing each of us.

I had never seen this done before and certainly, no one had ever spoken a blessing over me quite like that, but I felt the power of the words as they landed in my soul; it was as if, even as she spoke them out, they were fulfilled. Done. Sealed. Shari had a word from God that was unique to each woman, and though I couldn't for the life of me afterwards remember what she said, something shifted in me that night. Not only had I been blessed, but I had witnessed a whole other sort of bravery. This was a new, vulnerable expression of Christian friendship, and I was humbled.

My friend's example got me thinking. Perhaps I needed to go beyond my usual, 'I'll pray for you,' or 'I hope it turns out well for you,' when I talked with people. How had I not picked up that in a place where curses are openly spoken day after day, a blessing was what was needed most? What if I were to be that bold? What if I too, learned to speak out a blessing from God over the many people I interacted with each day? What if I caught an inkling of how very much God loves us, sees us and cares for us, and joined Him in blessing every person who crossed my path, even in the deeply divided city of Bursa?

77. The Children's Home
The German girls brought an unexpected blessing too; through their coming, the doors were about to open for foreigners to volunteer once again with the children of Bursa, and in the end, it all happened rather easily.

The students had spent a week settling into their new city when Ayşe called to arrange a meeting. 'I want to discuss opportunities for the German students to teach classes for children.' Ayşe's suggestion took me by surprise. 'We have a wonderful children's centre here in Bursa where we provide amazing programs for children from underprivileged backgrounds, and the German girls need to work with children to fulfil their university requirements. Why don't we set up a meeting with the Director?'

So it was that Ayşe and I met at the Children's Home the next afternoon, where we introduced the students from Germany. 'It sounds good,' the director replied without fuss, 'they can start teaching music classes next week.' It was that easy. 'Come,' she said, 'and I will give you a tour of the classrooms.'

It wasn't clear if the offences of the past had been forgotten, but now was a chance, I realised, for them to at least be forgiven, and so, as we toured the building together, I quietly repented for the wrongs of the past. *'Lord, I take my place as the representative of foreigners in this city,'* I whispered under my breath as we walked the corridors together, *'I ask forgiveness for all the harm that was done here. I wash these walls with your forgiveness, I wash these corridors . . .'*

The director and Ayşe chatted with the students as we walked, and with one ear tuned to their conversation and the other to heaven, I spoke words of blessing, nearly inaudibly, but still, out they flowed, down every corridor, into every room. This day had been a long time coming. Never again, I thought, must this city be subjected to humiliation.

The Germans started going to the children's home twice a week to teach music or English, or to do crafts with the children, and they did it all with joy and excellence. When it came time to write their first report, I found it an easy task. *'The students are reliable and professional; they prepare engaging and creative classes and deliver them with enthusiasm.'* I made a few extra comments about how well they related to the children and to the staff, and what a pleasure they were to work with. What I didn't write, was that the German students had, in their unassuming way, done so much more than they were asked. They had won back the trust of our city.

78. The Dormitory Boys

(Jeff writes) . . .

I had been visiting the Islamic dormitory for nearly a year by now. Most weeks the format stayed the same—tea, then conversation until the early hours of the morning, followed by a long but pleasant walk home. Every now and then, however, the young men conspired together to mix it up. One night they brought everything for a party to the classroom; another time we ended up down the road at some sort of café at midnight drinking ayran[1] and eating Turkish desserts. What a joy to be with them!

But all the while I was holding back. We had come to Turkey with a simple vision that people who might never otherwise meet a Christian, might have a Christian mate. Here I was living that dream, but of all the

---

1 A yoghurt-based drink

Turks we knew (and there were many), the boys at the dorm were the ones I cared for most. Their souls were constantly on my mind. I prayed for them, spoke life and light over them and contended for their blessing. But following the leading of the Holy Spirit, I had never mentioned my faith—a fact that was building in my heart as a constant irritant.

Out of the blue one day, however, the Lord placed a message in my spirit that I knew was for the boys at the dormitory. It was so anointed, so *right*, and I was excited about the prospect of sharing it. As I talked it over with God, I came away excited. I sensed that God was bringing no ordinary opportunity my way, and that I would know when the time was right . . .

Our lessons continued as normal for several weeks when I received an unexpected call from the man who organised activities at the dormitory. 'Could you come another time this week?' he asked. I questioned him to be sure I had understood the message correctly. 'Yes,' he assured me, 'We still want you to come for your usual Sunday lesson, but please come tomorrow night as well.' The time he specified was much earlier than usual, certainly before the last call to prayer. *Interesting,* I thought.

The whole situation felt uncanny from the start. I turned up at the specified time and could tell right away that nothing about the night ahead would be 'business as usual.' For a start, the coordinator took me to the 'important' conference room rather than the usual classroom, and soon we were joined by a group of middle-aged men. My usual students were serving us as if this were some kind of catered event, but still I could not work out what the gathering was about. '*What was the excitement I sensed in the atmosphere? What exactly was God up to that night?*'

And then I knew. God had prepared a wide-open door, and this was my moment to step through it!

After the refreshments were cleared away, my students sat down with us and indicated I should speak. 'Tell us more about yourself,' they asked.

'Up to now,' I began, 'I have talked a lot about the way I do business. But I have never shared with you one aspect, and that is *who I am when I am doing business.* I have a faith, like you do, and my faith plays a big part in how I do things. In fact, we have a story in the Bible that explains this. Would you like me to share it with you?'

The room was full of agreement.

Drawing on the insight God had given me for that very moment, I told them the parable of the three different types of soil. 'Jesus told this story,' I explained, 'to teach us about three things: the world, the flesh and the devil.'

Suddenly the group of men began talking among themselves. 'We have all of those as Muslims too!' they told me, and before I knew it, everyone was engaged and interested in the most delightful way.

Yay God!

I was careful to keep the conversation focussed on business. I talked about how Allah is gracious and compassionate, and how He wants to do kind and merciful things through us and our businesses. I talked about Him dropping seeds into our hearts and wanting us to respond in kind and generous ways. And then I explained how the system of the world, the flesh and the devil all try to hinder us from following through on what God has asked of us.

One by one, their faces lit up. I could see their minds processing the idea; in fact, for a moment it felt as if I could have been leading a church service or life group back home, they were so on-board with the message! I shared a few everyday scenarios and then we drifted into an open conversation. The students chatted amongst themselves, sometimes breaking into Turkish, but mostly, I lingered in this incredible moment when somehow our friendship had breached the unspoken faith divide.

That night I worshipped all the way home, humbled and overjoyed, aware that what had just happened was the culmination of more than a year of fruitful investment in those delightful young men.

79. Camping in a Blizzard

Our own boys, in the meantime, were feeling cooped up. But winter was behind us, and though the days were still cool, when Jeff suggested it was time for an adventure, everyone jumped at the idea. What better adventure, we decided, than spending a night in a tent? Camping was one of the few things we missed most; in Australia we often set off for a weekend, pitching our tent by a river, and enjoying the clear night skies and fresh air.

Why shouldn't we go camping in Turkey too? We had brought a tent with us from Australia with every expectation it would be put to use, and this was a good opportunity. Jeff would take the two boys up the mountain, we agreed, and the girls would enjoy a few days at home with me. Easy. That afternoon, with bags packed and spirits high, the explorers were ready to roll.

Mount Uludağ, here we come.

It wasn't exactly sunny with blue skies when the three of them left home, but a few clouds were nothing to worry about—the gondola ride would take them high above the cloud line anyway, we figured.

Jeff loved mount Uludağ. Back in the Spring he had taken Vangie all the way to the summit, coaxing her one piece of chocolate at a time, until they both reached the peak in triumph. Now it was Eric and Joseph's turn, and *what could be more exhilarating than camping on the mountain that loomed high over Bursa?*

Halfway up the gondola, that question was up for grabs. The weather seemed to deteriorate as quickly as their little capsule ascended the mountain, but '*this too shall pass*' thought Jeff with typical enthusiasm— and anyway, there's no turning back once you're stuck in a gondola. The boys agreed. Bad weather would only make for more of an adventure than they'd already hoped for.

Quite so, as it turned out. For a start, they stepped out of the gondola onto a sprinkling of freshly windswept snow. 'Let's pitch the tent over there near those boulders of rock,' Jeff was quick to make plans. 'At least that will provide some natural shelter if the winds come up.'

The boys were in their element as they hammered the stakes into the ground, set up camp and cooked their little stash of food over a gas burner.

Life is good.

Only, before they'd even unrolled their sleeping bags, the weather took a sudden turn for the worse. Snow and sleet and rain started swirling, the wind picked up, and looking over to the gondola, the realisation hit—the one means of getting back down the mountain had just closed for the day.

'This is exciting!' the boys began exclaiming, but then darkness closed in, and with it, what sounded like the howl of wild dogs—only they were not just *somewhere out there*—they seemed to be circling, closing in, and from the barking and cracking of branches, there seemed to be quite a pack of them. '*How long will it be until I have to go and face off with them?*' Jeff wondered, but he kept the thought to himself as the boys shivered in their sleeping bags.

The situation only got more tenuous as the night progressed, rain began pelting down, and a deepening pool of water accumulated in the rocky bowl that housed the tent, until it felt more like sleeping on a waterbed than on solid ground. And then the water began to seep in.

Suffice to say, it was a long night, cold and damp and dark and frightening, and as soon as there was the slightest hint of daylight, Jeff and the boys emerged wearily to assess the situation. Pulling down their sodden tent and throwing their packs back over their shoulders, they made their way back to the gondola station to await the first ride down the mountain. As minutes soon turned into hours, Jeff grew concerned. 'CLOSED due to bad weather' read the sign, and for all he could tell, the situation was not about to change that day. How on earth were they going to get back home?

Just at the point of desperation, Jeff noticed a figure walking through the fog and rain towards the gondola. 'What are you doing here?!' he asked when he saw the huddled little group. 'Quick, come with me!' With great relief, the boys and Jeff picked up their bundles and tried to keep up as the man led them through a little doorway, along a tunnel and into a room far beneath the gondola platform where a second man, when he saw the boys wet and shivering, could hardly believe his eyes! Had these three foreigners spent the night on the mountain?! 'Hurry, come in,' he beckoned, and soon Jeff, Eric and Joseph were sitting around a barrel stove, sipping hot chocolate and sharing the story of their night on the mountain with the two gondola operators.

'You cannot go down the gondola today,' the men explained. 'It's too windy. But don't worry, when our shift is finished, we will take you down the road instead.' And so, hours later, all five of them finally bundled into the front seat of a pickup truck, and made their way precariously down the mountain tracks until, relieved and exhausted, our three missing men arrived home talking of an adventure they would not soon forget.

80. What a Roof is For

Before long, summer arrived, and sitting on my balcony one afternoon with my feet resting lazily on the sun-warmed tiles, I pulled out my journal and wrote . . .

The long hot days seem to slow everyone down—there's no hurry to get home before dark, no wondering if the laundry we hang over our balconies will dry before the day has ended, no trying to keep warm without overusing the gas supply. And, no end of incredible produce in the markets. I can't get over the fresh figs. We buy them by the box, which costs about the same as a single fig in Australia or New Zealand—we scoop them over fresh yoghurt for breakfast. There's quince and pomegranate and raspberries, and the market holders arrange it all bountifully and deliberately, combining their love of commerce with their creative flair, and I can't help but buy some of everything.

The girls love coming to the markets too, where they are constantly handed samples—here, try this, says one old man, handing a ripe strawberry to Vangie; he hurries on with his work, but I see the pleasure in his eyes when she smiles and tastes the sweetness. Liberty, of course, gets passed around from one shopper or stallholder to another, each one filling her mouth with a little piece of fruit and pinching her cheeks with a 'maşallah.'

Today I looked out from our balcony to see the neighbours up on their roof. Four generations live in that home, from the baby to a great-grandmother in her eighties, and I had to look twice because for all the world it appeared it was the great-grandma up there with her black headscarf and hunched frame. The roof is rather steeply sloped, there on the third floor, but the women seemed undaunted as they passed sheets out the windows and laid them out on the tiles.

It was a few moments before I realised what they were doing. For these women, summer isn't just a season for relaxation; it's a time to prepare for the seasons to come. I watched as, for at least half an hour, they laid out all manner of fruit and herbs to dry in the heat of the midday sun.

I decided to pop over to Arzu's house to ask what they were drying. 'Oh, fresh thyme, parsley, oregano, basil, apricots, figs, tea,' Arzu teyze explained. We peered together at the women across the way and smiled, because at that moment they were passing cushions through the little window-like opening near the roof, and then, one by one, they climbed out onto the tiles and eased themselves into position. As I write, they have been sitting there on the roof for three hours, watching over their stash, shooing away any birds that come close, and waiting as the sun begins to do its glorious work.

81. Maintaining a Life Back Home

One of our biggest decisions as we approached moving to Turkey had been whether to sell our house in Australia or rent it out while we were away. Most people advised us to keep it—after all, we had no idea how long we would be gone for, or when we might need to unexpectedly return home.

Deep down, Jeff and I felt that it was probably best to sell rather than to try to juggle two lives at once, but the truth was, I was scared of having nothing to come back to—and, I had come to love our little family home with its lush quarter-acre block and terraced gardens Jeff had built by hand. When we heard of some old family friends who were preparing to return to Australia after living in Asia for many years and needed a house to rent, the decision seemed obvious. Perfect, we thought!

If only it had been that simple.

We had been in Turkey only a few months when our friends wrote to say that they had been offered a job in another city and had decided to take it. Within weeks, the house was empty once again, only now we had a mortgage, no tenants, and since we had rented our house privately, no property manager either.

Not to worry, we thought, and with a few phone calls, we appointed an agent to take care of finding new tenants. Only it never went well. The new tenants looked good on paper, yet seemed to have a policy of only paying their rent as often as needed to prevent us from legally being able to evict them. There was no problem with their income, the agent assured us, but there was little she could do. Two months would pass without rent being paid, and then, just when she was about to issue a letter of warning, they'd pay a few weeks—just enough to keep our hands tied for another few months.

The tenants also began submitting requests for maintenance jobs—all of which we were bound to assess and sometimes agree to. However, after eight months of a seemingly constant stream of requests accompanied by suspiciously high quotes from the agent's preferred maintenance company, we knew the whole arrangement was unsustainable.

Managing a property back home was made harder, of course, by the difference in time zones—and the fact that our property manager refused to take phone calls. Email was her only form of communication, and even that was sporadic. With non-paying tenants and an agent who seemed more concerned about filling her pockets than sorting out the real issues, it was no surprise when our bank manager got in touch. 'It looks like you have fallen behind a little with your mortgage repayments,' he said during what was to become the first in a series of three a.m. phone calls.

We explained the situation and that we were holding out until the end of the year when we could hopefully bring the lease to an end and appoint new and hopefully more profitable tenants. The reality was, though, that while our team of friends were doing a fabulous job of supporting our family, we were not looking to them to buffer our house repayments in Australia. Without a regular rental income, holding onto our home back in Australia had turned into a constant strain.

We had been praying about the situation for nearly a year. Why was it that God had looked after every area of our life so well and yet there was nothing but trouble when it came to our house? In any case, a decision had to be made to either take legal action to evict our difficult tenants or place the house up for sale—a decision not helped by the fact that I couldn't bring myself to talk it over properly.

Jeff understood, of course. The whole situation felt humiliating and nerve-racking and left us both on edge, but the reality was, neither of us could turn a deaf ear to those early morning phone calls. We had done all we could, but we both knew there just wasn't enough money to keep us in Turkey *and* hold onto our house in Australia.

With no real choice, we put the house up for sale. Until that point, the property market had been strong, house prices were up, and there were plenty of cashed-up buyers, by all accounts. Only our house attracted no interest at all. Nothing made sense—this was a sturdy family home on an incredible property in a highly sought-after location. It should have sold within days, if the indicators were anything to go by. And then it started raining in Brisbane. For sixty days, it rained. We watched in disbelief as news reports showed our home city of Brisbane under flood. Eight open homes came and went, but no one was even coming, the real estate agent told us.

Now we were stuck. Our life had been full of financial miracles, yet everything to do with our house in Australia seemed to be an exception to this. It was time to come up with a plan.

82. Getting Away

Jeff's plan involved twelve months of rations and then, he figured, we might break even, the property market might have moved, our loan would no longer be fixed, and we could take another look at whether we should sell the house. More and more, however, it seemed that the decision to hold onto our home in Australia could, in the end, be the thing that kept us from staying in Turkey. We'd even begun talking about a graceful exit strategy, should things not improve with our tenants.

We also decided to take some time to deliberately think and pray over our dilemma. Our boys were booked to attend a summer camp in Antalya the following week which presented us with the perfect chance to clear our heads and hear what God had to say. It would also give us the chance to visit one of the few international churches in Turkey. Perhaps there, we thought, perspective would come.

(Jeff writes) . . .

After a full two years of pressure, my soul felt dry. I missed having a church to attend and was desperately looking forward to a recharge in Antalya where the English-speaking church, we had heard, was vibrant and welcoming. The only problem was, when we turned up excitedly the following Sunday, there was hardly anyone there. I hadn't realised that the church basically shut down while everyone went to kids' camp, and to say I was disappointed was an understatement.

Anya, on the other hand, was not at all put-off. 'They still have their prayer meeting this week,' she said, 'why don't you go to that?' A Korean-Australian couple had come to live in Antalya to engage in prayer and worship, she told me; their prayer room was on the top floor of their apartment, overlooking the city with the sparkling Mediterranean just across the rooftops.

It took some effort to convince myself to go, but I arrived at the specified time, only to find that once again, no one else had turned up. 'Not to worry,' the couple assured me in their refreshingly laid-back Australian way. 'Let's go upstairs and pray anyway.'

How do I describe what happened that night, except that God Himself seemed to fill the place where we prayed, and, as we lingered for hours in His presence, I received the refreshing touch of heaven that I had craved for so long.

I returned to our apartment that night, strengthened in my spirit and filled with fresh hope once again. With renewed determination to get a breakthrough in our housing situation, I decided that I would begin to fast and pray.

~

That week was unusually quiet as I prayed and looked for ways to fight what was going on spiritually. Eventually it came to me in the form of a simple revelation: *'Goliath died by his own sword.'*

In that moment, I knew what was going on. If we were facing lack, I could overcome it with the same dynamic! Prophetically, I emptied my pockets, handed over my bank cards and gave the job of internet banking to Eric, our eldest son. I had taken up lack, in a sense, and with that unusual weapon, I determined to fast and pray until the matter was resolved.

I spent much of that week by the river near the botanic gardens, praying, and though I did not experience anything special—no glorious open heaven, no huge sense of the presence of God—I felt the urgency of the situation and the need to be persistent.

Seven days later, something shifted. In my spirit, I knew that the job was done. I had broken through. The house situation would be okay. I returned home that day hopeful and confident. It was time to break my fast. Now we would wait for the breakthrough to find its way into our ordinary lives.

Our miracle arrived just two weeks later when our bank manager in Australia called. 'Jeff,' he said, 'I've taken another look at your home loan and come up with a solution that will actually get you ahead again. We don't usually do this, but I am happy to unlock your fixed rate mortgage and change it so that you get lower interest rates and a more realistic repayment schedule.'

'Wow, that's awesome!' I agreed. God had given us a benevolent bank manager, and now the pressure was off. Feeling very blessed, we thanked the Lord and breathed a sigh of relief. Now we could turn our focus once again to the work that we had been given to do.

83. What to Wear

With the house situation resolved, at least for the time being, I should have been able to relax. The reality was, though, that on every other front, I was struggling to manage the demands. My diary was full to overflowing, what to do on any given day was not a given any more, and I was officially out of my depth. Formal engagements clashed with parent-teacher interviews. A visitor would turn up wanting to have tea, just when I was about to head out the door for a meeting. We had a roster of people coming and going from our house to support our little home-school co-op—the German girls two afternoons a week, Mildred one afternoon, my Australian friend on alternate mornings, and everyone staying on or coming early to have lunch together. While I spent most mornings with the children, the afternoons and evenings were crammed with social functions, newcomers to meet and greet, planning meetings, pastoral meetings, prayer meetings, and an array of parties that my ever-gracious team of twenty-year-olds still invited me to.

Jeff had a schedule of his own—teaching at the dorm, meeting with Ishan and other businessmen, following up contacts at the universities, and jumping through the constant hoops that allowed us to maintain our status as resident expats in Turkey; the mayor's office had also asked him to help draw up a strategic plan for the city, and the Director of Disability Services had invited him to speak at a meeting later in the month. All of it allowed us to bless the city in significant ways, but when we added in shopping, cooking, spending time together as a family and keeping up communications with our friends back home, the bottom line is, we were way beyond capacity.

To a point, we were okay with living at that sort of pace. What we were not okay with, was bad decisions, wasted opportunities, and being torn in two over who should be where. We wanted to be led by the Spirit of God who always operates with ease and purpose and with whom there are no scheduling clashes, but by this stage we were struggling, wanting to keep up with what He was doing but needing help to discern what was from Him, and what was unimportant in the greater scheme of things.

Until now, I had tried bringing the multitude of to-do options before the Lord, asking Him for a yay or nay on each one. That in itself took time, however, and still left me feeling unsure if I had to choose between afternoon tea with my Christian friends or the birthday party of my

Muslim neighbour—or, as had happened a few days earlier, I had taken two buses across town to attend a meeting that ended up being cancelled anyway.

And then, one day, I woke up with a ridiculous yet simple idea in my mind. What if I asked the Holy Spirit just one question each morning: *What should I wear today?* It was an outlandish thought, but I took hold of it rather tenaciously.

What if I just asked the question, and then got dressed in whatever came to mind? If it was my tailored pants and ribbed turtleneck or silk shirt, I would go into the office and work. If it was a jeans and sweater day, it was probably a day to stay home.

A week of implementing my new approach was all it took to get into the swing of it—and it worked! One day I got up and dressed casually, popping on my dark red flats just because I liked them, and decided it was a lipstick kind of day. Sure enough, a few hours later some students got in touch and asked if I could meet with them. 'Perfect,' I said, 'that works,' and with that I was ready to walk out the door.

Another day, when slippers seemed like the perfect choice and a message came through to my phone reminding me that the International Women's group were going to visit the Deaf School that afternoon, the decision was easy. 'My apologies,' I replied. 'I can't make it today,' and then I turned back to the jigsaw puzzle I was working on while I waited for a fresh loaf of bread to rise in the kitchen.

I was grateful that God had brought such a light-hearted, almost childlike approach to my sense of overwhelm, and I loved him dearly for helping me bring order to my days in such a personal, intimate way. The longer we could keep this up, I decided, the better.

84. Visiting Izmir

The same week I began my new approach to scheduling, Jeff received an unexpected invitation to have lunch with the directors of a new university which was about to open in Izmir. We had heard of this university and Jeff had made contact a few months earlier to introduce our company and offer to provide academic editing services to their staff and students. Now they had got in touch, and the meeting sounded promising.

The next day, Jeff set off before dawn. Travelling to Izmir would take five hours, and he wanted to arrive early. The restaurant they had planned to meet in was on the far side of the city, but Jeff found it easily and was soon joined by an impressive-looking group of men, all connected in one way or another with the establishment of this prestigious university.

Lunch consisted of a wafer-thin pide about a metre long which was brought out and set on an elevated dish in the middle of the table. 'It's a speciality dish from the Konya region,' one of the men explained to Jeff. With the meal served, the business discussion got right underway.

Jeff liked these guys. They were upright men, he later remarked. They also appreciated excellence and wanted their professors and students to publish their research in reputable international journals. They had come to the discussion with a big vision, and that, in itself, was refreshing. They were also extremely well-connected throughout the region and were keen to do business with our company.

Then came the clincher. 'The university is owned by . . . ' The man who was speaking mentioned the name of an Islamic organisation we were familiar with. 'We will require your company to openly align with our ethos,' the man explained, 'and if you do that, we can assure you that you will never have to look for work in Turkey again.'

It seemed a shame to walk away from the deal when we had tried so hard to find a sustainable way to make an income in Turkey, but in the end, we did. Although we had deep respect for the many expressions of Islam we encountered in Turkey, and these particular people had gone out of their way to build bridges with us, we were also aware of the political undercurrents these associations carried, and knew there was more to this allegiance than met the eye.

In contrast to more radical groups, these men represented a movement known for tolerance and peace, and above all a commitment to promoting Islam as an intellectually-sound religion. In the context, it was a breath of fresh air. But endorsing an Islamic movement just to get preferred status as a company? These people wanted more than our professional services—they wanted us to openly align with their branch of Islam. While we never wanted to be put in such a position, a line had been drawn in the sand, and it was one we decided not to cross.

We debriefed with our neighbours that night. 'Yes, I know what you are speaking about,' Omer Bey nodded his head. 'I have had a similar situation with my business.' He went on to tell us how his mechanic workshop had recently been visited by representatives of a different Islamic sect. For years, Omer had serviced his customer's cars without any consideration for what 'type' of Muslims they were. He ran a good business, his work was exemplary, and he had a reputation for being an honest man. Until now, that had been enough.

But a few weeks earlier, things had changed when an old customer had brought his car in for a service. When he came back to pick up the car and pay the bill, the man had quietly remarked, 'Omer Bey, you must build a prayer room in your workshop.'

The implication was clear to Omer. If he didn't offer a prayer room for his customers, this man would take his business elsewhere—and with it, every client who belonged to the same religious 'group.'

We were beginning to see how the system functioned beneath the surface—with quiet ultimatums that were not publicised or fussed over; word simply got around. Religious control was tightening, and though the whole country had been moving in that direction for some time, it was unnerving to see it happen in the world of commerce.

That merchant is one of us. That one's not. Comply, or you'll lose us as customers. Endorse us, or you won't even get a look in.

We wanted no part of it. We had seen how it worked. The principle applied to foreigners as well as locals: *subscribe, submit, or we'll starve you out.* Thank God we had friends back home who were committed to supporting us. We had wanted to transition into being completely self-sufficient by now, but it was not working as we had planned. We were grateful our Team of Friends was there for us, and now their love and support shone even brighter against the backdrop we were now living in.

As we gathered the family around the table the next morning, Jeff explained to the children the events of the previous day in Izmir. Together we agreed that we would choose to live above it all, that we didn't have to function the way the world around us did, and most of all, that we would continue to lean on God, who had promised to supply all our needs.

85. Air Force Academy

The following week a colleague at the city council came to me rather quietly, and with an unexpected request. 'Here in Bursa we have an elite Air Force academy,' he said. 'It is a military high school with students from all over the country who are being prepared for a career in the Air Force. It is important that they learn English from a native speaker. Could you recommend someone, perhaps? As a city we like to support the academy and they have asked for help to find English teachers.'

My mind went immediately to Jeff. 'Yes,' my colleague looked pleased. 'Jeff would be perfect. We were hoping you would suggest him.'

That week Jeff stepped into the role of English teacher to the next generation of Turkish fighter pilots. The whole setup was intriguing and rather awe-inspiring. Two days a week, a minivan loaded with civilian military staff stopped in front of our house to pick Jeff up for the drive across town.

The academy itself was a restricted military zone protected by high fences and security booths and signs declaring 'No Admittance.'

Once Jeff had been issued with a pass and taken through a short orientation with the Director of English Studies, he was introduced to his students—two hundred and fifty high school age boys in total, all hand-picked from around the country and brought to Bursa, where they lived on-campus and received one of the most sought-after educations in the nation. Jeff's job, he was told, was to get the boys speaking confidently in English so that within a few years they could communicate with air traffic controllers anywhere in the world. Apart from conversational English, every other subject was taught by Turkish nationals, mostly military officers.

Jeff only had to open the door to his first class to realise this was an exceptional institution. On entering the room, twenty-six boys dressed in impeccable military uniform rose to their feet, snapped to attention and saluted. A student representative made a loud announcement, introducing the class to their new teacher, after which the students shouted in enthusiastic unison, 'Good morning, sir!'

(Jeff writes) . . .

The boys remained standing until I instructed them to sit, making the entire experience feel like quite the power trip. Whenever I said a boy's name, he would promptly stand to his feet and answer as if I were a sergeant major. 'Yes, sir!'

I had ten classes in total. These boys were the nation's best and brightest and they were a pleasure to teach. I put a lot of thought into the topics we discussed and decided to start with family scenarios. It was riveting to hear the boys talk about family life from their perspective, and to hear their often-skewed perceptions about foreigners. On one occasion a student confidently declared that Westerners did not wash frequently or even wear pyjamas! I gently suggested that this was not the case, but still he looked doubtful. Time to change topic, I decided.

Some of the boys were nearly fluent in English while others struggled, and though I tried to engage them all, it was when we began talking about football that things started going especially well. Acting out a game tended to be the best way to teach, and once the students realised they could abandon their usual standards of discipline, they all started pitching in, using English with greater freedom, and having a lot of fun in the process.

Before long, we began speaking about flying. All these boys were training to be air force pilots and they were fanatical about aircraft. Now I really had their attention. At home, I researched flight-related topics and created scenarios for the boys to discuss—planes, payloads, navigation, the idea of a single point of failure—and soon we were conversing in class about strategic situations these boys might one day face.

~

It was a pity how short-lived the whole thing turned out to be. The reality was, though the students were passionate, and the other English teachers were great company, tensions soon emerged elsewhere.

A particularly strange conversation occurred one day, where an officer took me aside and began venting his political opinions, comparing Turkey with other Western countries. Given the troubled history between the military and the government, I knew better than to take sides; still, the whole conversation left me feeling ill at ease.

The difficulties between the military and the Turkish government impacted the employment of all the conversational English teachers. Understandably, the government was uneasy about bringing foreigners into their military environment, yet it was undoubtedly the most effective way to provide the level of English instruction their recruits needed. The situation soon came up in conversation. 'We have had trouble with the government in Ankara,' an officer told us one day. 'This makes it difficult for us to pay you on the books. We are no longer allowed to allocate any of the military academy budget to foreign teachers.'

The teachers looked at each other, unsurprised. 'But do not worry . . .' the officer said brightly, 'we have come up with a plan.' I was intrigued as the details unfolded. 'There is a store on campus,' the officer explained, 'where the academy boys go to buy snacks and simple necessities. The profits from that store are off the record, so we have decided to pay you in cash from the proceeds of the store. From now on, if you go to the store every Friday afternoon, you can pick up your wages. We will place them in envelopes behind the counter.'

'Okay,' we agreed, and I was once again thankful for my current perspectives on freedom in the face of ethical dilemmas. Little did I know, however, just how strained relations were between the government and the military—or how far Ankara's scrutiny reached, until one day I received a call from the foreigner's police. 'Jeff,' the police chief said, 'we have to tell you that what you are doing is illegal. I'm sorry to say that you are not allowed to work for the military.' The irony of the whole situation was not lost on either end of the phone. 'Let me call the academy and I will get back to you,' I replied.

But now the military commanders had a dilemma on their hands. They had requested foreign teachers in the first place, the city council had been keen to assist, and there was no easy way to smooth the situation. I figured it was the Turkish Government's problem to figure out how to get along with itself and decided not to overthink things. Having been invited in, I felt fearless despite the tight spot we found ourselves in. The other English teachers agreed as well—best to let the Turkish officials sort out the technicalities among themselves.

In the end, there was no easy answer. My boss called me into his office the following week and waited for coffee to be served. Over the past months, we had become friends, and as we sat together, the officer shared his concerns. 'I am afraid, Jeff, that if you continue teaching for us, things will not go well for you with the police.'

'I'm not too worried,' I replied. 'It's up to you. If you still want me to teach, I will.' Looking down at his polished black shoes, my boss replied, 'We want you to continue here, of course . . .'

But I had caught the look of defeat in his eyes.

'How does the situation seem to you?' I asked gently. 'You know the issues better than I do. Would it be easier for you if we brought our arrangement to an end?' The sigh of relief from behind the desk was audible.

'Why don't I talk to the students?' I offered.

'No, I will do that,' the officer replied, and as we stood to shake each other's hands, I saw the sadness in my friend's face, a look of defeat that will stay with me forever. With a sense of profound disappointment, knowing that I would miss both the teachers and the students, I said goodbye, picked up my pay, and walked out through the security gates one last time.

86. A Culture of Honour

It was inevitable, I know, but it still came too soon when three of my core working group team told me they would soon be leaving. Ben was a highly intelligent, quiet, trustworthy individual from Russia, while Taylor and Lynn had come from China to study business in Turkey where they soon figured out how perfect they were for each other. There are times you just know two people are made to share a lifetime, and Taylor and Lynn were a great example. Ben, Taylor and Lynn all had bright business minds and were unfailingly reliable, and losing them would reduce my core team from six people to three. With over fifty people now part of our working group, I knew I would need to replace them quickly.

First though, I wanted to honour our friends properly before they set off on their new endeavours. When I ran my idea past President Semih Pala, he warmed to it quickly. 'I would like to give everyone who works on my team a formal reference to take with them, as well as a certificate of appreciation signed by myself and the city council officials.' I explained, 'and not just for these three. I would like everyone who volunteers in my working group to be honoured like this when they leave.'

We made the first presentations at an official supper at the Convention Centre. It was low-key—just a sincere thank you, handshakes all round and a team photo presented along with the lovely framed certificates, but I felt particularly pleased about this simple initiative as we acknowledged the character and success of the humble yet hardworking people I had been privileged to lead.

And, the idea obviously took off, because just a few days later, as I walked past the office of the council's graphic designer, my eye was drawn to two more certificates lying on the desk—only the logo was changed! Other working groups had picked up our template and implemented the idea of rewarding and thanking their volunteers too—and suddenly a huge wave of joy came over me, because the atmosphere was shifting, and I was pretty sure it had just become normal for people to be honoured for the beautiful yet quiet contributions they made in this city we loved.

87. The Boy from Brazil

For all the foreigners who moved on from Bursa, others continued to arrive. It was a short email that ushered a young Brazilian man into our lives the following week.

> *Dear Mrs. President,*
> *I have recently come to Bursa and I have some problems.*
> *Please can I meet to discuss these with you? I hope your group*
> *can help me. Sincerely, Victor.*

I had met with so many newly-arrived expats, hopeful young souls who came for good and valid and sometimes courageous reasons only to find the reality was nothing like what they had been led to expect. Yet somehow, they would hear about our group and seek us out, hopeful for answers or advice, or that our respect and standing in the community might make a difference if we would only mediate for them. I had said 'yes' to every request so far, and every time, there had been a human story I wished the world could hear. As I might have expected, Victor's was no exception.

He was in his hometown in Brazil, when he met a wonderful Turkish girl online, he told me. 'I know it sounds crazy,' he said, 'but there was something amazing about her. We talked all the time. After some months we realised we loved each other.' And so, Victor proposed, and the girl, a twenty-year old from Bursa, accepted.

Sometimes I was surprised by how open-minded families in Turkey could be. Apparently, her family was delighted. Here was a well-educated, honest Brazilian man who had found their daughter online and had done the right thing—he was going to marry her. In fact, he'd left his family, his country, his whole life, and was here now, a son in their home. Turks are very good at showing hospitality.

But Victor hadn't come to tell me how wonderful things were, I was sure of that, and so I let him do the talking. 'When she said yes, she asked what religion I was,' he continued. 'I told her I was a Christian, and she told me she was Muslim. We were both okay with that. It doesn't matter,' he said in his Latino accent.

Only, it had mattered enough that the next day, Victor paid a visit to his local priest, just to make sure. 'Is it okay for a Christian to marry a Muslim?' he asked. The priest was busy that morning, but he took a minute or two to tell Victor that, no, it wasn't really okay. Yes, maybe they did love each other, but they must share the same faith. Otherwise the marriage would be very difficult. And that was that.

As Victor left, he was deep in thought. The priest had said they should have the same faith, he reasoned, but he hadn't said which faith it needed to be. He didn't want to ask his fiancée to become a Christian, so . . .

So Victor found himself walking to the other side of the city, until he came to the open doors of a mosque.

'An imam was near the entrance, and saw I didn't know what to do,' Victor told me. 'He came over and put his arm around me. We sat for a long time, and I told him my problem. He was very understanding.' Victor spoke quietly now. 'When I finished talking, he asked if I would like to know about Islam. I said *yes please*, and the more the imam talked, the more peaceful I felt. He asked me if I would like to learn how Muslims pray. I said *yes*, again. I wanted to know everything.'

But Victor learned more than simply how to pray. He learned to wash before praying, he learned how to stand facing Mecca, he learned to repeat some words in Arabic, and by the time Victor left the mosque, he had converted. He was now a Muslim.

'So what is the problem you mentioned in your email?' I asked. *These two people love each other, they share the same faith, the parents are happy, what could possibly have come up?* Inwardly I was simultaneously amused and astounded by the naiveté of these kids; they were all the same, all hopeless optimists. But oh, how I admired their sincerity; I respected this boy for what he'd done and how he loved this girl.

Still, I know a heartbreak in the making, and this was one of them. I still hadn't heard why Victor was here, meeting with me, but already I wanted to invite him and his girl to come home for a meal, to meet Jeff and the kids, and come, be part of our family. I wanted to bundle them both up and hold them close and tell them how brave they were, and that *yes, it's a tough, tough world, but some love stories are meant to be, and of course, we'll help . . .'*

But the issue was that Victor wasn't having any luck at getting work. Without work, he couldn't rent an apartment, and without a place to live, he couldn't get married. He'd been in Bursa three months by now, living with his fiancé and her parents; they didn't speak English or Spanish, and he couldn't speak Turkish, and it was all getting very tense.

'Now her parents are saying I am not a real Muslim, that I only became a Muslim to marry their daughter, and they're not happy about it,' he told me, as much with the desperate expression in his eyes as with his words. 'Besides, if I can't get work, how can I look after her? At the start they treated me like a son, but I don't feel like a son anymore.'

Victor was feeling helpless, and *'please, do you know where I could find a job?'* he said. *'I'm an engineer,'* and though I knew the likelihood of finding work was close to zero, my heart was moved by the humility and sincerity of the guy; all he wanted was love and faith and a place to call home, and it wasn't working out.

If Jesus were here, I thought, he'd look on this young man with compassion. In my spirit, I knew what to say next. Looking into his eyes, I quietly asked, *'Are your parents happy for you?'*

And suddenly, his deep, sad eyes overflowed with tears; he didn't know where to look, so I passed him a serviette from under the coffee cup and with a quiet 'grazias' he told me that *his parents loved him so much, and his brother and sisters too; they just wanted him to follow his heart, but now he missed them . . .*

I told Victor I would certainly ask around, that I would let him know if any opportunities came up that might suit him, and I assured him that his problem was the same as most foreigners in Bursa faced—so few work opportunities, hardly anything that came with a work permit, but 'let's see,' I said, knowing we needed to stay hopeful.

What I also knew was that I'd just sat across the table from a man who thought he needed a job, when what he really longed for, was home.

88. The Girl from Iran

It wasn't just the lack of work that made living in Turkey difficult; it was the spiritual environment too. My next meeting for the day was with Leila, a young woman from Iran. As we started sharing our stories, my heart went out to her as well.

'Anya, I am a Christian. I love Jesus so much,' she said. 'I came to Turkey because I thought there would be opportunities to work in a good company and to further my skills. It hasn't turned out that way. I have worked long hours in very bad conditions, and I don't think it will get easier.'

'Are you thinking of going back home?' I asked her.

'Yes,' she said. 'In fact, I'm leaving tomorrow. I'm going back to Tehran.'

I wondered why Leila had asked to meet with me if she had no intention of staying in Bursa. 'Oh, I wanted you to pray for me!' she said, 'and I want to pray for you. You see, it's not just the job that makes me desperate to go home. The other problem is that here in Bursa, when I pray, I can't find God anymore. It's as if the heavens are closed above Turkey. I can't live here. In Iran, it's easy to pray. In Iran,' she said, 'the heavens are wide open!'

I knew what she was talking about, and suddenly a part of me wanted to get out too, to join Leila at the airport the following morning and go anywhere else, anywhere but under the heavy, oppressive atmosphere I felt in Bursa. Instead, we prayed and hugged and said goodbye; I blessed her, and she blessed me. I never imagined it would feel so good to wave a young woman off to Iran, given the likelihood she would end up in prison for her faith, but she was ready to go. 'Don't worry,' she assured me as we parted, 'I want to encourage the Christians there. I want to serve the Lord in Iran.'

89. Sick and Sorry

But we weren't leaving, we were staying, and now it wasn't only as if the heavens were dark above our heads; on the ground, we were worn down too. It had been rare that any of us had been sick since moving to Turkey, but for the week that followed, I was completely wiped out. It didn't help that the word 'sick' in English sounds like a swear word in Turkish—so I couldn't explain to the neighbours or those who called that *'I'm not well and no. I don't want to come over for coffee,'* because I didn't know any alternative word.

Instead, with a roaring headache and every muscle hurting, I went into Jeff's study, found a pillow, laid down on our extra-long corduroy couch and gave in. My body was run down, my mind was tired, and I didn't care if it was only five o'clock in the afternoon—I needed sleep, and maybe days of it.

I drifted off, glad that the kids were quietly playing downstairs and thankful for Jeff who assured me he'd sort out a meal and get everyone settled for the night. *'Just sleep,'* he said.

And then, sometime around ten o'clock, when the sky was dark and the last call to prayer had sounded, Jeff came into the room, tucked a soft quilt around me, and going over to his computer, he clicked on a site that had become somewhat of a spiritual lifeline for us all.

Livestreamed from Kansas City, teams at the International House of Prayer worship and pray and speak out Scripture twenty-four hours a day, seven days a week—and that night, *all night*, as I slept, those incredible people with one foot on earth and one in the heavens, sang and interceded, and I can't explain it, except to say that the most profound peace filled the room, the darkness was pushed far away, and when I woke the next morning, I was a new woman. My head was clear, my capacity was back, and I was once again healthy and well.

90. The Glitch in Our Marriage

Two years after being in Turkey, however, it was not only our strengths that had come out—so had all our uglies, and they showed up most in our marriage.

On one hand, Jeff and I were functioning at our absolute best. I couldn't have been prouder of how we'd handled the whole adjustment to Turkey, how we'd navigated endless pressures and taken on every possible opportunity. There was no denying we were caught up in a God-story far bigger than ourselves. But despite all that, we'd hit a serious glitch; for no good reason at all, it seemed, our relationship was self-destructing, and the biggest problem was that we couldn't put our finger on the issue, we had nothing to work with.

If there was a wrong way to take each other, we did. Everything we said seemed to provoke a frustrated response, and now we were left wondering how two people could possibly love each other so much and yet seem unable to function on the most basic level.

Was it possible we might return home from Turkey with an amazing God-story, and no marriage?

Neither of us could live with that kind of hypocrisy. Either our whole life needed to come back into healthy alignment, or we needed to go home and get sorted.

One of the issues, of course, was that our life never seemed to slow down. When on earth were we meant to get time to work it out? We were at capacity just trying to keep up with all that was going on, so much so that by the end of the day, we had very little care-factor to work with anyway.

Who wants to spend the only twenty sane minutes together at the end of the day going around the same old mulberry bush?

So, not knowing what else to do, we found ourselves hardly speaking, both of us at an absolute loss to know what the problem even was.

91. Ramadan Drummer

When it comes to timing and bringing people and situations and solutions together for breakthrough to occur, no one does it better than God. He's the perfect strategist, setting answers in motion before we've even been able to identify the problem. And so it was that two seemingly random events converged to not only restore our marriage, but, as it turns out, to restore *me*.

I never realised I was so broken, had no concept of the wounds I carried or the strongholds that had built up over the years, silently holding me captive, in a sense, until I was well and truly lost and only some poor resemblance of the real me remained. While the rest of the world seemed to draw out the best in me, those I loved most, it seemed, got the worst.

The first random event was that I was loaned a book with a prayer written in the back that was unlike anything I had come across before. The moment my eyes fell on that prayer, I knew that was exactly what I needed to pray.

A second prompt came the following morning, when, at four a.m., the erratic, exuberant beating of a great bass drum woke me from sleep, and I suddenly remembered it was the first day of Ramadan. Back in Ottoman times, before alarm clocks and cell phone alerts, enthusiastic young men would rouse the people of the Empire well before sunrise throughout the forty days of Ramadan, so that everyone might eat their breakfast before the first call to prayer rang out from the minarets and the long day of fasting began.

The tradition of the Ramadan drummer was certainly alive and well in twenty-first century Bursa; fit young men were right now, running up and down the streets; lights in bedrooms and kitchens were flickering on, and in that moment, I knew what I needed to do.

If the locals could seek God for forty days in prayer, so could I.

I was tired of trying to fix my marriage, tired of trying to fix myself, and right then I decided that enough was enough. That Ramadan, I wanted a God-story of my own.

And so, as the noise of the drums receded, I found myself slipping out of bed, tiptoeing down the marble staircase until I reached the basement, and right there, on the ornate blue Turkish rug, as Jeff and the children fell back into a deep sleep, I kneeled down, placed the prayer[1] I had found so intriguing in front of me, and bowed my face to the ground.

'My dear Lord Jesus, I come to You now . . .' and that's as far as I got before I started sobbing—great sobs of love, relief, and pure desperation.

I pulled out a journal and began to write every word I said to God and every word He said back.[2] Before the first morning was over, one thing was clear. It wasn't my marriage that was broken. It was *me*. I was a mess. It was time for Him to take the lead.

~

Three weeks later, our marriage seemed in far less of a crisis; we both realised how strategic the devil had been, causing us to use each other's brokenness against each other, and we were still feeling very tender about it all. We decided the way forward was to simply share communion every night before we went to bed.

We didn't say much as we took bread and wine together, but in a

---

1 Daily Prayer for Freedom (www.ransomedheart/dailyprayer)

2 Anya's journals are published under the title 'Feels Like I'm Breathing.'

tangible, visible way, we declared that Jesus had overcome all the works of the enemy and that our marriage was not up for grabs. Now something powerful was taking place, not only in our marriage but in our hearts and minds. We had finally realised that the Gospel was more glorious than we'd ever imagined.

92. Night of Power

Of course, I wasn't the only one praying my heart out during Ramadan. The locals had been extra-fervent too, persevering through the scorching summer days without as much as a glass of water, and though tensions were high, so was the sense of expectation. Now everyone's focus had turned to the final night of Ramadan. 'It's called the Night of Power,' our Muslim friends told us. 'On that night, when we pray, Allah listens and grants us all our requests. On that night, miracles can happen.'

For them it was a serious but joyful evening; by ten o'clock, the mosques of the city were overflowing with men and women, babies and children—no one, it seemed, wanted to stay home when the heart of Allah was turned towards His people. Back in Australia, our friends were praying too, that miracles would indeed break out, that Jesus Himself would come to our city with healing and salvation.

(Jeff writes) . . .

It was after dark when I arrived at the Green Mosque in the centre of the city. The carpeted space was already crowded with men standing shoulder to shoulder, and behind them, with a narrow walkway in between, hundreds of women stood or knelt in prayer, packing the mosque to capacity.

I felt abnormally self-conscious as I slipped off my shoes and walked slowly between the two masses of humanity; my heart was burdened for these people. I wanted to be there to stand beside them, praying for them as they fervently supplicated Allah for their many needs.

I settled quietly right on the edge of the tenuous no-man's-land and watched as one by one the men in front of me alternately stood and then bowed themselves low. It was hypnotising in its repetition, like gentle waves on the seashore. I prayed with my eyes open, reading the earnestness on the face of one and then another, praying for each man who caught my eye. I was fascinated by the mosquito-like movement of the children zig-zagging back and forth between their fathers at the front and their mothers at the rear; it was as if they were no threat to the solemnness of the occasion at all—in fact, they seemed to be adored, accepted as a natural part of the proceedings.

After a few hours, my whole body ached. When I want to spend time in prayer I walk and talk to God, but that night, I was hemmed in, challenging both my body and soul as the long hours passed. Eventually, though, the sun rose, and the crowds made their way home.

I was thankful for what I had been part of that night, knowing nothing is as powerful as praying the name of Jesus over people He desperately loves. I was also aware, however, that I had witnessed a level of tenacity and fervour that night that is uncommon in our part of the world, a sense of desperation before God that touched my heart in a humbling kind of way.

93. Pancakes for Breakfast

With Ramadan finally behind us, the German students came up with a plan. 'We want to make pancakes for breakfast to share with your family,' they announced, and right then, I couldn't have loved those girls more. Not only were they fun and generous, they loved hanging out with us as much as we enjoyed being with them.

At eight o'clock sharp the following Saturday, they arrived, not with ingredients for the batter, as I'd expected, but carrying huge trays absolutely piled high with pancakes they had already made! I laughed as I watched them help each other through the front gate, balancing baskets of toppings and ice cream, and laughing as they tried to keep the aluminium foil covers from flying in the wind.

Our kids were hyped, and so were the Germans. They'd got up three hours earlier because they only had one small frying pan and a gas burner to cook on, they said, and then they described the great lengths they had gone to, to keep the pancakes hot and fresh while they travelled across town on the bus. I laughed—there were only six of us and four of them, yet here they were with enough pancakes to feed a small army!

But in the end, quantity was exactly what we needed, because somehow word had got around that there was breakfast to be had at Jeff and Anya's place, and soon, students, most of whom we had never laid eyes on before, began showing up at our door. By nine o'clock, our lounge room was packed—our Afghani friend was there, and a couple of Albanians, some Polish and Greek women, and a Palestinian too. They took our offer literally and made themselves right at home, sitting anywhere they could—on the floor or the stairwell, at the table, on couches, and helping themselves with abandon to platefuls of pancakes.

Someone remarked about how we foreigners knew how to celebrate the end of Ramadan better than anyone, and soon everyone was talking about their experience of the month that had just passed. Sitting across the table, a few girls asked what Ramadan had been like for me, and that's how I ended up sharing the story of how I decided to seek God over the past few weeks, and how during those early morning hours in His presence, God had changed me.

I told them how just being here in Turkey seemed to bring out all the best in me but also all the worst, and how I wasn't okay with that, how desperately I felt the need to be made whole, to not keep living as if I were two different people. I told them how I'd asked Jesus to forgive me of my sins at the age of four, that I'd loved him all my life, and yet how powerless I felt here in Turkey to overcome my own personal issues— issues like bouts of anger or depression or apathy.

The young women were leaning in now, hanging on my every word— they were desperate themselves, it soon became obvious—and I noticed the chatter around the room slowly peter out until everyone, as if by instinct, had silenced their own conversations in order to listen.

I told them how I had started each day by closing my ears to every lying spirit and even to my own random thoughts, how I declared that I was only going to listen to the Spirit of God. I told them how I wrote down every word I said to God and every word He said to me, for three solid weeks. I shared how Jeff and I had been at each other for no good reason but that we weren't okay with that, how we loved each other yet seemed unable to get to the heart of the problem.

The students knew exactly what I meant—some of them were in relationships; most had experienced something similar in their own lives too. The spiritual dynamics at work in Turkey had impacted everyone in the room, and as I spoke, a niggling feeling began to surface, like the realisation that we had all been robbed of something good in full daylight.

We talked about how Jeff and I had been through our family with a fine-tooth comb before we ever left for Turkey; how we'd renounced generational curses and learned to spiritually cleanse our home, and how we'd got good at dealing with demons and summoning angelic help. Who would have thought it would be our own private brokenness that would threaten to take us out of the game?

Until now, the students had only really seen me in my public role, when my joy and confidence were at their peak; now, they were seeing into my heart. I told them how every time I asked God why I behaved the way I did, he had shown me the root of it, giving it a name I would never have imagined—Fear. Neglect. Guilt. Intimidation. Desolation—and how, one by one, those fortresses came down, how they had no power over me anymore, how before I did this, I prayed and asked for help, but it never seemed to work that well, but how now that I'd got to the root of things, the enemy couldn't mess with me so easily. Now I had what it took to overcome it all! Now, the provocations weren't bigger than me; instead of sin having power over me, I explained, I had power over it!

The room full of students clued in quickly. *'So you can actually be more like the real you?'* they asked, and I nodded, because, *yes, exactly! That is precisely what had happened. Strip the power from anger and fear and guilt and sorrow and whatever else life has thrown your way, and what's left is the beautiful life God planned all along!*

I bared my soul that morning.

The leftover pancakes were cold by now, but the students didn't care. 'What did you do next?' they wanted to know, and I told them how the Lord led me, how not once had He held back on me during these early morning hours, how it was as if He was even more eager to get me sorted than I had been myself. I told them how He never left me in the lurch—as soon as He showed me the root of an issue, He told me what to do, what to say, how to wield the scriptures like a sledgehammer—and how together we dealt with one thing after another until, three weeks in, the most amazing thing happened.

'I was down in the basement one morning,' I told them. 'I started out as I had done every other morning, reading my Daily Prayer, lingering at the words the Holy Spirit was drawing me to, asking God to show me the real issues and dealing with them in Jesus' name. I was beginning to wonder if there was any end to this whole process, if there was any part of me that *wasn't* messed up!' I told them how finally I'd dealt with one particular stronghold. This one was nasty and complex, but I shared how God and I set to work, and finally rendered it powerless in my life.

'I looked up after I dealt with that last thing,' I explained, 'and I actually said out loud: "Oh my goodness, God! Is this what it *feels like* to be born again?!"'

The students looked at me in amazement. My soul felt alive as for the first time I told the story of what God had just done for me. 'It was as if a weight I never knew I had been carrying was lifted off my shoulders,' I continued, 'like I'd just taken my first breath of spiritual air! Who would have thought that, here in Turkey, I would finally be set free?!'

Settar, the young man from Afghanistan, needed a cigarette, so Jeff went out onto the balcony with him and sat as he sucked in deep and then breathed the smoke into the cool morning air. Settar was an atheist who told Jeff he wasn't at all convinced there was a God. But evil? Settar had seen plenty of evidence for that, and Jeff and Settar were in deep conversation. If Satan was real, maybe God was too.

One by one the students turned back to their conversations, some went to the kitchen to brew fresh coffee or refill their plates, and a few started playing hide and seek with our girls.

The sacredness of the moment had passed but a song had been let loose within me. I'd just shared my God-story! One I didn't even have until I came to Turkey! *Oh, the irony.*

Truth is, I was still taken aback myself. I knew the Gospel was powerful but now that word hardly began to describe what I had experienced. Was *this* the message the whole world was craving, that there is healing for broken hearts and freedom from bondage and oppression?! If so, I'd just had the chance to share it, right there in my lounge room!

Later that day we played a round of cricket, and by mid-afternoon our unexpected breakfast guests began leaving in dribs and drabs. What Jeff and I were left with, though, was a fresh insight into the longing of all humanity to be restored, to be made whole, and ultimately, to be set free.

94. Collapse

The Working Group kicked off the second half of the year by offering free Turkish language courses to any expat or foreigner living in Bursa.

Over the summer, I had met with Turkish university students who were training to become English teachers, figuring some would be keen to get face-to-face teaching experience. One girl had volunteered right away, and the rest were weighing it up, but in the meantime, the response from the foreigners had been huge.

These classes brought a level of vulnerability to us all. The Turkish students felt intimidated by the idea of teaching foreigners, and the expats needed all the humility they could muster to attend a class where some were fluent and were hoping to hone their already-strong language skills, while others were complete beginners.

It was clear on the first night that we would need to split the class according to ability—from the following week, I decided, we would run three classes simultaneously, which meant finding two more teachers. But for now, at least, everyone seemed thrilled that we had simply made a start.

And then, at the half-time break, one of our students went missing.

Betsy had recently arrived from England, having come to Bursa for three months to serve in any way she could at the small Christian church. I admired her for coming to language classes when she was in Turkey for such a short span of time. For a seventy year old woman, navigating unfamiliar public transport at night was a challenge to start with, but, precious woman, she'd arrived at class that evening completely out of breath—she'd got a bit lost, she said, but now she was here, and as she pulled out a fresh notepad and began taking notes, I smiled to myself. Some people just keep on learning and growing and making the world a better place, and Betsy was one of them.

Only, when we all regrouped after our ten-minute break, Betsy didn't return to class. 'Maybe she's in the bathroom,' I thought, but fifteen minutes later, when she had still not appeared, I began to feel uneasy. I had sent a text to Betsy's phone and waited, but there was no reply. Scenarios began traipsing through my mind, perfectly good explanations, but the bottom line was, she hadn't said goodbye, had given no indication she was leaving, and even if it turned out nothing was wrong, I needed to locate her. Slipping out of the class, I began searching the corridors nearby.

Within minutes, I heard a muffled sound that seemed to be coming from the ladies bathroom. Opening the door, I could hear a woman moaning as if in pain; I knew it was Betsy, yet I couldn't make out a word she was saying. Gently, I tapped on the door of her cubicle and called, 'Betsy, it's me, it's Anya.' The moaning grew louder as I prised open the lock—and when I finally got in, there was Betsy alright, sprawled and slumped, half sitting on the toilet, half leaning against the wall, and it didn't take my years of training as a physiotherapist to figure out what was happening. Betsy was having a stroke.

I called for help, but my voice sounded weak and no one was within earshot. Betsy was a heavy woman; now she was clearly paralysed as well. I couldn't leave her, but neither could I move her. Propping her head up on my shoulder I sent a text to one of the students: 'Please call an ambulance—first floor bathroom.'

Within minutes, the ambulance arrived and together we got Betsy into a wheelchair. I dropped into the classroom to ask Adnan, a young Moroccan from the working group, to take care of locking the rooms once the language class was finished for the night, sent another message to one of Betsy's colleagues from the church, and climbed into the waiting ambulance. I took Betsy's hand in mine and noticed how heavy it felt, but her eyes held mine, and suddenly my heart went out to her. How scared she must be, I realised.

'*The Lord is my Shepherd. I shall not want . . .*' I began to whisper, but the paramedic interrupted to give me his assessment of the situation. 'She is just dehydrated,' he said, and right then I cut him off. 'No,' I replied, 'she's having a . . .' but I didn't know the word for 'stroke' and pointing out the obvious clue that her mouth had drooped to one side and her body was limp didn't seem to change his mind.

The ambulance driver, on the other hand, was more concerned about insurance. 'Yes,' I assured him, although it was complete presumption on my part, 'I'm sure she has medical insurance.' 'Okay,' he shouted from his front seat, 'then we will go to the German Hospital.' The medic beside me suddenly looked a bit more anxious and began preparing a drip to insert into the arm of his foreign patient.

I'm not sure how word travelled so fast, but by the time we pulled into the emergency driveway of Acibadem hospital, two official black cars waving state flags were already parked, and standing beside them was the Mayor of the city, President Semih Pala and two of their staff. 'We heard there was an emergency,' one of them said. 'Is everything okay?'

'I think she's had a . . .' The Mayor's assistant helped me with the translation, '. . . a stroke.'

'*Let's go inside,*' Semih Pala said gently, '*we'll take care of things. Don't worry.*'

Later I heard the details, how President Semih Pala and the Mayor had been hosting a special dinner nearby when an urgent message came through from the security guard at the council headquarters. '. . . *an emergency . . . foreigners' group . . . Acibadem hospital . . .*' and that was all it took—the two men had excused themselves right away and there they were, waiting, like kind father-figures, ready to help however they could.

And they did. *Betsy was to get good care, someone should contact her family back home, and the city would foot the bill, please.*

When Betsy was stabilised in a treatment room, they turned to me. 'Would you like us to take you home?' the offered.

I thanked Semih Pala but said I would prefer to wait until Betsy's friends from the church arrived, in case she took a turn for the worse.

'*Of course,*' the President said, and then added, unexpectedly, '*we will wait with you.*'

The hospital staff were baffled. Why were the leaders of the city sitting patiently in a public waiting room for a foreign woman? In the meantime, I sat beside Betsy, watching her vital signs flick across the monitor screens and praying that she wouldn't die. *Not on my watch, Lord. Please, not here in Turkey, not on our first night of class . . .*

And she didn't. Betsy's friends stayed with her through the night, and sure enough, she began to improve. Within a week she was back on the plane to England. I, on the other hand, was chauffeured home that night in a black limousine with little flags of Turkey and Bursa waving on the bonnet, much to the bewilderment of the entire neighbourhood.

95. Love your . . .

The International Women's Association had scheduled their Christmas party for late November, and this year I wasn't particularly looking forward to it. Although I deeply admired the women and their work and was blessed with many dear friends among them, I also found myself regularly being put on the mat, so to speak, about what I was doing at the city council, and, indeed, in Bursa. Quite frankly, it was getting to me. Having never had a real enemy in my life, suddenly it seemed as if one or two of my fellow-expats were determined to humiliate and discredit either me, my working group, or my family.

But the provocation was about to get personal—and public. And neither Jeff nor I saw it coming. I was standing near the door on the night of the Christmas party, keeping an eye on the children as they played and jostled together in the crowded room. Their excitement was high as they waited for Santa to arrive and start handing out the much-anticipated presents.

That's when I noticed Janine; the mulled wine had clearly taken some effect on her already, when suddenly, she began making a beeline towards Jeff and his friends who were standing at the edge of the room. Barging into the circle of men, she got straight to the point. Glaring at Jeff, she demanded in front of them all, 'What exactly are you doing here in Turkey?' followed by, 'and tell us, where do you *actually* get your money from?!'

The men around Jeff couldn't hide their shock and embarrassment; the implication was obvious. We all knew that Turkish people often suspected foreigners of working either for the CIA or for missionary organisations, but to be so blatantly confronted by a fellow-expat was unheard of.

The mere suggestion was enough, though, and she knew it. Those two questions had the power to dismantle and embarrass every relationship we had, every aspect of our working life, and potentially, our ability to continue living in Turkey.

96. When Apparently the Solution is Golden Syrup

The angst in my spirit was short-lived, however, thanks to an unexpected encounter that put an end to every hard feeling I harboured and left me rather humbled in the process.

I was merely pushing a trolley around a supermarket when I spotted a shelf of Golden Syrup. In the nearly two years we had been in Bursa, I had never seen golden syrup for sale. I'd enquired, of course, because Anzac slice is every Australian mum's go-to recipe, and making it properly calls for a decent quantity of Golden Syrup. But I'd always been met with confused looks. 'No. There is no such thing in Turkey. Perhaps if you ask in Istanbul, but not here in Bursa.'

Yet there it was, on the shelf of my local supermarket, *Lyle's Golden*

Syrup, mind you, straight from Great Britain, two small stacks of the same shiny green and gold tin it was first marketed in way back in 1885. The moment I saw it, the Spirit of God stirred my heart with what I needed to do. With Christmas coming, surely even my British 'enemy' would jump at the chance for some good home-style baking. Right there and then, I decided to buy Janine a gift.

Just as quickly, my mind rebelled. How absurd. Her remarks had reached a new low that week; a few days earlier it had taken all my resolve to keep from tossing this whole Bursa-assignment in, leaving the city to her once and for all.

But wisdom had come to me, and as I stood there with my hand on my shopping trolley, I knew that this one tin of golden syrup could turn the tide of bitterness that had been pounding me day after day.

It was reduced from thirty-two Lira to just nine, a helpful little prod that I probably needed to follow through with the purchase, and I bought a second tin for ourselves just for good measure. The next morning, I sent a text to Janine. *'I've got something for you—can I drop past your place soon?'* She replied right away. *Yes, she was home.* We made a time to meet, and I told her that, no, unfortunately, I wouldn't be able to come in for tea; in fact, if she could meet me on the street, that would be great.

I can't deny the fact I was being a complete coward. To make up for it, though, I wrapped the tin carefully in Cellophane, tied a lavish bow and hand-wrote a little message wishing her a very merry Christmas.

That simple act of gift-giving called for every ounce of effort and emotion I possessed—my heart was racing and my words were stilted as I passed the present to her through the window of the car—the best I could come out with was that *I'd seen the golden syrup in Migros and thought of her, and no, I'm so sorry, I did need to keep going, but I hoped she enjoyed a little treat from home . . .*

My awkwardness was not lost on either of us, but for once it was Janine who was completely at ease—kind, even—and I for all the world, felt foolish. Had I got this whole thing out of proportion? Did she have any idea the courage I'd mustered just to follow through with this one simple act?

My hands trembled as I reached again for the steering wheel. I'm sure she noticed, and in a rare, gracious moment, she said nothing of it. But did her expression soften a little? Had she too, been thinking the worst of me, thinking perhaps that I was hard-nosed and arrogant, not realising that I so often battled uncertainty, that her undercutting of me had hurt more than I wanted her to know?

Obviously though, my courage was short-lived. With a poor excuse for a smile, I said goodbye and Merry Christmas, then drove around the corner where I pulled over until the shaking that had just engulfed my entire body, subsided.

97. Second Christmas in Turkey

We were not the only Christian family to encounter suspicion—many of our friends from other countries dealt with it too, and, bless them, they included us in their Christmas celebrations that year. At the end of twelve months of pressure and mounting hostility, it was good to be together on Christmas Eve.

I was beyond thankful for the invitation. This Christmas, I had no desire to be with anyone other than those who shared our faith on a heart-level. By now, our family was longing only for safety and simplicity, and that's exactly what our friends gave us.

There's something wonderful about shared traditions from around the world—just stepping into a room with Christmas carols playing, a tree all adorned with advent-decorations, and little bags of sweets on the tables helped to lift the weight that had settled recently on our hearts. By the end of the night we all felt grounded again, wrapped up in the love and festivity of our favourite time of the year.

It never ceases to amaze me how, when Jesus' people get together anywhere in the world, it's heaven on earth. It's family. For one whole wonderful evening, it felt like we had come home.

The Third Year

98. The Family Hammam

We had come a long way since our first awkward hammam experiences. In fact, the Turkish baths had become a semi-regular escape for our family, particularly when everyone was a bit stressed out or over-wrought. We'd even discovered a hotel that had private hammam rooms for hire! The historic baths in town were segregated into men's and women's, but at this hotel, there were family hammams, where, for a small cost, the six of us could relax together, away from the eyes of the outside world.

Visually, this hammam was stunning. The door opened into a small room lined with blue tiles from floor to ceiling; there was a bench around the edge to sit or lie on, and six small taps were spaced around the walls, each with a copper bowl underneath for filling with warm water and pouring over each other. The kids lay down on the benches and Jeff and I sloshed water over them, rubbing them down and massaging their backs as they soaked up the warmth of the marble tiles. In the adjacent room was a private pool; this one had marble flooring around it, and naturally heated mineral water gushed from the mouth of a bronze lion's head mounted on the wall at the end of the room.

The effect was incredibly soothing. Gentle splashes of water muffled all other sound, and for a wonderful hour, we were away from it all—the people, the sights, the never-ending noise, even our own responsibilities and concerns. In the hammam, it was just the six of us resting and recuperating and relaxing until we could barely keep our eyes open. And then, when the warmth had worked its way right into our bones, and our muscles were loose and every pore squeaky clean, we emerged, blinking at the sunlight outside, and made our way home like brand-new people.

99. Tintin in Turkey

Speaking of time out, we had anticipated the release of 'Tintin—the Movie' for weeks and finally, there it was, showing in our local cinema, and in English too! It had been a long time since all six of us had been to the movies together; now we made our way in the chilly afternoon air to the mall, where we waited at the ticket office, bursting with excitement.

'Two adults and four children to see Tintin,' I told the man behind the glass pane. But my smile was not returned by the ticket-seller.

'I'm sorry,' he said with a frown, 'no children allowed.'

'Excuse me?' I asked. 'Why on earth not? Who is Tintin for, if it's not children?!' My tone already had an edge of incredulousness in it, because, well, this was Turkey, and sometimes stupid things did get to ruin the day, but *not today*. Today was a chance for my family to have some light-hearted fun in their own language, and goodness knows, I wasn't about to give in.

'Tintin is rated 18+,' the man explained. 'Not suitable for children. Only eighteen years and over.'

Now, we had been baffled many times since coming to Turkey, but this was absurd. 'Who decided that?' I asked.

'Ministry of Culture in Ankara,' said the ticket-man, with the little flick of his eyebrows that everyone in Turkey knows means: *Sorry, not sorry. Nothing I can do. Not my problem.*

I stood there speechless. 'You want to buy two adult tickets instead?' the man persisted, and I believe the word *imbecile* may have passed through my mind. What did he think we'd do? Sit our four kids down in the foyer with a bucket of popcorn while mum and dad went to watch a two-hour long children's movie? It was time to pick a fight.

'Why is the movie rated 18+?' I questioned. 'It's a children's movie!'

The ticket-salesman humoured me by looking up a review on his computer screen.

'Oh yes,' he said, eventually finding what he was looking for. 'It's because the movie has alcohol in it, therefore it is not suitable for children.'

'Here we go', I thought, 'Islam at its best. It's okay for kids to feast their eyes on nudity and porn at school and to sit through excessively violent battle-themed movies—but alcohol? *Forbidden*. 'Still,' I reasoned with myself, 'it wasn't actually Tintin they had a problem with. It was Captain Haddock. *What shall we do with the drunken sailor?* Slap an R-rating on him, that's what we'll do, and make sure this nasty foreign influence doesn't sully the innocence of our Turkish youth.'

The kids were begging me not to make a fuss. 'It doesn't matter, Mum. We can get it out on DVD later.'

But in the moment, it did matter. The moral superiority of the whole nation had got under my skin; these kids of ours had given up a whole lot of normality for a very long time, and in my mind, we were going to see this movie one way or another. 'Then we will buy six adult tickets,' I told the ticket-man. Surely that would solve his problem and ours.

'No. Not possible,' came the reply.

'Then we will buy two adult tickets, and you can go and make a coffee or check your emails or something, because we would like to take our kids to see Tintin.' The guy decided to ignore me and at that point, Jeff stepped in. *When would I learn?* I should have simply hung back with the kids, let him take it from the start, and we would have all been seated in the theatre by now.

'Yes, yes,' Jeff was agreeing pleasantly with the man, 'It is very good that your government protects children. R-rating is very suitable, very good.' I rolled my eyes, but Jeff knew what he was doing. 'The Ministry of Culture is doing the right thing,' he said, 'but R-rating is only for Turkish citizens, not for foreigners. Your government wants to protect your young people, I'm sure you understand. It's okay. We will decide for the foreign children.'

And with that he handed over thirty lira, told the kids to walk right on in, and by the time he had the tickets in his hands, we were seated.

We had the entire theatre to ourselves, and for the next few glorious hours, we were not in Turkey at all—we were dodging our way through markets and rolling around on the high seas and plodding across deserts and laughing uncontrollably at the ridiculous Thomson and Thompson, and that movie did more for us than any holiday could have.

In those wonderful hours, we didn't hear a word of Turkish, we had no one watching us, and the fact that we'd overridden the Ministry of Culture along the way, was simply the cherry on top.

100. Igloo and Architecture

It was the new year holiday season once again, and that year, our city was covered in gleaming white. With lovely, firm, white snow right in our own backyard, our kids were thrilled. Joseph went straight into building mode; ever since we had arrived in Turkey his eyes had taken in the incredible architecture all around us, the way tiles were laid to create the best effect on the front of a building, or how a dome was constructed in a new mosque. Now, he had his own project to work on, right outside our house.

Jeff and the kids wasted no time in setting to work, making piles of snow-bricks and assembling an igloo that would make an Eskimo proud. From early morning until dusk, they laboured out there on the central lawn while the neighbours looked on in complete disbelief. Maybe they wondered why anyone would put so much effort into something that was going to melt away, or maybe they didn't appreciate the way we disrupted the snow and spoiled the smooth white blanket that covered the grass. Perhaps they wished *they* were out there enjoying the fun of it all.

In any case, the finished igloo was packed tight and strong, and the neighbours certainly smiled when they saw me carry out trays of hot chocolate and pass the steaming mugs one by one through the low arched entryway to the proud young builders inside.

The igloo served its purpose well for a few weeks; even though the temperatures eventually rose and melted all the snow around it, the igloo remained, an edifice of snow-construction excellence. Eventually the bricks of icy snow began to soften—of course, we'd known it wouldn't last forever—but then, in a greatly peeving moment, the gardener turned up, walked over to the remaining igloo, and started hacking it down, stomping on the bricks and raking them into the grass until there was nothing left but a wild and fun-filled memory.

101. Care Packages

The thoughtfulness and generosity of our team of friends continued to take our breath away, and on one particular day in December, a parcel arrived from a young family back in Australia. Inside, to my delight, was a selection of wonderful, hardcover cookbooks, all in English! These friends had also lived abroad; they knew how even something simple like a familiar recipe brings its own sense of comfort. Although I could pull up any recipe on the internet, I had always enjoyed sitting on the couch, thumbing through cookbooks, and with the arrival of that parcel, my love bucket was topped right up.

Then there was the package that came addressed to our children, a gesture that touched us deeply. Our kids knew that their mum and dad were proud of them, yet seeing firsthand that others believed in this adventure too, affirmed them in a way that even we could not. We laughed together as the girls sprawled out in their pyjamas in the living room that night, poring over a picture book and beaming at the inscription a young couple had written in the front: *'Happy bedtime, McKee's . . .'*

I guess it must have been the week for allowing goods from Australia into Turkey, because only a few days later, another box arrived, and this one was full of gluten free treats. That parcel, we noticed, cost far more in postage than even the value of the contents, but when we caught a glimpse of the lavish love that surrounded every carefully-selected item, the boost to our souls was immense, and let me tell you, there's nothing like the kindness of friends when you're a long, long way from home.

102. Books from Bulgaria

Speaking of parcels, it looked as if we were about to receive a shipment that would revolutionise our entire city. An English-language library in Bosnia was closing down after many years of serving the expat community there, and the director had got in touch to offer our working group the entire stock! *A whole library of English language books! In Bursa!*

I could picture it already—a community hub, complete with book clubs and special interest groups, even story time readings for the children. A library was one thing every Western foreigner missed, and we had just been gifted hundreds of titles to establish a library of our own!

Our contact in Bosnia also happened to be an Australian woman, which made the conversation between us even more fun. 'Great,' she said when I explained our vision, 'I'll send you through an inventory. Just choose which books you want.' With it came a generous offer— the expat community in Bosnia had agreed to pay to send the entire shipment to Bursa as their way of helping to get our library started.

Why on earth I didn't just take whichever books they wanted to send? Instead, I spent the next few days scrolling through pages of book titles. I researched each title to see if it was one our expats would enjoy. I tried to calculate how many books would fit on a pallet. In short, I obsessed. It had obviously been too long since I'd stepped into a library, and now I was deliberating as if the literary future of my city depended on it.

Eventually I narrowed the list to three-hundred or so books. Now, all we needed to do was obtain some library space, appoint someone to oversee the setup, and be there to collect the books when they arrived.

By the time we were notified that our boxes were ready for collection at the customs office in Bursa, everything was in place.

My working group was thrilled, and the next morning, Jeff and I ordered a van-sized taxi and made our way out to the port, where we followed the signs to the customs office and presented our consignment slip to the manager in charge. That was the moment my grand designs began falling to the ground.

The customs officer looked at the packing slip and raised his brow. 'Books?' he asked. 'Yes,' I smiled broadly, 'I represent a Bursa City Council working group. We are going to open a library for the foreigners in Bursa.'

No we weren't, in fact, only I didn't know it yet.

'We cannot possibly release the boxes to you,' the official told me. 'All books must be approved by the Ministry of Culture before you bring them into Turkey.'

So this was another Tintin scenario—movies, books, any kind of media that might carry a message—it all needed to be classified and signed off as suitable for Turkish consumption.

'Oh,' I said with relief, 'they're not for Turkish people. These books are just for foreigners to read. They are all written in English. President Semih Pala has approved the library.' I only had a few more sentences of Turkish to reason with and I wasn't getting far.

'We must see which books they are,' said the officer.

'No problem,' I said. I handed over the list of books we had selected.

'Çok problem,' responded the officer as he flicked through the pages in his hands. 'Big problem. It is not only the Ministry for Culture that must approve these books. Also, the Ministry for Education must agree. The only way you can proceed is to send the books back to Bulgaria. When the Education Minister approves these books, you can bring them to Turkey again.'

It was then that I realised we were never going to get our library.

'And what happens if we don't send the books back?' I could hardly bring myself to ask.

'The boxes will be destroyed,' came the reply.

In that moment I felt like the greatest fool on earth. Why had I just presumed we could ship books to Bursa? Goodness, I couldn't even download a book on my Kindle without getting the message, 'this book is unavailable in your region.'

I thought of the hours I'd spent deliberating over titles, how carefully I'd selected each one. I thought of the requests we'd made for shelving space, of the excitement that this was one project we could pull off that would last well into the future. And I thought of the generous souls in Bosnia who had given so much stock from their precious library in order to continue their legacy in Turkey.

I couldn't bear it anymore. 'Thanks,' I whispered as Jeff and I returned to the van, and I guess something must have died on the inside that day, because what I really meant was 'thanks for nothing.'

103.   A Room of Our Own

Our disappointment over the port debacle was well and truly alleviated later that week, when, over a tray of Turkish tea, Ayşe announced that our working group had been allocated our own office space, a seemingly small thing that meant the world to me.

The four largest working groups at the City Council were referred to as Assemblies, having grown in their influence and contribution to the point where they had been given their own dedicated meeting rooms in the congress centre. The other fifteen or so working groups, of which ours was the most recently-formed, scheduled their meetings around the use of a shared conference room in the centre of the building.

It wasn't until my team and I stood there unlocking the door to our new office that I realised what an honour this represented. Now we had a room where our people could get together throughout the week to collaborate on projects and work in their subgroups; it allowed our team to meet when it suited them best, or to come in to work spontaneously, rather than having to pre-plan and arrange everything. I was especially thrilled because having our name on the door also gave us another level of legitimacy in the eyes of the city—and it spoke a great deal about how the city council viewed us. As a group, we were not a trial idea anymore. We had been recognised as a permanent working group, and on top of that, had been given a privilege usually reserved for the Assemblies.

I deliberately kept the ribbon-cutting low-key because I was aware that there were many other working groups who would have loved to have space of their own, and I didn't want to stir up contention over a room. So with a quick text message, I announced that if anyone wanted to come early, before our next formal meeting, we would meet on the first floor to officially open our new room.

President Semih Pala was there, along with his media representative and staff. A ceremonial red ribbon, I noticed, had been strung across the door. The occasion called for a brief speech—one in which I took the chance to praise the working group, acknowledge the City Council, and thank Semih Pala.

Then, with my eclectic young team clapping and patting each other on their backs, I cut the ribbon, opened the door, and cheered as everyone rushed inside, joked about how squashed we were but how great this moment felt, and then, like typical students anywhere in the world, filled their plastic cups and drank Pepsi in celebration.

104. The Media Shoot

Shortly after, President Semih Pala came to me with an idea. 'Would you be happy to do a press interview?' he asked. 'It would be good to run a story about your family in the local newspapers.' That sounded fine me, and so once again, all six of us scrubbed up and headed into the council headquarters.

The president met us at a staff café where we waited for the reporters to arrive. 'Choose any drink you like,' he encouraged the children as they took their seats around the table.

To call what we were about to participate in, an interview, however, turned out to be too generous. For a start, it was clear that the journalist had not been prepped for his task.

'Where are you from?'

'When did you come to Bursa?'

'Do you like living here?'

They were benign questions, to say the least. If I'd thought this might be an opportunity to showcase the achievements of the working group, or talk about the way our family had adjusted to life in Turkey, or even offer a foreigner's perspective on living in Bursa, I was clearly mistaken. In fact, the journalist bypassed Jeff and myself completely and honed in exclusively on Eric, presumably because he was the most competent of us all when it came to speaking in Turkish. But even Eric was given very little scope to give a personal opinion or response.

'What are your favourite foods?' the reporter began, 'Lahmucan?

Köfte?' Ice cream?'

'Evet,' replied Eric. '*Lahmucan seviyorum. Köfte seviyorum. Dondurma seviyorum.*' I like, I like, I like. Eric knew enough by now to choose from the range of expected answers and nod agreeably.

'And what is your opinion about Turkish people?' the reporter went on. 'Very friendly, yes?'

I could almost hear the sigh from my son's spirit. 'Evet. Turkish people are very friendly,' he replied for the record. Cameras clicked all around us as the sham interview proceeded. 'Now let's go outside,' the journalist said. 'We would like to take some pictures of your kids playing in the park.'

The meaninglessness of the interview became even more apparent when, coming across a group of boys kicking a ball between each other, the reporter decided this was the perfect opportunity to capture a show of friendliness between foreigners and Turks. '*Go on, join in,*' President Semih Pala encouraged. One of his staff patted our boys' shoulders. 'Yes, just kick the ball with the other kids while we get some photos!'

The cameraman adjusted his tripod ready to capture the scene as Eric and Joseph walked towards the group of friends. 'Can we play soccer with you?' they asked hopefully. The unashamed disdain in their reply caught us all off-guard. '*Yabanci*', they spat on the ground in disgust, and turned their back on Eric and Joseph.

The president's aide made his way over to the young soccer-players; I saw him look each one in the eyes as he addressed them, but there was no fixing the scene. The interview was over. The whole thing had been a farce, leaving us all somewhat confounded. The reporter, however, was happy; his story would be featured in the following day's papers, the incident in the park would never be mentioned, and with handshakes all round, we gathered the kids, ignored the weight that had come upon our hearts, and headed for home.

105. Intimidation

It didn't take long for the hostility to follow us home. I was working in the kitchen a few weeks later when I noticed one of our neighbours chatting with our girls in the garden. I smiled. The lady they were speaking with had, over the past few years, become one of my dearest friends in Bursa.

'Mummy,' the girls came running in, 'the neighbour invited us to play at her house. Can we go? Can you come too?' And so we all ended up in my friend's lounge room together, playing with her delightful ten-month old baby and drinking coffee, and just when I was thinking how heart-warming it was to be hanging out with Turkish friends in typical Australian-style—sitting on the floor, surrounded by toys and baby wipes, husband relaxing on the couch, all of us barefooted and happy—I was brought back to reality again.

'How did your holiday go?' my friend asked. She knew our family had been away for a few days earlier in the week, visiting with friends in Istanbul.

'Lovely' I answered, 'Istanbul is wonderful, and it was good to catch up with friends.'

My friend looked down for a moment before she spoke. 'While you were away, the police came to our door,' she said. 'They talked to the manager of the housing complex first, then they came to all the neighbours. They asked some questions about your family and asked about what you do.'

I couldn't hide the range of emotions that crossed my face. My throat felt nearly choked. 'Really?' I responded quietly. 'I thought the job of the police was to keep law and order. I don't think we cause any disturbance, do we?'

But there was nothing to be said, except that by now we were weary of being watched, of being held in suspicion simply because we were foreigners. Why on earth couldn't the police have brought their questions directly to us? It took the shine off a wonderful morning.

106. Paranoia and the Police

If the police intimidation had ended there, we may have shrugged it off, but instead, it accelerated. The next appointment for our visa renewal was coming up, and this time, Jeff found out, we were in for trouble— our family had essentially been red-flagged.

The first thing Jeff noticed as he sat across the table from the police chief was that our dossier was thicker than usual; a quick glimpse was all it took to realise that the authorities had tapped into our email accounts, because, there, in the file, were copies of our personal correspondence, all stamped and collated on the desk in front of him.

We knew that my phone calls had been monitored for a while—I'd noticed it a few times—muffled voices in the background when I was midway through a call. Once I'd even heard a distinct 'click' just before I'd hung up.

But there was more to come, and it hit us unexpectedly in the midst of a beautiful spring day right on the cusp of Easter. As Christians around the world prepared to celebrate the holiest week of the year, I came across a song on YouTube that moved me to tears with love for Jesus. The fact it was sung in Spanish only made the words sound even more tender, and if it impacted me so deeply, I figured, why not share it with my expat friends who, I'm sure, were also feeling isolated from their usual traditions and communities this Easter?

On the morning of Good Friday, I got up early, made a pot of tea, and prayed that whoever listened to the song might be encouraged and strengthened, wherever in the world they might be. And then, I posted the video—only to be completely taken aback, when less than twenty minutes later, my link was suddenly blocked right across Turkey. Anyone who clicked on my post was now greeted with an official message:

THIS VIDEO IS PROHIBITED IN TURKEY UNDER THE NATIONAL SECURITY ACT

Jeff and I looked at the screen in shock. Whoever had been assigned to keep an eye on my posts was not in Bursa after all; they were probably operating out of the nation's capital, and it had taken less than twenty minutes for my post to be noticed and censored.

I decided to take the situation straight to the City Council—not to the President, because it would put him in the impossible situation of having to side with either myself or the authorities in Ankara—but to Ayşe, my friend and advisor. Sitting opposite her, I opened my laptop and showed her the message. 'Ayşe,' I said, 'it's just a song. I know it's a Christian song, and yes, it's about Jesus, but it's in Spanish! Only expats are really going to understand the words anyway. How can this be a threat to national security?'

Ayşe was baffled and shocked, but she remained diplomatic—and for that, I admired her so well. There was, of course, nothing she could do, except to acknowledge the increasing scrutiny we were facing here in Turkey.

I came home that day, looked out of the fourth-floor bedroom window to the street below, and for the first time since arriving in Turkey, something close to paranoia gripped my mind. Down on the road beneath me, a yellow taxi made its way down our street, slowing noticeably as it passed our house, and suddenly, even that troubled me. We'd heard that the local taxi drivers were, more often than not, 'retired' policemen—were we now under some sort of surveillance? I needed perspective. I needed reassurance. If nothing else, I needed to hear the voice of a friend. I needed to call home.

That call, I believe, will stay with me forever. My friend in Australia picked up the phone. 'Anya?!' she asked, 'are you at home? Let me call you right back.' And when she did, the mounting strain of the past few months poured out in tears and sobs. 'I don't know what to do, Sharon, they're watching me. They're listening to my phone calls. They've got my emails. There's a taxi going up and down our street . . .'

If she thought I'd lost my mind, she never let on. This was the friend who had spoken truth to me as I raised two toddler sons in Canberra, she'd welcomed my baby girl into her arms the day she was born, and now her gentle, gracious words reached around the world and soothed my tumultuous soul.

'Anya, are you safe?' she began.

'Yes,' I stammered, and then she reminded me that it was God who had brought us to Turkey, that He had promised us peace and safety, and that His love would not fail us now. Then she prayed a kind, motherly prayer, and by the time she finished, every troubled thought in my mind had been stilled.

I'll never underestimate the impact of that call. I could see it now— the enemy had well and truly got inside my head, speaking fear and inciting panic—and in the face of quiet, faith-filled encouragement, he simply up and fled.

107. The Email that Shifted things

The following week, Jeff decided to take the kids up Mount Uludağ. Although the days were getting warmer, the snow still lingered high on the mountains around the city, and the children were excited to enjoy the slopes one last time before the ski season ended.

It was a rare treat to have the house to myself, and I was determined to soak up the quiet. Truth is, it had been a tough night; once again I hadn't been able to shake the sense that we were somehow being threatened. Jeff too had become concerned. That morning, before we got out of bed, I had rested my head on his shoulder as he prayed, 'Lord, please relieve the pressure we've been facing. We're asking you to do something about it. Sustain Anya, strengthen her, carry us through this time . . .' I'd added my agreement, and with a quieted mind and renewed trust, we had got into the day.

Funny though, how when everyone had left, kitted out in their gloves and hats and backpacks loaded with flasks of hot chocolate, I wished I'd gone too. Perhaps it had been too long since I'd had a day to myself—in any case, I didn't know what to do with the hours ahead of me. In the end, after pottering around a bit, I turned on some music and sat down to flick through emails. And then, I stopped flicking, stopped breathing, I believe, because I knew that feeling, the sudden recognition in my spirit that this was a moment on which the future could pivot.

The email had been sent to a wide group of Christian expats living throughout the country.

'We are looking for a family to sublet our apartment in Antalya for one year while we are on leave in Australia,' I read. 'The apartment is currently set up as a House of Prayer—we would prefer to lease our home to people who can keep that focus in our absence.'

I'm sure details followed, but already I had reached for the phone. I was convinced and excited and reeling all at once, and the patchy cell phone coverage must have made it only more difficult for Jeff to make out what I was saying.

'Jeff!' I exclaimed when he answered the phone, 'I've just seen this email and it says they are looking for a family . . .'

Jeff calmly told me that it sounded interesting. 'Let's talk about it when I get home,' he said.

~

Jeff told me as we lay in bed that night that he was on the slopes, trying to keep two little girls upright on their skis when he took my call, but the jist of the message had got through, and by the time he got home, Jeff had done what he does so well—connected the dots and come up with a plan.

We knew something had shifted as Jeff had prayed that morning;

we'd felt the pressure lift, the rising tide of animosity recede a little. But what neither of us expected was that God's ultimate answer might be to take *us* out of the picture—move us on, perhaps. And yet, with that one email, there it was, an unexpected answer, and suddenly the timing made perfect sense. Could it be that our assignment in Bursa was coming to an end? 'Yes,' Jeff agreed, 'let's enquire about the apartment in Antalya.'

108. Time to Resign

The move to Antalya was soon confirmed. In the meantime, however, I had come to realise that, regardless of whether we stayed in Bursa or not, the time had come to hand over my role at the city council.

(from Anya's Journal)

I sense that my time as president of the working group is coming to an end. It's not a decision as much as a feeling within me—but it's a feeling I now trust.

On a rational level, though, I've worked tirelessly, day and night for nearly two years. I've met with hundreds of people—foreigners, locals, students, business owners, government officials, men and women of so many nationalities. I've taken in a lifetime's worth of stories and situations. I've poured everything I have into my vibrant and capable team, and they have risen to every challenge.

Against all predictions, we've pulled off projects galore—the first photofest, where foreigners joined with local artists to showcase Bursa through the lens of their camera; an emergency plan so foreigners can be informed and find help in a crisis; we've united people from all kinds of backgrounds and cultures through our bus tours and picnics and cultural events; we've supported foreign students on campus and opened pathways for volunteering in our city once again. We've lifted the standard of English in tourist brochures and information centres, lobbied for an affordable international school and a multi-language library, become a point of connection and friendship for newcomers to our city—and most importantly to me—we have gained the trust and respect and the sincere friendship of the leaders of our city.

I've come alive—no doubt about that. I'm not much good at forward planning or strategizing, but we've been maximally productive and effective anyway. I remembered when I first took on the role, asking Jeff to tell me the basics of how to scope out and manage a project. I tried to take it in, I really did, but no less than a week later I found myself reverting to intuition, to going with the natural connections, to following the paths as they opened before me, and it's worked.

Relationally, these two years couldn't have been richer. Semih Pala Bey and his team are relieved, I think. He took a big risk, in this country, letting foreigners have a say, valuing us and allowing us to be in public view. I think he's more than relieved, actually. He's proud. And so he should be. This is the first municipality in all Turkey to have foreign representation, and we've become not only a model for other cities, but a source of enlargement and learning and joy for us all.

But I'm tired. Jeff and the kids have shared me with such a multitude of people that they've missed out to an extent. They don't resent it—in fact, they love to see me rise—but I can't sustain the pace or the level of responsibility forever.

And then there's the police. I've got too big for their liking. When I speak, the hearts of the people are with me. They're seeing the news reports of my leadership and they're always there at big events—either sitting in the front row, or dispersed strategically through the crowd, or standing with tight expressions at the back.

My influence has become threatening to them. The closeness, the familiarity I have with the city leaders is something I have never been able to cultivate with the Yabanci police. Under their handshakes and polite meetings, they don't trust me. They don't trust any of us foreigners, and though I suppose that's their job, I have remained idealistic, hoping the outward show of cooperation would eventually turn into something tangible.

But every project we have attempted with the police has come to nothing. We've had token meetings, agreed to collaborate on issues that have been dismissed from their agenda before we've even left the room. Still, we've tried. The city council has tried. At the end of the day, the Yabanci police are working for Ankara, and there's every chance they have only ever been playing along to save face and keep their finger on the pulse of all us rascally expats who they seem unable to pin down.

I get on well with nearly all the women from the international community, but a couple have remained peeved about my role and the rapport with which I'm held, and I'm tired of managing their hostility, of answering their provocative questions, their jibes. I'm starting to find myself awake at night, unable to shake them from my mind. It's time to move on.

I love how God never leaves us in limbo for long. When my spirit knows the job is done, it's best to step out sooner rather than later.

I know who should lead the group after me. I recognised him as soon as he walked into the room. Adnan, the Moroccan student-cum-entrepreneur, with his open smile, clear thinking and ability to mix easily, like a chum with the students, and yet he can don a suit and give a sincere handshake and carry himself with all the deportment of a diplomat. Most of all, he knows how to show appropriate honour to the President and Mayor and their officials without any pretence or show. He's a good man, I believe, and he's got a healthy ambition to serve for the good of the city.

The first day I stared my job here, I prayed that whenever it came time to leave, I would do so with every relationship intact, that I would finish well. Now I'm glad I covered that off, right from the start. God has woven together so very many variables, protected me and my reputation, and prospered every connection. It's with great gratitude and confidence that I find myself ready to hand my precious team and the future of the foreigners working group, to Adnan.

Only, I don't get to choose. As when I became president, there needs to be a vote, and I will not be part of it. My position is open to anyone, and although I can encourage Adnan to put himself forward, I don't get to pull any strings. Tomorrow at our meeting, I will simply announce my intention to resign and call for a vote the following week.

109. Voting a Successor

Every Foreigners Working Group meeting was advertised, but I was not expecting anyone new to come along the following week, especially since we had let people know that this meeting would simply include a wrap-up of unfinished business, some words of farewell from me, and the vote for the new president.

As I arrived, however, I was greeted by two unfamiliar faces. I introduced myself and shook their hands. They were Palestinians, here to study at university, they told me without a hint of warmth in their expression. Strange, I thought. Most newcomers turned up with a bit of first-time enthusiasm; these two, on the other hand, were dismissive of me and seemingly uninterested in what we were doing. Not to worry. That night, welcoming newcomers was not my priority. I wanted to be fully present. I had prepared an official speech which I would give from my heart, and then I would honour the selection process by taking a back seat.

As it turned out, three people put their names forward as my potential successor—the first was Ilir, the incredibly likeable Albanian student of history and theology and languages who had been with us from the start. I was glad he was standing. Then there was Adnan from Morocco, who had taken my leadership suggestion humbly but sincerely, and Janine, who I guess saw her chance to have what she had wished for all along. I felt for her that night, to be honest.

I was surprised, however, when, as soon as the three nominees were announced, Ilir immediately withdrew his name, openly aligning his vote with Adnan and offering to support him, should he be elected. And that is how it went. Adnan was elected, we all clapped politely, and the outcome was tabled in the meeting minutes. Janine left without comment or fuss, and I had no reason to believe she would trouble herself with the working group any further.

As the meeting concluded, President Semih Pala came into the room, accompanied by Cüneyt, his offsider, and Ayşe, who had first welcomed me to the city council nearly two years earlier. Standing in front of the flags of Turkey, the Municipality of Bursa and the city council, they thanked me for the job I had done, handed me a framed certificate just as I had done for so many of my volunteers, and with it, a genuine hand-painted tile from Iznik, a small village just outside the city precinct.

The significance of the gift was not lost on me. You see, it was in Iznik that the Emperor Constantine, in 325AD, called together the heads of Christian churches cross the world, in what is now known as the first council of Nicaea, a forum which resulted in an historic declaration that Jesus was indeed, God.

As I stood and received the gift, my heart exploded with gratitude to the Lord, and with silent words that I'm sure only my spirit could articulate, I prayed that the truths of the Nicaean creed had also found a home, nineteen centuries later, in the heart of the city I had come to love.

I would spend the next few weeks handing over to Adnan and his team, and as I headed home on the train that night I felt completely at rest.

~

At seven o'clock the next morning, the Foreigners Police knocked on the door of Adnan's apartment, waking him up and hauling him down to the police station.

'We heard you have become the new president of the Working Group,' they said, 'We are here to tell you that we will be watching you very closely.' And with that, they let him go.

Adnan wasn't phased in the least, but when I heard of it, the faces of the two Palestinian students flashed through my mind. Those two young men had not been at our meeting of their own accord, after all.

So my gut feeling had been correct; with this new dynamic in the mix, I was even more grateful that God had gone ahead and opened a door for us to leave. The truth was, I was glad to be free, glad that it all fell to Adnan now with his thick skin and delightfully carefree spirit.

110. Jeff's Goodbyes

With only weeks to go, the biggest concern on Jeff's mind was to spend as much time as possible with his boys at the dormitory. Their final evening came too soon, and as they sat around together, it felt like the end of an era. The boys had brought snacks and Cola to share—*Turk-Cola,* that is, because Turks would rather produce their own version of the beverage than support a foreign company—but the night was relaxed and happy, and when it was time to leave, the boys insisted on walking home with Jeff despite the fact it was one-thirty in the morning.

The walk back to our house took an hour or so, enough time for God to surprise Jeff by adding a magnificent postscript. Suddenly free of all restraint, the students peppered Jeff with questions. 'What's it like to be a father?' they asked. 'What happens in your family?' These were unusually intimate and personal questions, and, after quickly recovering himself from his surprise, Jeff began to share about fatherhood, family and faith, and the way they all mixed together.

'Let me tell you about my son, Eric,' Jeff said as they walked together, and soon he was sharing the story. 'One day he was on a bus and he heard God tell him to get off and pray in front of a particular mosque . . .'

In great detail, Jeff spoke about how he had taught Eric to hear God's voice, and in the early morning hours, it was as if the young men were by proxy hearing a father share with them how to hear God for themselves.

They walked Jeff all the way to our front gate that night, and as he turned to say a final goodnight, his heart was overjoyed. God had worked in ways that were 'immeasurably more than all we could ask or imagine.'[1]

111. Heaven Touches Earth

A few weeks had passed when Ayşe called me into her office. 'I know you're tidying up your projects and getting ready to hand everything over, but I want to ask if you would do me a favour?'

And suddenly my mind went back to the sidewalk outside our real estate agent's office.

Would you stay here in Bursa?

Would you do me a favour?

I pulled my thoughts back into the moment. 'Of course,' I answered. 'What is it?'

'We have just received a request from the music department at Uludağ University,' she said. 'A handbell choir from a college in America are coming to Bursa for one week. They will conduct workshops and share some cultural experiences with our students. The Director of Music contacted me to ask if the city council would give them an official welcome. We'd like it if you could help us host the group and organise a concert for them at the Convention Centre.'

'What's the name of the college?' I asked, and sure enough, in her soft Turkish accent, she replied, 'Clearwater Christian College.'

Oh God.

It's a wonder I didn't break down and sob right there in her office. Had it only been two and a half years since I had sat in my first Foreigners Working Group meeting? The enormity of what we had pulled off struck me, the friendships we had made, the enduring relationship we had established with the city council, the hundreds of people who had contributed to our cause, the incredible goodwill we had been shown.

---

1 Ephesians 3:20

But my role had carried a sort of loneliness that wasn't easy to put into words, the pressures had been constant, the scrutiny had never let up, there was opposition from within the group and from outside, and now, just when we were leaving, God had sent a group of Christians from the other side of the world to bless our city.

Two weeks later, sure enough, they came. Phil, the teacher who had initiated the tour, was sitting at the edge of the room when I entered. An official welcome was underway, and his students were already seated, interspersed with Turkish students from the local university.

I leaned over and whispered, 'I'm Anya. I'm with the foreigners working group here at the city council. We're so pleased to have you here.'

And you know, there are people who identify as Christians, who may have been born into a Christian tradition, or perhaps have an interest in the Christian faith, and then there's those who have, at some point in their life, been absolutely transformed by the love and life of Jesus, and when Phil turned to shake my hand, I was left in no doubt that here was a man full of faith and full of love, in every sense of the word, one of us.

~

For the next few days our family joined in like tourists with the Clearwater and Uludağ students—visiting the historic Ottoman village of Cumalıkızık, sharing an official dinner hosted by the Mayor, and, on the final night, we gathered with the crowds at the Convention Centre for the much-publicised handbell concert.

The whole concept of handbells was new to the Turks. Most had never heard of the instrument, let alone a choir of them, but huge banners had been strung across the main street: Bursa City Council and Uludağ University, along with the Foreigners Working Group are pleased to announce the 'CLEARWATER CHRISTIAN COLLEGE HANDBELL CHOIR'—along with details of the time and place. Everyone was invited. This night was a gift from the city to all its citizens.

I took my place on the front row that evening beside my council colleagues. In the program that night we had included the children from the Children's Home—the German girls had taken some of the Clearwater students there earlier that week, and in just a few sessions, the enthusiastic children had learned to make incredible music together on their bright new set of coloured handbells. Now, here they were, all dressed up, their hair done and shoes shining, excited to perform in front of their proud parents.

I cannot describe what happened in the hour that followed, except to say that from the moment the music director stood to welcome the audience, a hush of expectation fell on everyone in the room. First, the handbell choir from America would perform a combined piece with the music students from Uludağ University, she said.

The music was beautiful—all those handbells in perfect unison, ringing out like a summons into the very heavens. Phil honoured every person possible that evening, weaving stories and highlights of their visit to Bursa in amongst the various items. The longer the concert proceeded, the more graciously and generously he spoke, until something incredible happened. I perceived a softening, a tenderness coming upon the Turkish people around me, and in that moment, it was as if we were all one in heart and mind.

It wasn't until Phil stood to play a solo piece on his French Horn that I realised how tender my own heart had also become; the clear, rich sound filled the room like the sound of heaven—in fact, it *was* the sound of heaven, because as he played, heaven opened, I felt it! The skies above Bursa had finally parted, and it was as if Jesus himself had come and was right there in the room with us. Tears rolled down my cheeks as my whole spirit was moved; the tune Phil had chosen to play was an old, familiar hymn, and *Dear God, how did You pull this off?* was all I could silently pray.

What I didn't know, was that the grand finale was still to come.

112. Grand Finale

The children sang and played their instruments, the students from abroad demonstrated how handbells should be played, and all the while, the mutual friendship between our group of foreigners and the people of Bursa was beautifully on display.

Now it was time to bring the concert to a close. 'To finish the night,' Phil addressed the audience, 'we will play for you a song that means a lot to us. We pray it will bless you, and we offer it as our gift to your city.' His eyes shone with the love of God as he surveyed the crowd.

He turned to his students, who lifted their bells in unison, and as he raised his conductor's baton, a song began to ring out, one that we had loved for years: *As the deer pants for the water, so my soul longs after you.*

I glanced over my shoulder to look for Jeff among the crowd, because if we'd been sitting together in that moment, I would have reached for his hand and squeezed it tight out of love for him and for our city, and for all that God had done.

Then I saw him. He'd slipped down the back, where he'd taken off his shoes and now stood to his feet in worship. I couldn't hold back my emotion; it was as if a whole host of heaven's angels had suddenly joined us, and as the music rose in stunning honour of all God had done, I realised, *this was His grand finale! His moment of glory!*

Perhaps only a few human hearts perceived it, but I believe that heaven spilled over to earth that night, and as the concert came to an end, I could hardly contain the joy in my soul. An ocean of peace had flooded my heart, and with it the realisation that our assignment in the City of Silk had come to an end. Jesus had been enthroned in Bursa.

113. Goodbye Bursa

It's a big thing to realise the assignment God gave you is over. We had come to Bursa with no agenda but to live as expats and follow the Lord and now, there we were, some three years later, realising the job was done. All that was left was to pack a house, say our goodbyes, and relocate into a new season and a new city.

Perhaps we underestimated the intensity at which we'd lived the past few years. Maybe thinking about the concerns of a city and a family had left me incapable of even the most basic decision-making. Whatever it was, our final week in Bursa found me on the second floor of our nearly empty house, absolutely paralysed. We'd packed up the kitchen, the schoolroom and most of the bedrooms and done just fine—but what to do with the last stray pieces of Lego, the unmarked keys that emerged from under the dresser, the pile of children's drawings? Had we really come this far only to be overwhelmed by *this?*

It was then that God brought friends to pull us over the finish line. Shari and Kerry were the first on the scene, and they knew exactly what to do. 'The job just needs to be finished,' Shari said, and then she set up a system, sorted everything into three piles, and within the hour, the job was done.

Kerry, bless him, was down on the sidewalk, his hand resting on Jeff's shoulder in brotherly solidarity. The boxes were piled high, ready to be loaded onto a truck, and the furniture was yet to be moved. It would take a good few hours to pack the load, and Jeff still had a seven-hour drive to our new location in Antalya ahead of him.

And then, from down the street, six men appeared, and a smile as wide as any I had ever seen broke out on Jeff's face. It was *his boys*, the young men he had grown to love; they'd come as a pack from the dormitory with their sleeves already rolled up, and there they suddenly were, greeting Jeff and Kerry and Eric and Joseph with a kiss on each cheek. There was no chance to be overwhelmed with gratitude though, because within minutes every one of them had removed their shoes, walked into our house, and had started carrying our furniture out the front door. Sometimes the blessing is not just in getting the job done; it's the mere fact that someone turned up to do it with you, and on our last day in Bursa, we were surrounded by people who loved us and wanted to help us on our way.

We had said as many goodbyes as we could over the previous few weeks—coffee with Elif and Nurcan, farewell dinners with our expat friends, a last cup of tea with the taxi drivers in their tiny booth, another round with Ishan in his little shop at the bottom of the hill, a visit with the Director of Disability Services, and the Lieutenants at the Air Force Academy. . .

We were physically and emotionally spent. Still, nothing could lessen the grief when we said goodbye for the last time to our beloved house cleaner, Cadriye. I didn't think I had overlooked her. I just presumed she would do one last clean, and then we would hug and thank each other, and it would be hard, but we'd say goodbye with what little language we could garner. What I never expected was that she would sit down on our front steps, hold her covered head in her beautiful hands and sob from the bottom of her heart. Liberty climbed into her lap, and Cadriye alternated between hugging her tight and pushing her away. I knew how dearly we had loved Cadriye Teyze; now I realised how deeply she also had loved us. I sat down beside her, put my arm around her shoulders and cried my heart out too. *Is this how every great story ends? With tears and goodbyes?*

But the parting was about to get even harder. Arzu Teyze and Omer

Bey, who had been like grandparents to our children and like parents to Jeff and me, stood on their front porch watching the whole scene. *What do you say when there are no words?* These were the people who had looked beyond the usual prejudices and fears, thrown their own reputations to the wind and loved us, cared for us and watched out for us from the moment we arrived. We'd shared tea. We'd sat on each other's balconies. I'd stood in Arzu's kitchen and learned to make lentil soup. Omer Bey had advised us and helped us understand the many situations that left us confused; they had shared our Christmas meal and shared their Ramadan food with us. God Himself couldn't have given us more wonderful neighbours. Now none of us knew how to bring it to an end.

'You're always welcome at our house.' 'Thank you for everything.' 'We love you.' But words could never convey the depth of emotion between us all, and in the end, we just hugged and cried and bundled the kids into a taxi, and the whole thing seemed cruel and harsh and there was absolutely no way to make it gentle on anyone.

Thankfully, Fatih had had the foresight to say goodbye a few days earlier. He had come over late one night, as he often did, to drink tea and eat fruit and talk—and to give us a gift, he told us as he stood to leave. I wondered what it could be. I'd wracked my brains to think of a present for Fatih and Anna, but whatever I came up with seemed far too meagre.

It turned out that Fatih had prepared a gift more beautiful and priceless and heart-wrenching than I could have ever imagined. Sitting down at our piano he said, 'I wrote a song for you,' and then he played it, note after note, depicting all we had left behind in Australia, all this city had come to mean to us, and the joy we had found in our friendship. It was classical and jazz and everything rolled into one, just as our time in Bursa had been. Fatih, of all people, had shared our ups and our downs, our victories and our losses; he was the one Turk who knew us best, and as the notes faded into silence, we simply hugged him and thanked him and knew that what we'd experienced could well turn out to be one of the most satisfying and rich friendships of a lifetime.

114. One Last Visit

We soon arrived in Antalya and began settling into a sixteenth-floor apartment with a rooftop balcony that looked out in the distance to the Taurus Mountains and the sparkling waters of the Mediterranean Sea.

Before long, we found the local playgrounds and shopping malls and enrolled our children in the international school. It wouldn't take long, we realised, to feel at home in Antalya, with its large expat population and tourists from all over the world.

And then, out of the blue, I felt a strong sense that we needed to return to Bursa one last time—specifically, it was in my heart to visit Semih Pala. We'd said all our goodbyes in Bursa, finished well with our neighbours and friends and the working group, but when it came to President Semih Pala and his staff at the City Council, I felt it had all been too hurried. Now, I wanted to properly honour the people who had most honoured me. And so, we packed the family into our newly acquired van, filled the tank with gas, and drove seven straight hours, back to the city we'd left only a month earlier.

We were racing the clock, having timed our journey to arrive after lunch but before mid-afternoon when many of the staff would leave to attend the Friday prayers at the mosque nearby, and so, on arriving in town, we headed straight to the city council chambers.

Jeff waved to me. 'I'll take the kids outside so they can run and play and stretch their legs,' he said. 'You take your time.' And off they ran across the same lawn where we had held our foreigner's picnic right back just a few years earlier. My heart was full as I reflected on the many memories, the privilege it had been to work with these city leaders.

I walked into the building which had become my second home of sorts, not knowing if the staff would be in meetings or at some event or another, or even if they'd have time to talk now that I was not there in any formal capacity.

It was Semih Pala himself who saw me first; his face lit up and softened the moment he looked my way, and my heart warmed as, with a few words, he summoned his closest colleagues—Ayşe, Murat, Başak and Cüneyt—the team I'd worked so intrinsically with for more than two years. Semih Pala led the way. 'Let's go!' he said. 'We'll have tea together across at the Congress Centre.'

There, in the vast grand foyer of the congress centre, we sat like family in a lounge room on the leather couches. A tray of fresh tea was soon brought out and placed on the table between us. We spoke of Cüneyt's wife, soon to give birth to their first baby, and how happy we all were for them. Ayşe reminisced about her holiday in London, Başak nodded and said how she was looking forward to going there too, soon, and Murat was relaxed and ready for the weekend . . . as for Semih Pala, he looked for all the world like a father surrounded by his children. Leaning back contentedly, he sipped his tea and told us that he too was going away for a few weeks, to see his son, in America.

When a second round of tea had been drunk and the time was coming to a close, I thanked my friends again for the privilege of working together over the past few years. 'It was a great honour,' I said. 'Thank you.'

Semih Pala leaned forward and smiled. 'This city is your city,' he said, 'and your family are my family. You are welcome at my home any time.' And then he said the words I have treasured ever since. 'Thank you, my sister.'

Did Semih Pala just call me sister?

Yes, indeed, and the weight of those words did not escape me for a moment. The man of peace who had first welcomed me in, had just blessed me as I left. With a full heart and just a few tears, we said goodbye and I went outside to where Jeff was waiting with Eric, Joseph, Evangeline and Liberty. It was time to say goodbye to Bursa. It was time for our next adventure.

AND NOW . . .

The legacy of those years in Bursa continues to this day. Five years after this story took place, the Foreigners Working Group was officially recognised as an Assembly. Early initiatives such as language classes, picnics and city tours, and the 'Grand Bursa Foreigner's Night' are now well-established and go from strength to strength.

My working group core team are now spread across many different countries and are well established in their own careers, where their skills and leadership continue to shine.

As a city, Bursa continues to thrive and was recently recognised as one of the 'main rising economies' across the entire region. The fact that Bursa prospers today gives us great joy.

One of our most satisfying moments, however, came when we met with another expat now living in Turkey. 'Oh, a lot has changed since you were there, 'she said with a laugh, 'these days, *everyone* wants to live in Bursa!'

Acknowledgements

To Janine. The tussle between us was nearly unbearable for me at the time, but I am quite sure that reflects more on my own sensitivities than anything else. You had beaten the odds and established yourself in Bursa long before I had ever heard of the place. For that, and for the many contributions you have made since, you have my utmost respect.

To Fatih. You can't imagine our relief when we met you. Your amazing gift for languages and basketball and jazz still blows me away. Thank you for being our interpreter, our advisor, the one who helped us make sense of things, and most of all, for being our friend. It's not everyone you share tears and frustrations and laughs with. For loving our children and being 'Uncle Fatih' to them, thank you. The music you composed for me when we left stays with me still. You and Anna will always be family to us.

To Nurcan. You are one of the most gracious, intelligent, hardworking women I have ever had the privilege of knowing. You were friends with religious and secular, educated and uneducated, old and young, rich and poor, and thankfully for me, with locals and foreigners alike. Your friendship was one of the greatest joys of my years in Turkey. I pray every imaginable blessing on you and Yunus and your beautiful children.

To the Foreigners Working Group. I laid down my life for you, and it was worth it, in every sense of the word. To see you thriving today as a full-fledged Assembly brings me a great deal of satisfaction.

To Başak, Cüneyt, Murat and all the city council staff. It was one of the greatest pleasures of my life to work with you. Thank you for welcoming me into the family.

To Ayşe, for every time we shared coffee in your office at the Bursa City Council, I am deeply grateful. Your guidance allowed me to shine. Thank you for being by my side, ready to offer advice and insight while I was president of the foreigners working group. Thank you for sharing your hopes and dreams with me too. It's very few people who are both colleagues and friends, and in you I found both.

To President Semih Pala. You were a man of peace, the father of a city, and by any country's standards, a wonderful leader. You invited a stranger in and because of your trust and grace, I was privileged to contribute to your vision of a welcoming, prosperous city. Thank you for coming up with the idea of a foreigner's working group. You loved the city of Bursa and left a legacy that will always be remembered.

To the Christian expats of Bursa. Jeff and I speak your names with great respect. Every one of you are faith-filled heroes, and our time in Bursa was rich because of your friendship. We can never speak highly enough of you all.

To Mildred. That a twenty-year-old home-schooled girl from rural America would listen to me share my story around a table in Istanbul and then move to Bursa just to help us, still blows me away. You made one of the toughest gigs on the planet look easy. I know that countless men and women, from the largest cities in Turkey to the most remote villages, attest to the joy that follows you wherever you go. For sharing your love of the natural world with our children, thank you. You were so much more than a tutor to them. You were a friend and a colleague and even as I write this story, I still aspire to your lightness of spirit.

To our parents, grandparents, siblings, aunts, uncles and cousins. We counted the cost but you, in so many ways, footed the bill. Thank you for all the times you have waved us off even when it made no sense and hurt too much. You've lived amazing lives too, and the best times are still when we're all together.

To our Team of Friends. Not one page of this story was written without you in mind. You believed in us and for us before we ever set foot in the City of Silk. Thank you for supporting us every day we were in Bursa and thank you for being there, every one of you, as we made the even greater transition of coming back again. Your faithfulness is rare in this world, and for every expression of your kindness and care to us over the years, we rise to our feet and applaud you. This story is, in every sense of the word, your story.

To our children, Eric, Joseph, Evangeline and Liberty. We couldn't be prouder of how you handled Turkey. It's not everyone who takes their kids to live in a Muslim country for who-knows-how-long. Only kids with your depth of love and honour for us could have pulled it off so well. For all you gave up so that your parents could live out what was in them, thank you. For the times it was a bit over the top, we're sorry about that. Our story is now your heritage. That you four get to take this family forward and build a dynasty of faith from here gives us great joy.

To Jeff. Publishing this book is our joint labour of love. Thank you for the chapters you wrote, and for covering for me so that I could be free to write. There's no doubt that I would be at a constant loose end without you. *We did it!* Thank you most of all for having the courage to uproot a family and follow a call to the other side of the world. The very fact we get to do this life together makes for the best story ever.

To our precious Father in Heaven. Words can't describe how much we love you for taking us to Turkey. You watched over us, believed in us, and took us in hand to reshape us so we could face the impossible. Thank you for letting us join you in Turkey.

THE MCKEE FAMILY

For one year after we left Bursa, our family lived in Antalya, a province in the South of Turkey. After living in a rooftop city apartment for six months, we moved to a tiny village on the outskirts of town, where we provided pastoral and prayer ministry to Christian expats and locals from around the region, and supported refugees fleeing the unrest of the Arab Spring. Our children attended an international school but spent most of their spare hours walking through the forest, exploring old ruins, and raising six abandoned puppies.

And then, one morning, Jeff woke up with the words, 'Go home,' clearly in his heart, and this time, it came with a sense of urgency. That's been another God-story, of course, but later that year, holding onto a few fresh but powerful promises, our family returned home, not to Australia, as we might have presumed, but in fact to New Zealand, the land of Anya's birth, and where we all now live as dual citizens.

As a result of our own journey, and following on from hundreds of hours of prayer ministry, pastoral care, mentoring and speaking, we established a wonderful ministry called Torn Curtain Collective, where our passion is the same as ever—to equip and inspire people to operate as confidently, naturally and effectively in the spiritual realm as they do in the natural, and to simply keep up with what God is doing.

The McKee family and Grandma arriving in Istanbul.

The gateway to our home in Bursa.
Fatih's parents lived on the left and we lived on the
right-hand side.

Playing street soccer with the local boys.

Loading up our furniture at the second-hand market.

Fatih, our neighbour, with Vangie.

Foreigners picnic in Merinos Park.

Anya, Semra and Riada

Cadriye (our gorgeous housekeeper)
taking a well-earned break with Liberty.

Vangie and Liberty heading to school.

Celebrating New Year's Eve with our Turkish-Australian friends.

Saturday morning soccer with the local boys.

Jeff with the students from the
Islamic dormitory.

Ishan and Jeff hanging out in his shop.

Our neighbours, Arzu and Omer,
relaxing on their front porch.

Anya presenting her speech at the Foreigner's welcome night in Bursa, with Ayşe translating.

Eric and Joseph's preferred way of getting into the house.

A home school morning in Bursa.

The McKee family overlooking the City of Bursa.

The German Girls and Mildred with our kids at the end of term.

Eric and Joseph taking a traditional tea break
on the balcony.

Vangie and her friend from across the garden,
with their slow-melting igloo.

Ready to set off for Mount Uludağ and an unforeseen
night in a blizzard.

Liberty being doted upon by Arzu and Omer.

President Semih Pala (second from R) with Ayşe (Far right) and members of the Foreigner's Working Group core team.

Aşure pudding made by a neighbour.

Ayşe presenting Anya with a farewell gift (a handmade Iznik tile) from the city.

Leaving day when all the boys from the dorm
turned up to help.

The six of us, ready for the next adventure!

Thank you for reading our story. We'd love
you to share how it impacted you!

To get in touch or to invite Anya to speak at your
church or community event, please email:

anya@torncurtainpublishing.com

or follow along on socials at:

f @anya.mckee.7

⊙ @anyamckee

#foreignersinthecityofsilk

BOOKS BY ANYA

Feels Like I'm Breathing
The Theatre (Illustrated Children's)
The Story of the Daughter of Zion*

Includes Discussion Guide for group and personal use.

DAUGHTER OF ZION
RETREATS

The Story of the Daughter of Zion is a conference or day-retreat experience suitable for women of every culture and generation. In three compelling sessions, Anya combines this biblically-rich spoken word drama with worship and prophetic insight to minister healing, freedom and spiritual confidence to women around the world.